PREACHER

WAR IN THE SUN

Garth Ennis
writer

Steve Dillon
Peter Snejbjerg
artists

Grant Goleash
Pamela Rambo
colorists

Clem Robins
letterer

Glenn Fabry
original covers

PREACHER created by
Garth Ennis and Steve Dillon

PREACHER: WAR IN THE SUN

Published by DC Comics. Cover and
compilation copyright © 1999 DC Comics.
All Rights Reserved. Originally published in
single magazine form as PREACHER SPECIAL:
ONE MAN'S WAR, PREACHER 34-40.
Copyright © 1998 Garth Ennis and Steve Dillon.
All Rights Reserved. All characters, their
distinctive likenesses and related indicia
featured in this publication are trademarks
of Garth Ennis and Steve Dillon.
VERTIGO is a trademark of DC Comics.
The stories, characters, and incidents featured
in this publication are entirely fictional.

DC Comics, 1700 Broadway, New York, NY 10019
A division of Warner Bros. -
A Time Warner Entertainment Company

Printed in Canada. Second Printing.

ISBN: 1-56389-490-4

Cover illustration by GLENN FABRY
Original covers by GLENN FABRY
Publication design by MURPHY FOGELNEST

What's happened so far?
Well, thereby hangs a tale...

Reverend Jesse Custer was your run-o'-the-mill Texas minister preachin' to the simple folk of Annville, Texas on Sundays and crawling inside a bottle the rest of the week until GENESIS—a spirit conceived in a union between angel and demon—broke free of its bonds and charged outta Heaven like a fiery comet...straight toward Jesse and his flock. Two hundred people died in Annville...all except Jesse, possessed by Genesis and wielding the Word of God. When Jesse spoke, he could make anyone do as he said.

Fate or a divine hand reunited Jesse with his long-lost lover Tulip O'Hare and linked 'em both to Cassidy, an Irish vampire with a taste for whiskey. Jesse decided it was high time God was made accountable for his sins, having abandoned his post in Heaven to walk the earth. And Jesse aimed to find the Almighty to do just that.

For his troubles, Jesse met the Saint of Killers, an awakened angel of death sent by Genesis' keepers in Heaven. The Saint's aim was always true, and he left a bloody trail in his wake. And then there was Herr Starr, an agent of the Grail—a secret society dating back to the Crucifixion—which had designs on just what mankind's path *should* be in the face of the coming Armageddon. Starr plotted to replace his order's flawed messiah with...well, someone like Jesse Custer, a charismatic figure who spoke with the voice of God. To do so, Starr captured Cassidy and led Jesse on a bloody chase from San Francisco to the Grail's mountain fortress of Masada in France. The Saint of Killers, of course, was about two steps behind.

In the end, the Saint pretty much took out the entire Grail army. Starr dropped Allfather D'Aronique, leader of the Grail, out of a helicopter and right on top of the Grail's retarded messiah. Jesse and Cassidy got away...as did Starr. Meanwhile, the Saint of Killers was buried under a mountain, but he's had worse to deal with in his life and death.

Just recently, Jesse took part in some good ol' New Orleans voodoo to mine the memories of Genesis. And he got some of what he needed, learning the tragic origins of the Saint of Killers and just who was behind the Saint's damnation. But Jesse knows that for the whole truth, he's gotta access GENESIS directly. And he knows that the answers lie somewhere West.

Starr, now Allfather of the Grail, vows that Jesse will be the Grail's messiah if it kills him.

In Monument Valley,
Jesse and Starr converge for
an apocalyptic showdown...

REVEREND JESSE CUSTER

Possessed by the entity GENESIS—a child born of a union between Heaven and Hell that should never have existed—

Jesse Custer's on a quest to find God and the reason He's abandoned his post. Because of GENESIS, Jesse's voice is the literal Word of God, commanding those who hear him to do whatever he says. Jesse drinks too much, smokes too much and has a peculiar habit of taking advice from the spirit of John Wayne.

TULIP O'HARE

Five years ago, Tulip and Jesse were pretty much joined at the hip—that is, until Jesse was hauled back to his childhood home of Angelville by good ol' boys Jody and T.C., disappearing on Tulip. Since that time, Tulip made a bungling attempt to be a paid assassin to pay the bills and forget about Jesse Custer. Guns came easy, forgetting Jesse didn't. Jesse's promised to love her until the end of the world. Tulip aims to make him keep his word this time.

CASSIDY

A hard-drinkin' Irish vampire nearly a century old, Proinsias Cassidy has been with Jesse and Tulip since Tulip tried to steal his truck after a botched hit in Texas. He's promised to stay with them until Jesse's found God— mostly out of friendship...and mostly because he's in love with Tulip, a fact he's kept hidden from Jesse. Call him Cassidy, Cass, or even a total wanker. Just don't ever call him Proinsias.

THE SAINT OF KILLERS

Once, the Saint's hatred snuffed the flames of Hell and left it an icy wasteland. For that, the Devil flayed the skin from his bones. But even that didn't stop the Saint from hating, and so he replaced the Angel of Death and was sent forth to be the patron martyr for all who take up the gun, leading the dead to the afterlife—above or below. The Saint shot the Devil before he left Hell. Now, he stalks Jesse Custer for the secret he has.

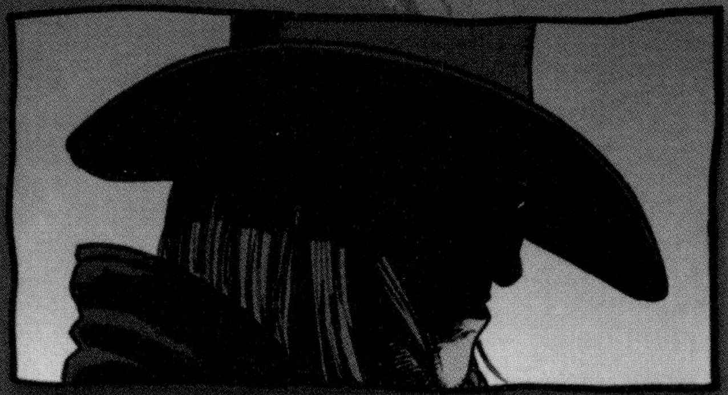

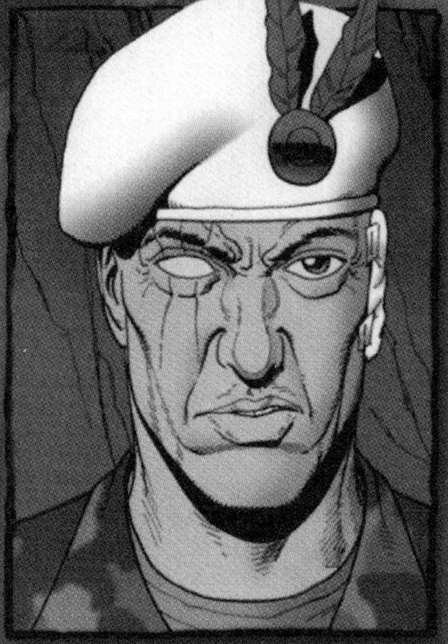

ARSEFACE

Sheriff Hugo Root's only son decided life wasn't worth livin' when Nirvana frontman Kurt Cobain up and killed himself. His father's 12-gauge missed all the vital stuff, and six operations rebuilt the rest. Arseface blamed

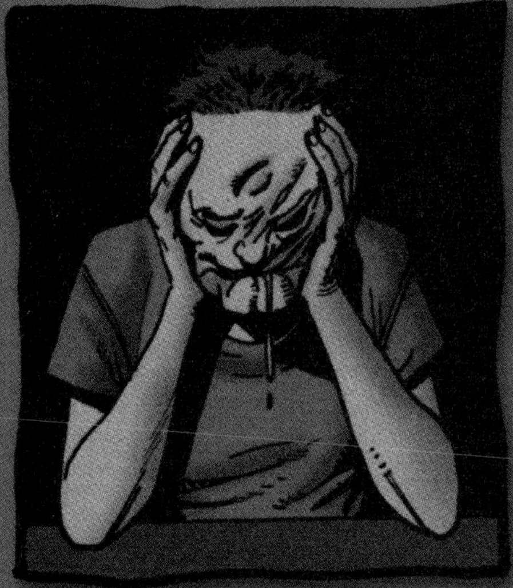

Jesse Custer for Sheriff Root's suicide, but Jesse and Cass convinced him otherwise. They even got him laid, and helped him land a recording contract. Now he's a pop icon...with a face like an arse. Go figure.

STARR

Recruited by the centuries-old Grail, Starr rose through the ranks to become the order's most respected agent, answering only to Allfather D'Aronique. Starr killed D'Aronique, realizing that the Grail's efforts were wasted on a tainted messiah. In Jesse Custer, Starr sees the future of the Grail...a future the newly risen Allfather Starr would gladly kill to see a reality.

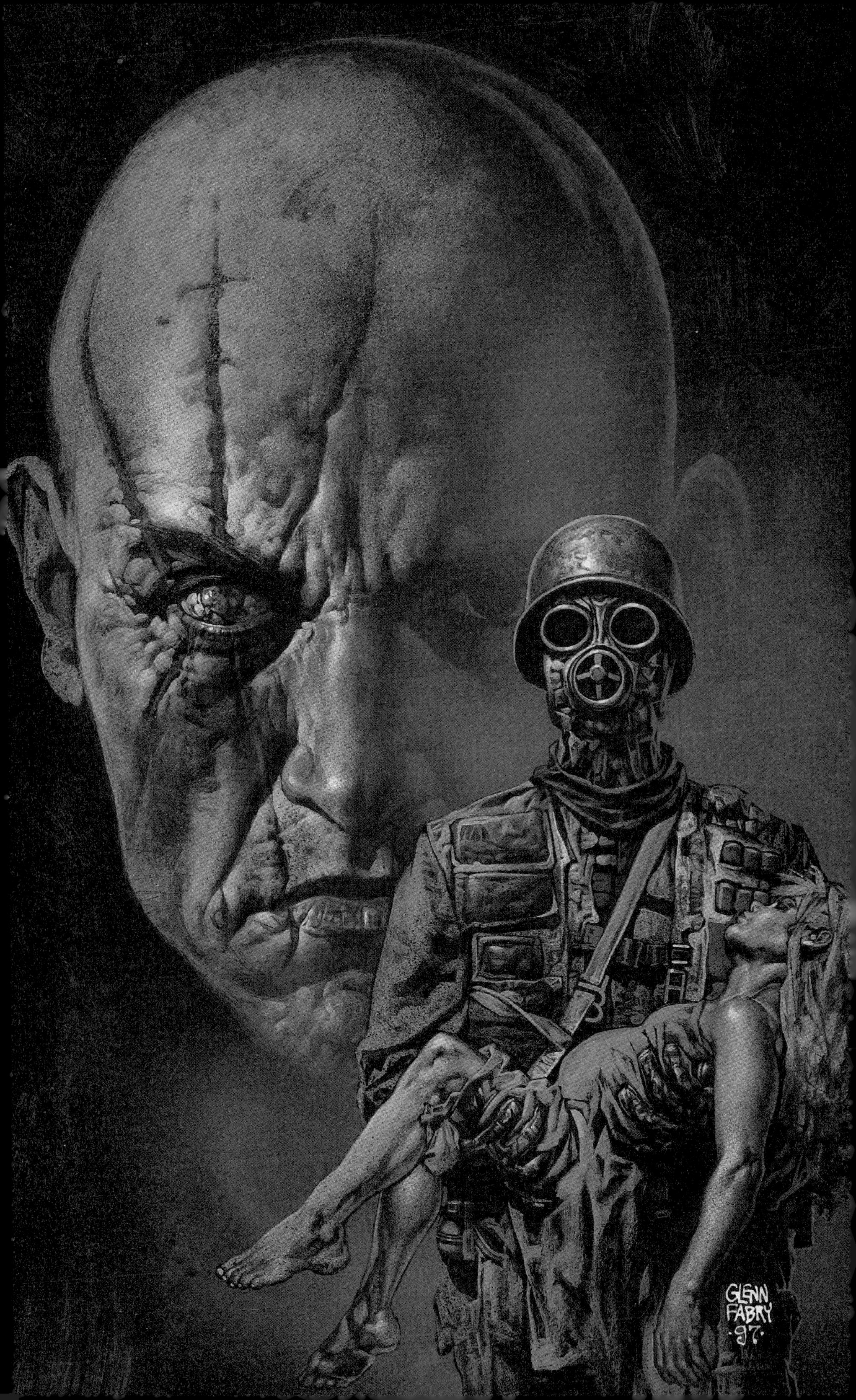
GLENN
FABRY
·97·

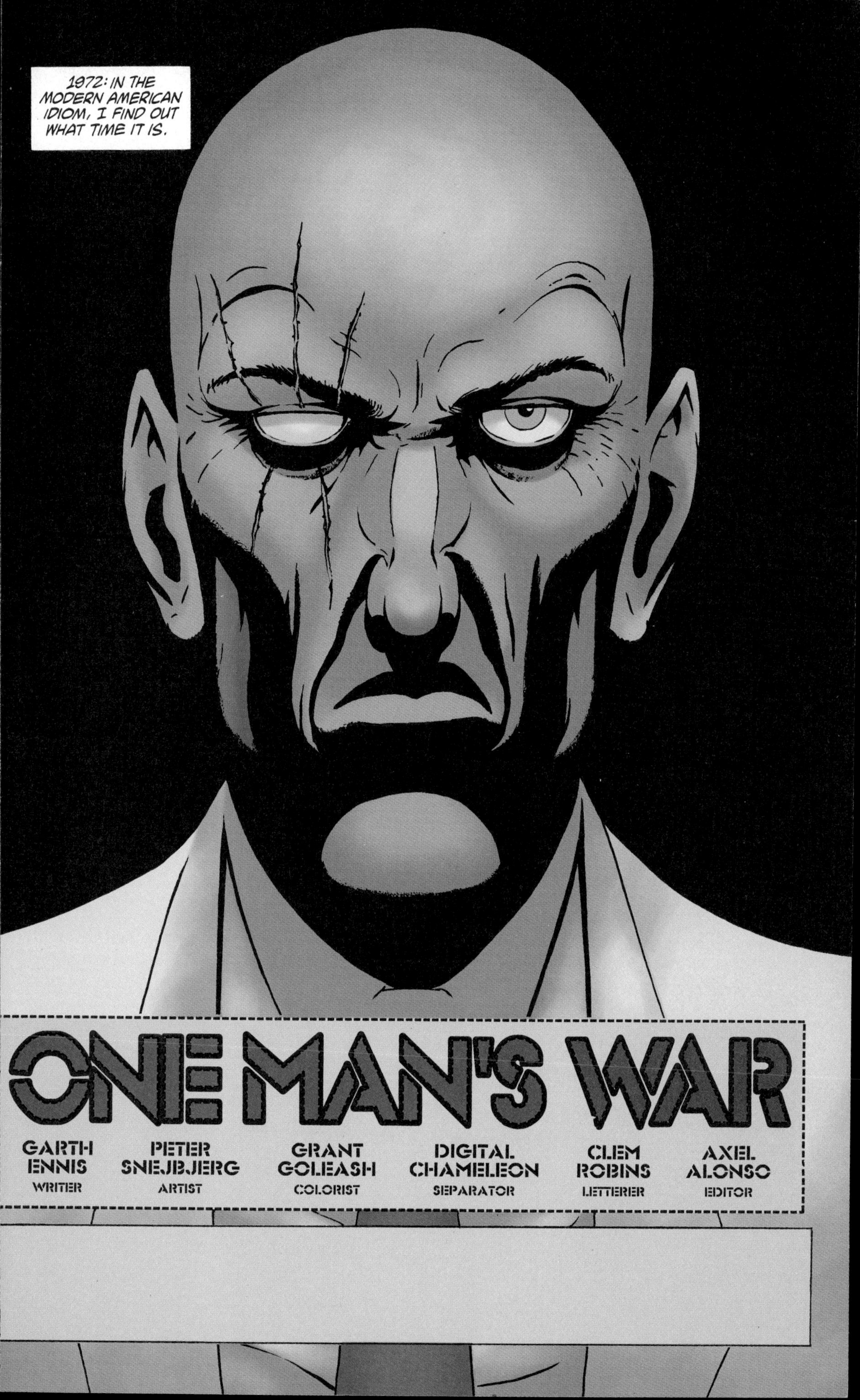
1972: IN THE MODERN AMERICAN IDIOM, I FIND OUT WHAT TIME IT IS.
ONE MAN'S WAR
GARTH ENNIS WRITER
PETER SNEJBJERG ARTIST
GRANT GOLEASH COLORIST
DIGITAL CHAMELEON SEPARATOR
CLEM ROBINS LETTERER
AXEL ALONSO EDITOR

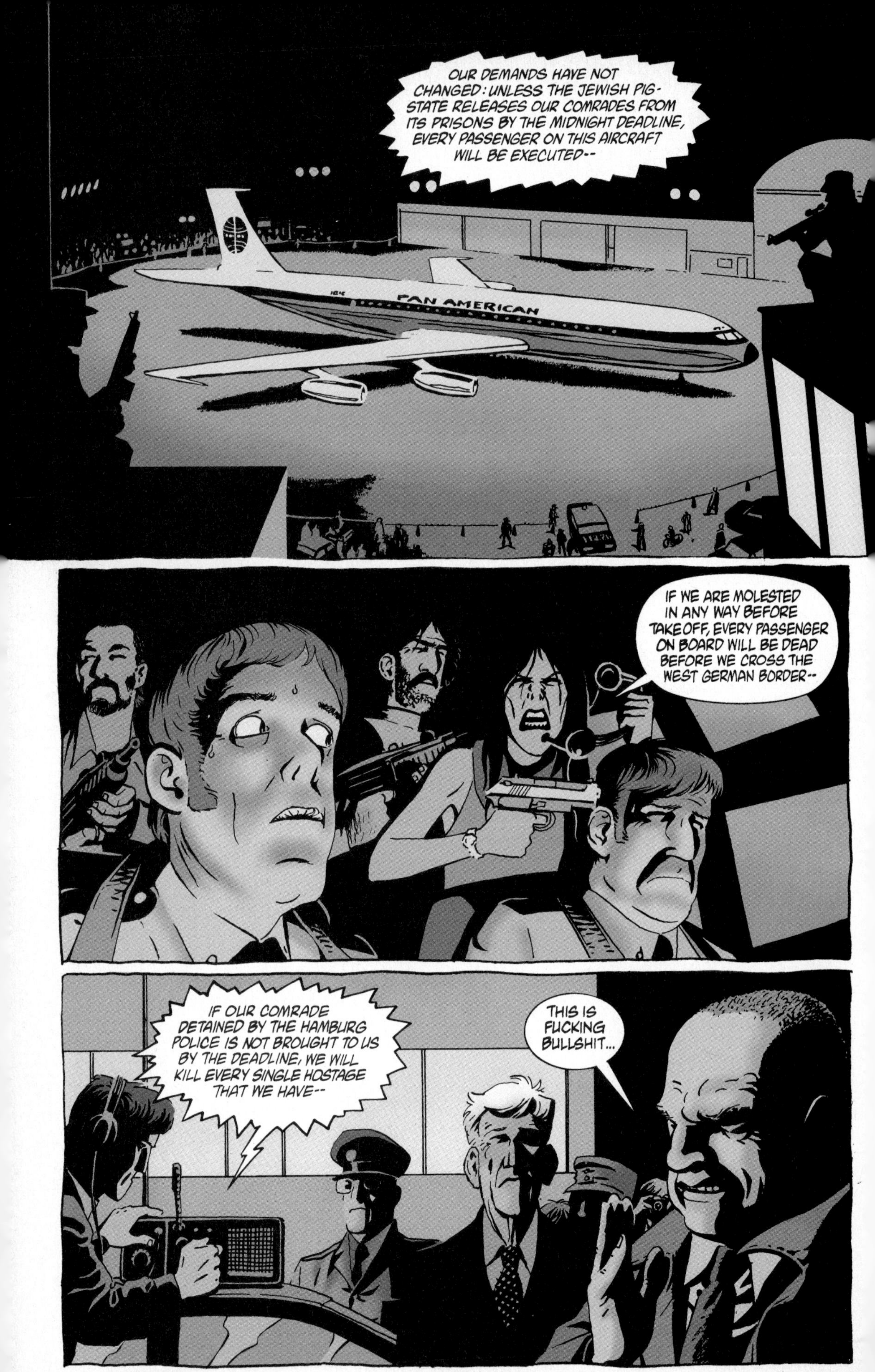
OUR DEMANDS HAVE NOT CHANGED: UNLESS THE JEWISH PIG-STATE RELEASES OUR COMRADES FROM ITS PRISONS BY THE MIDNIGHT DEADLINE, EVERY PASSENGER ON THIS AIRCRAFT WILL BE EXECUTED--
PAN AMERICAN
IF WE ARE MOLESTED IN ANY WAY BEFORE TAKEOFF, EVERY PASSENGER ON BOARD WILL BE DEAD BEFORE WE CROSS THE WEST GERMAN BORDER--
IF OUR COMRADE DETAINED BY THE HAMBURG POLICE IS NOT BROUGHT TO US BY THE DEADLINE, WE WILL KILL EVERY SINGLE HOSTAGE THAT WE HAVE--
THIS IS FUCKING BULLSHIT...

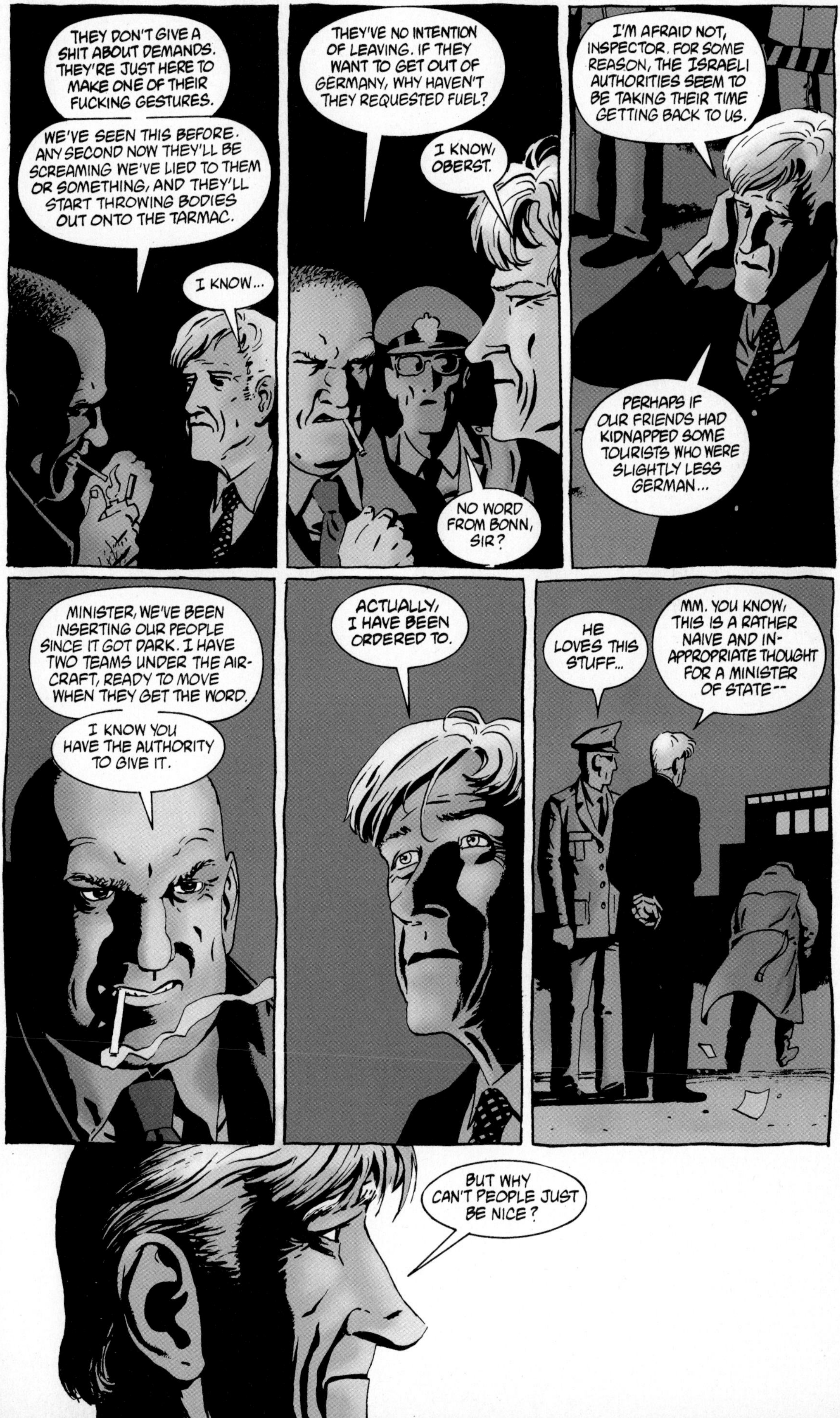
THEY DON'T GIVE A SHIT ABOUT DEMANDS. THEY'RE JUST HERE TO MAKE ONE OF THEIR FUCKING GESTURES.
WE'VE SEEN THIS BEFORE. ANY SECOND NOW THEY'LL BE SCREAMING WE'VE LIED TO THEM OR SOMETHING, AND THEY'LL START THROWING BODIES OUT ONTO THE TARMAC.
I KNOW...
THEY'VE NO INTENTION OF LEAVING. IF THEY WANT TO GET OUT OF GERMANY, WHY HAVEN'T THEY REQUESTED FUEL?
I KNOW, OBERST.
NO WORD FROM BONN, SIR?
I'M AFRAID NOT, INSPECTOR. FOR SOME REASON, THE ISRAELI AUTHORITIES SEEM TO BE TAKING THEIR TIME GETTING BACK TO US.
PERHAPS IF OUR FRIENDS HAD KIDNAPPED SOME TOURISTS WHO WERE SLIGHTLY LESS GERMAN...
MINISTER, WE'VE BEEN INSERTING OUR PEOPLE SINCE IT GOT DARK. I HAVE TWO TEAMS UNDER THE AIR-CRAFT, READY TO MOVE WHEN THEY GET THE WORD.
I KNOW YOU HAVE THE AUTHORITY TO GIVE IT.
ACTUALLY, I HAVE BEEN ORDERED TO.
HE LOVES THIS STUFF...
MM. YOU KNOW, THIS IS A RATHER NAIVE AND IN-APPROPRIATE THOUGHT FOR A MINISTER OF STATE--
BUT WHY CAN'T PEOPLE JUST BE NICE?

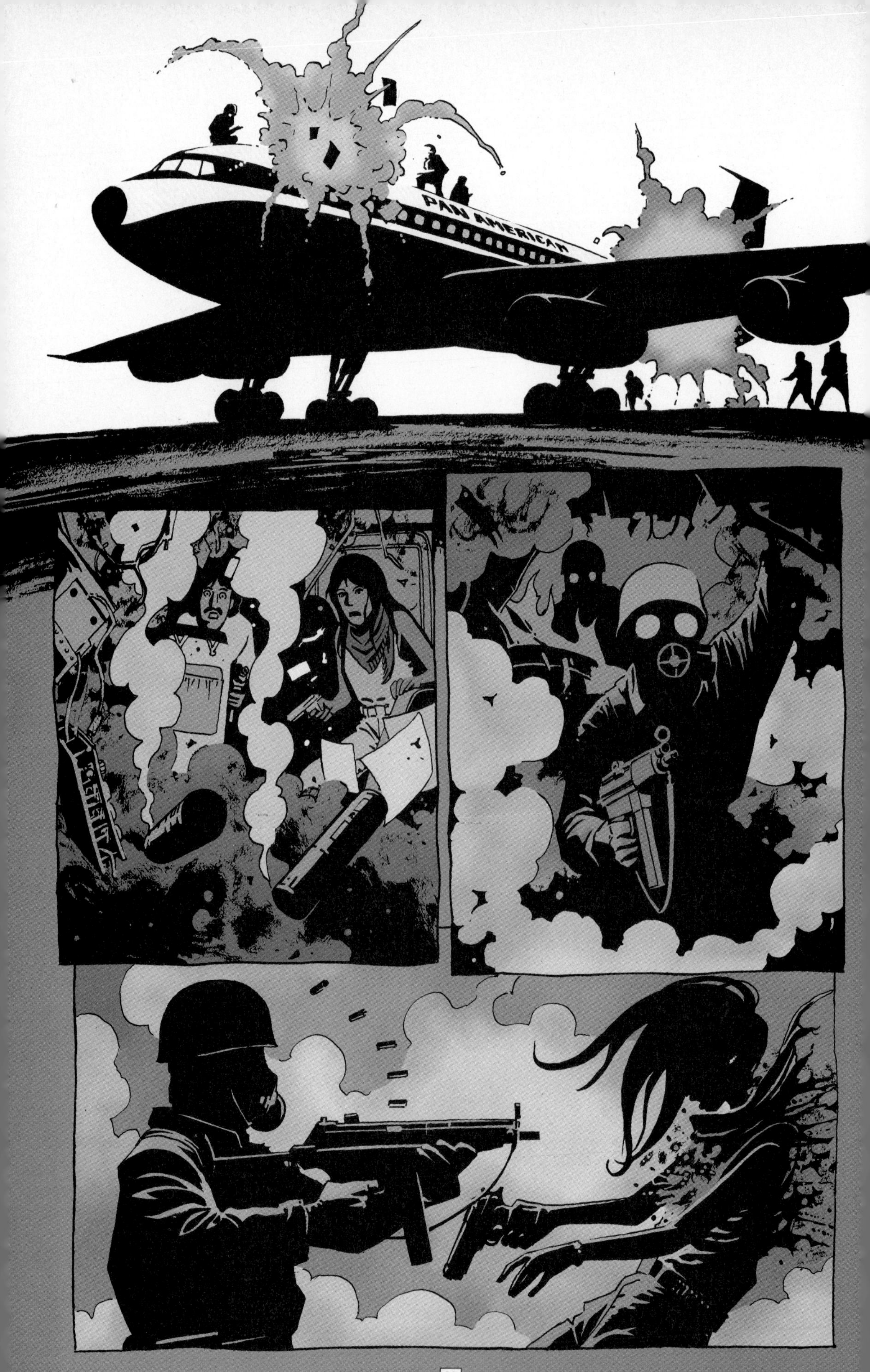
PAN AMERICAN

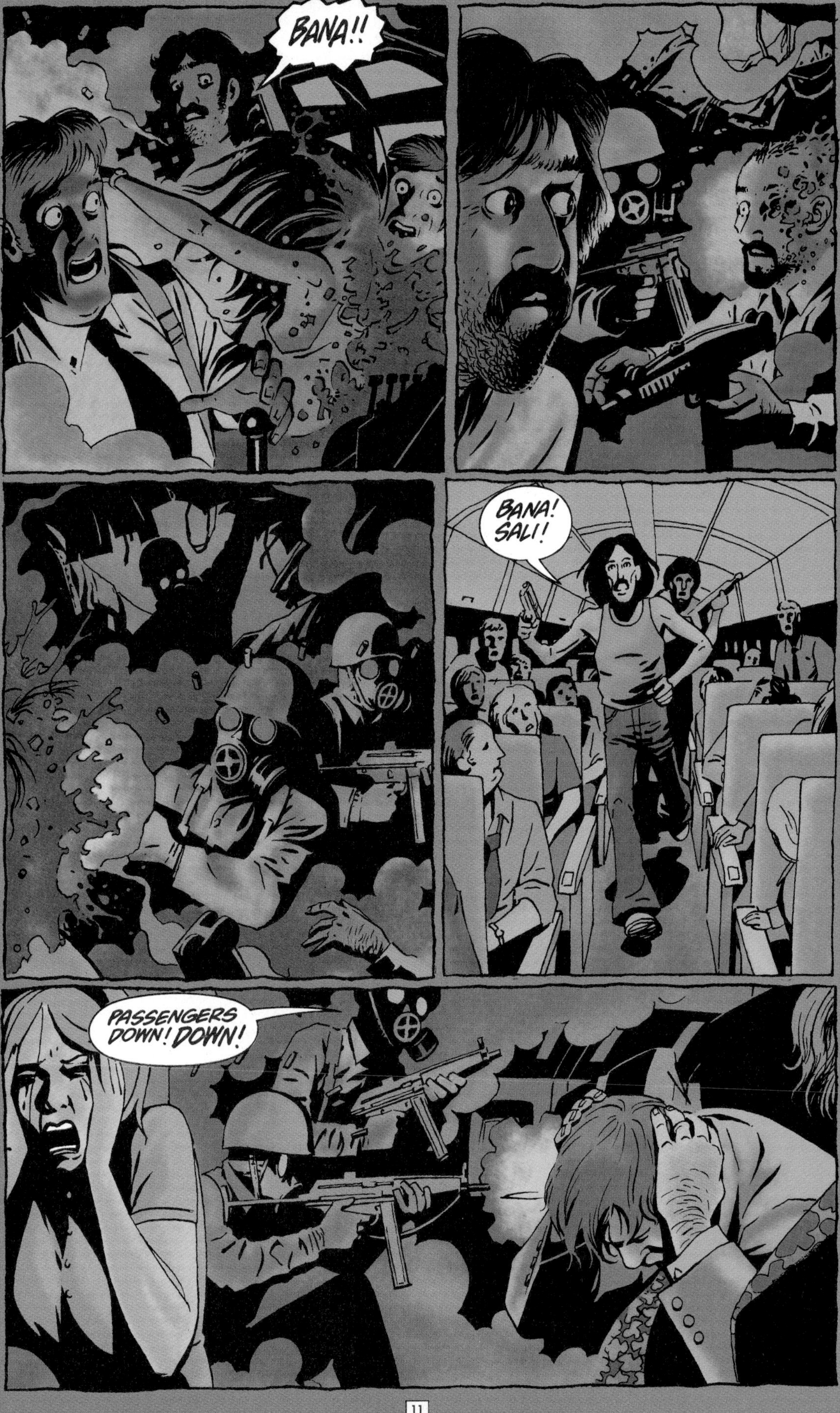
BANA!!
BANA!
SALI!
PASSENGERS
DOWN! DOWN!

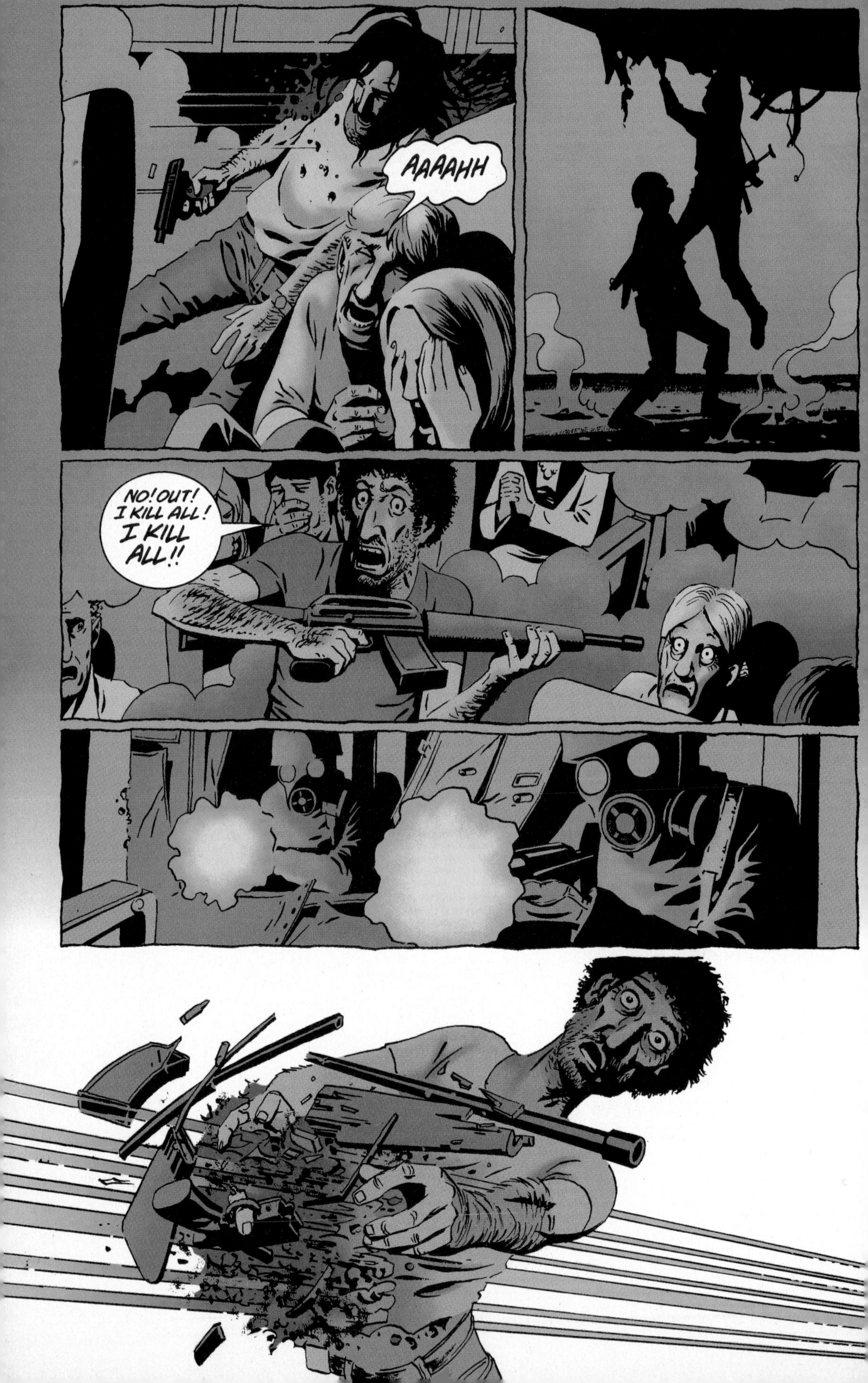
AAAAHH
NO! OUT! I KILL ALL! I KILL ALL!!

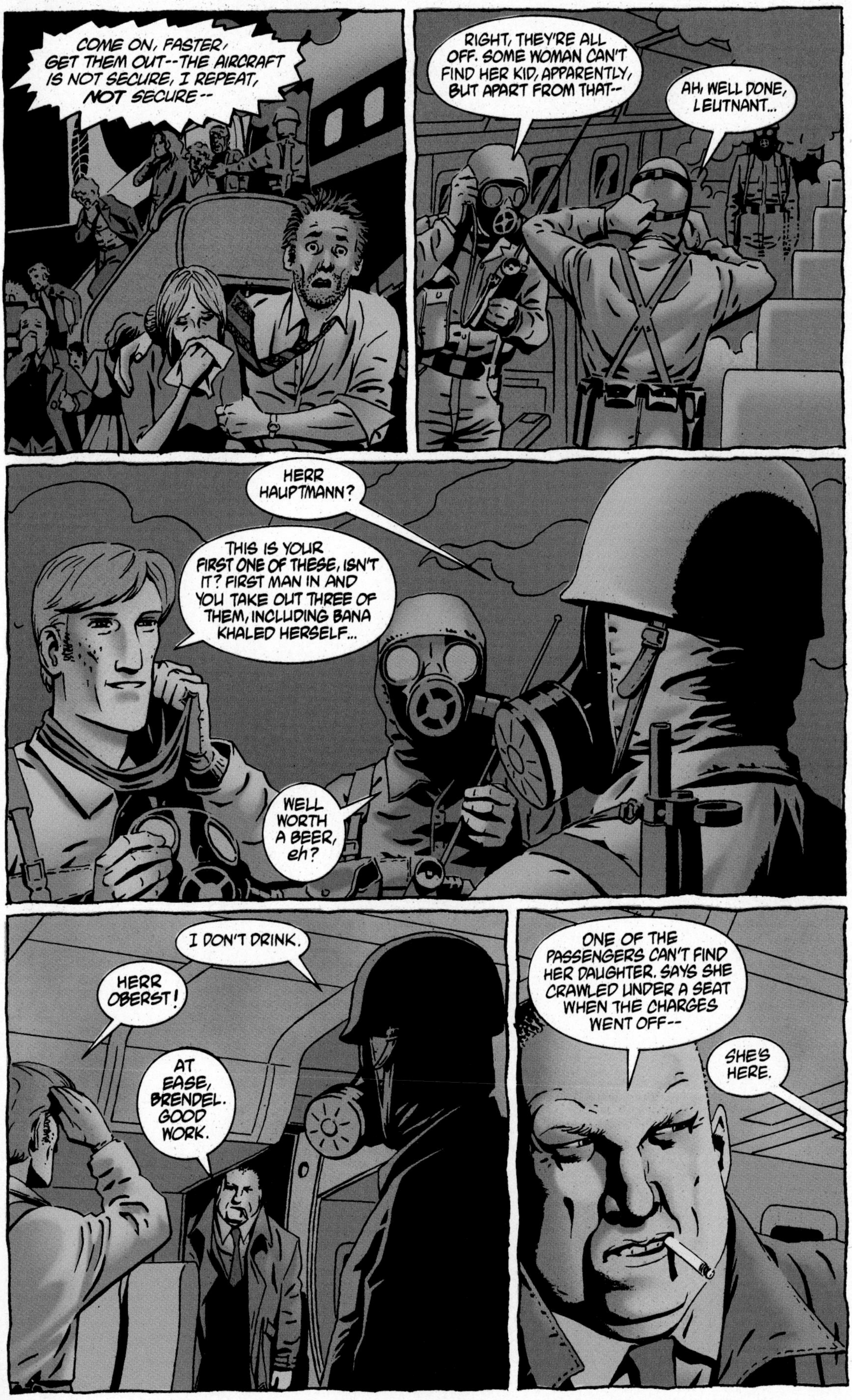
COME ON, FASTER, GET THEM OUT--THE AIRCRAFT IS NOT SECURE, I REPEAT, NOT SECURE--
RIGHT, THEY'RE ALL OFF. SOME WOMAN CAN'T FIND HER KID, APPARENTLY, BUT APART FROM THAT--
AH, WELL DONE, LEUTNANT...
HERR HAUPTMANN?
THIS IS YOUR FIRST ONE OF THESE, ISN'T IT? FIRST MAN IN AND YOU TAKE OUT THREE OF THEM, INCLUDING BANA KHALED HERSELF...
WELL WORTH A BEER, eh?
I DON'T DRINK.
HERR OBERST!
AT EASE, BRENDEL. GOOD WORK.
ONE OF THE PASSENGERS CAN'T FIND HER DAUGHTER. SAYS SHE CRAWLED UNDER A SEAT WHEN THE CHARGES WENT OFF--
SHE'S HERE.

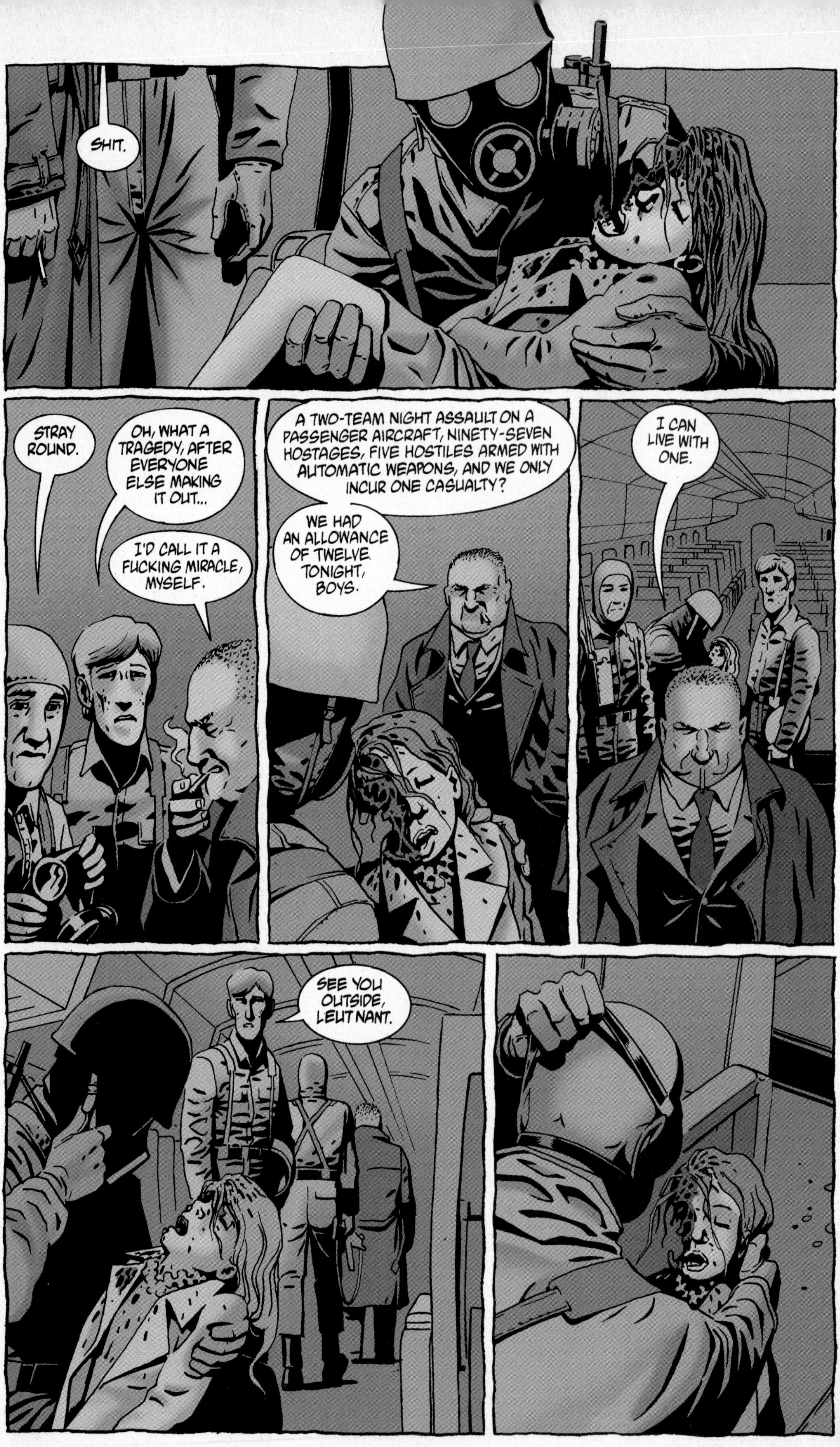
SHIT.
STRAY ROUND.
OH, WHAT A TRAGEDY, AFTER EVERYONE ELSE MAKING IT OUT...
I'D CALL IT A FUCKING MIRACLE, MYSELF.
A TWO-TEAM NIGHT ASSAULT ON A PASSENGER AIRCRAFT, NINETY-SEVEN HOSTAGES, FIVE HOSTILES ARMED WITH AUTOMATIC WEAPONS, AND WE ONLY INCUR ONE CASUALTY?
WE HAD AN ALLOWANCE OF TWELVE TONIGHT, BOYS.
I CAN LIVE WITH ONE.
SEE YOU OUTSIDE, LEUTNANT.

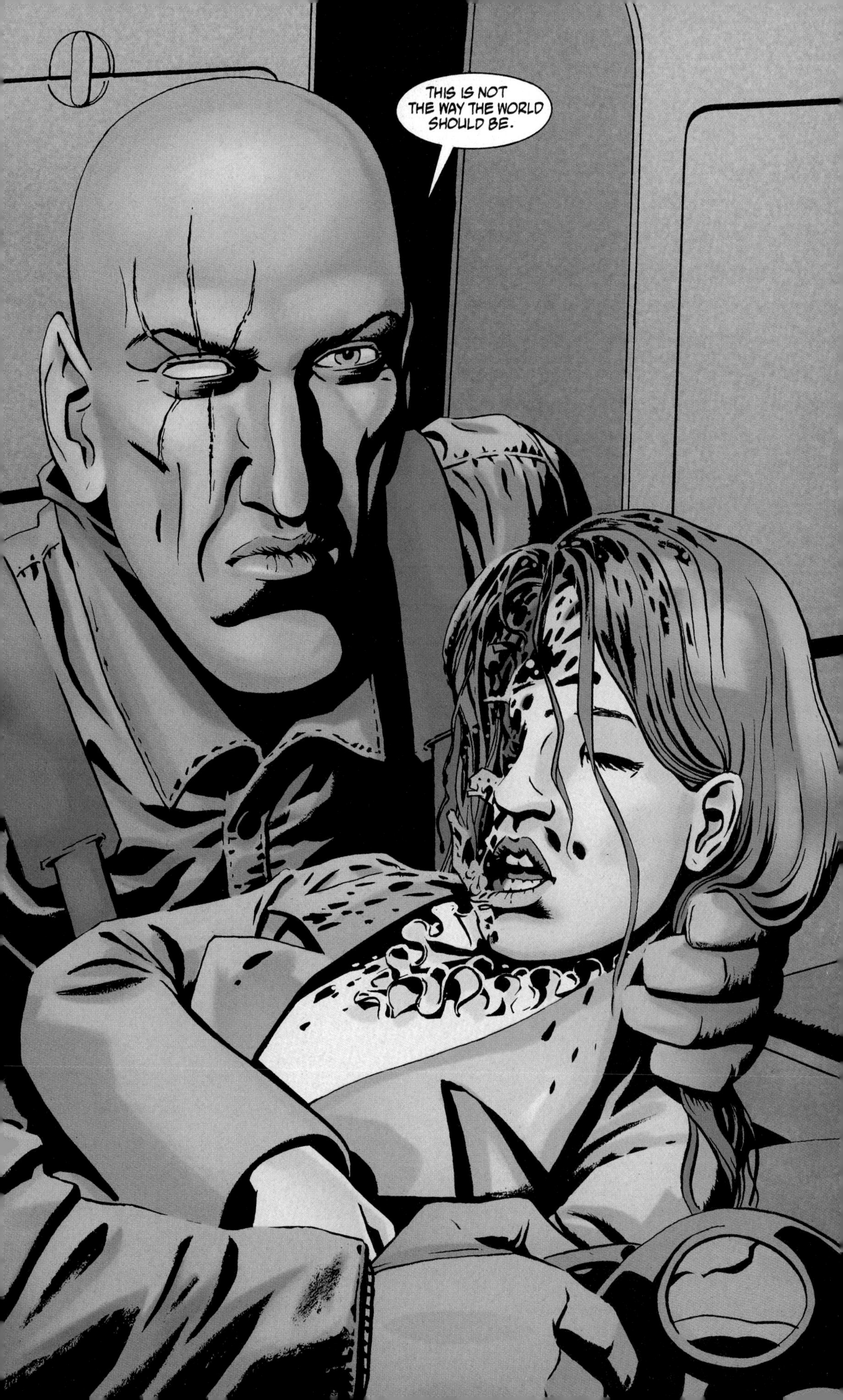
THIS IS NOT THE WAY THE WORLD SHOULD BE.

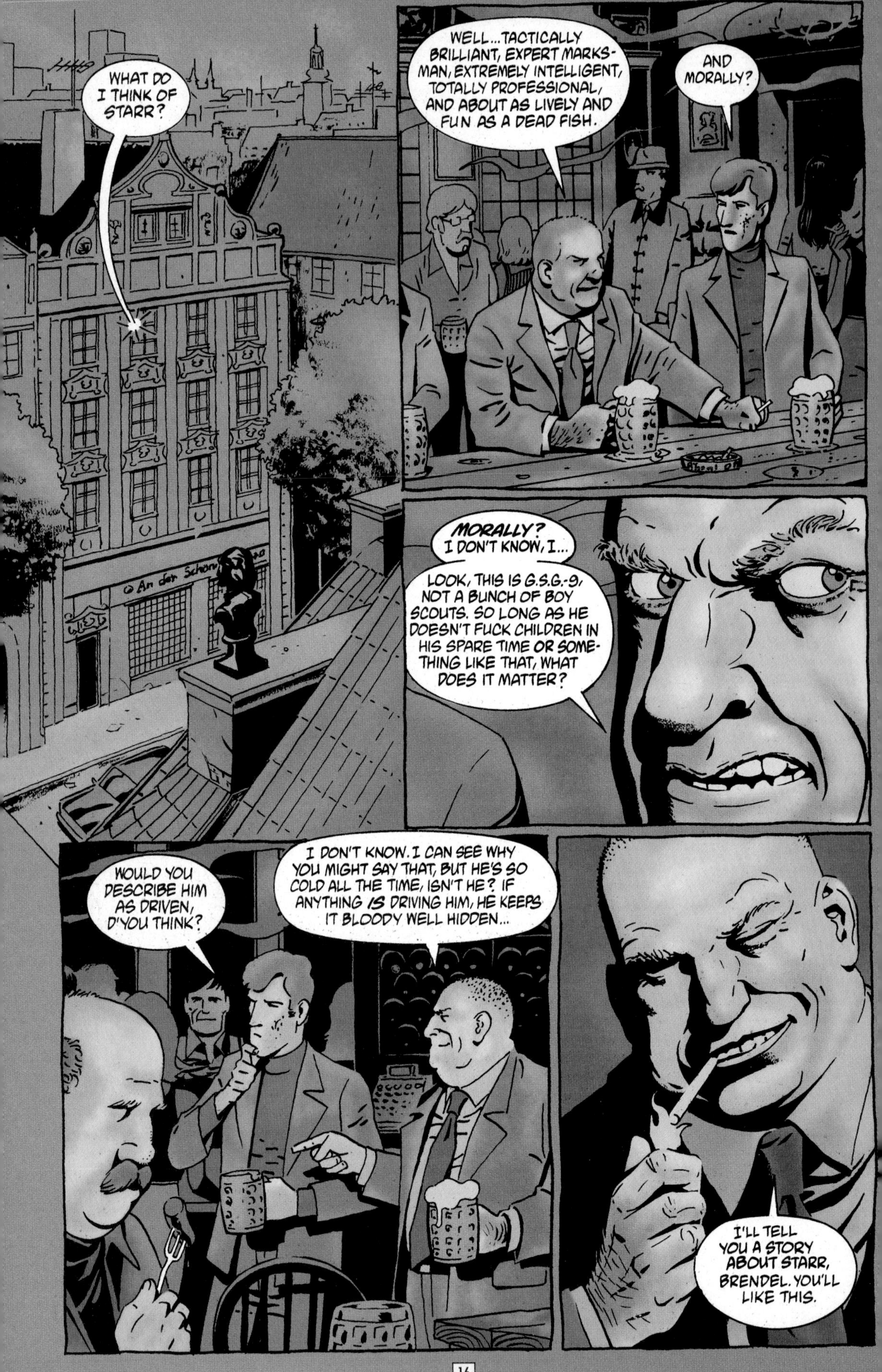
WHAT DO I THINK OF STARR?
An der Schön
WELL... TACTICALLY BRILLIANT, EXPERT MARKSMAN, EXTREMELY INTELLIGENT, TOTALLY PROFESSIONAL, AND ABOUT AS LIVELY AND FUN AS A DEAD FISH.
AND MORALLY?
MORALLY? I DON'T KNOW, I...
LOOK, THIS IS G.S.G.-9, NOT A BUNCH OF BOY SCOUTS. SO LONG AS HE DOESN'T FUCK CHILDREN IN HIS SPARE TIME OR SOMETHING LIKE THAT, WHAT DOES IT MATTER?
WOULD YOU DESCRIBE HIM AS DRIVEN, D'YOU THINK?
I DON'T KNOW. I CAN SEE WHY YOU MIGHT SAY THAT, BUT HE'S SO COLD ALL THE TIME, ISN'T HE? IF ANYTHING IS DRIVING HIM, HE KEEPS IT BLOODY WELL HIDDEN...
I'LL TELL YOU A STORY ABOUT STARR, BRENDEL. YOU'LL LIKE THIS.

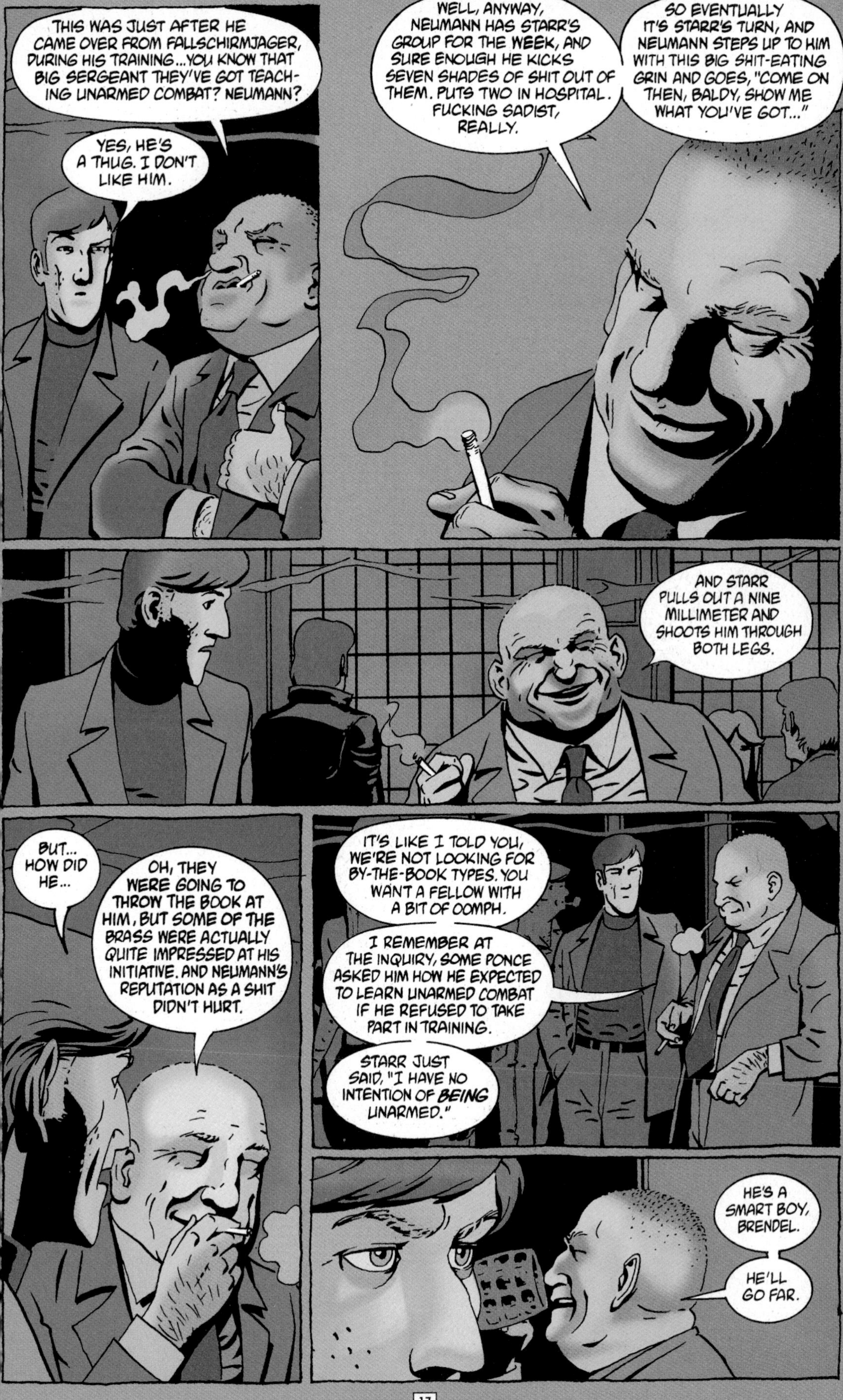
THIS WAS JUST AFTER HE CAME OVER FROM FALLSCHIRMJAGER, DURING HIS TRAINING...YOU KNOW THAT BIG SERGEANT THEY'VE GOT TEACHING UNARMED COMBAT? NEUMANN?
YES, HE'S A THUG. I DON'T LIKE HIM.
WELL, ANYWAY, NEUMANN HAS STARR'S GROUP FOR THE WEEK, AND SURE ENOUGH HE KICKS SEVEN SHADES OF SHIT OUT OF THEM. PUTS TWO IN HOSPITAL. FUCKING SADIST, REALLY.
SO EVENTUALLY IT'S STARR'S TURN, AND NEUMANN STEPS UP TO HIM WITH THIS BIG SHIT-EATING GRIN AND GOES, "COME ON THEN, BALDY, SHOW ME WHAT YOU'VE GOT..."
AND STARR PULLS OUT A NINE MILLIMETER AND SHOOTS HIM THROUGH BOTH LEGS.
BUT... HOW DID HE...
OH, THEY WERE GOING TO THROW THE BOOK AT HIM, BUT SOME OF THE BRASS WERE ACTUALLY QUITE IMPRESSED AT HIS INITIATIVE. AND NEUMANN'S REPUTATION AS A SHIT DIDN'T HURT.
IT'S LIKE I TOLD YOU, WE'RE NOT LOOKING FOR BY-THE-BOOK TYPES. YOU WANT A FELLOW WITH A BIT OF OOMPH.
I REMEMBER AT THE INQUIRY, SOME PONCE ASKED HIM HOW HE EXPECTED TO LEARN UNARMED COMBAT IF HE REFUSED TO TAKE PART IN TRAINING.
STARR JUST SAID, "I HAVE NO INTENTION OF BEING UNARMED."
HE'S A SMART BOY, BRENDEL.
HE'LL GO FAR.

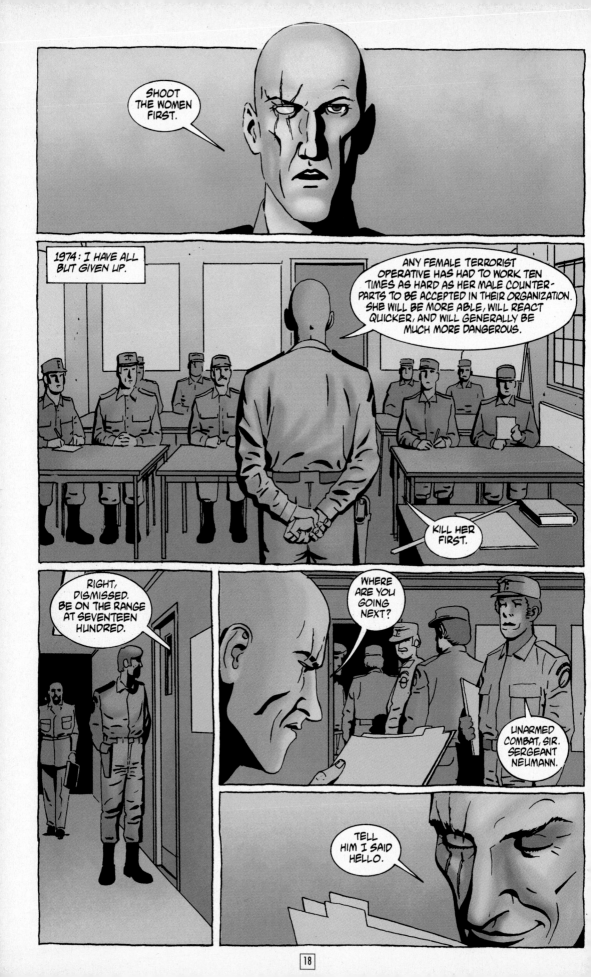

SHOOT THE WOMEN FIRST.

1974: I HAVE ALL BUT GIVEN UP.

ANY FEMALE TERRORIST OPERATIVE HAS HAD TO WORK TEN TIMES AS HARD AS HER MALE COUNTER-PARTS TO BE ACCEPTED IN THEIR ORGANIZATION. SHE WILL BE MORE ABLE, WILL REACT QUICKER, AND WILL GENERALLY BE MUCH MORE DANGEROUS.

KILL HER FIRST.

RIGHT, DISMISSED. BE ON THE RANGE AT SEVENTEEN HUNDRED.

WHERE ARE YOU GOING NEXT?

UNARMED COMBAT, SIR. SERGEANT NEUMANN.

TELL HIM I SAID HELLO.

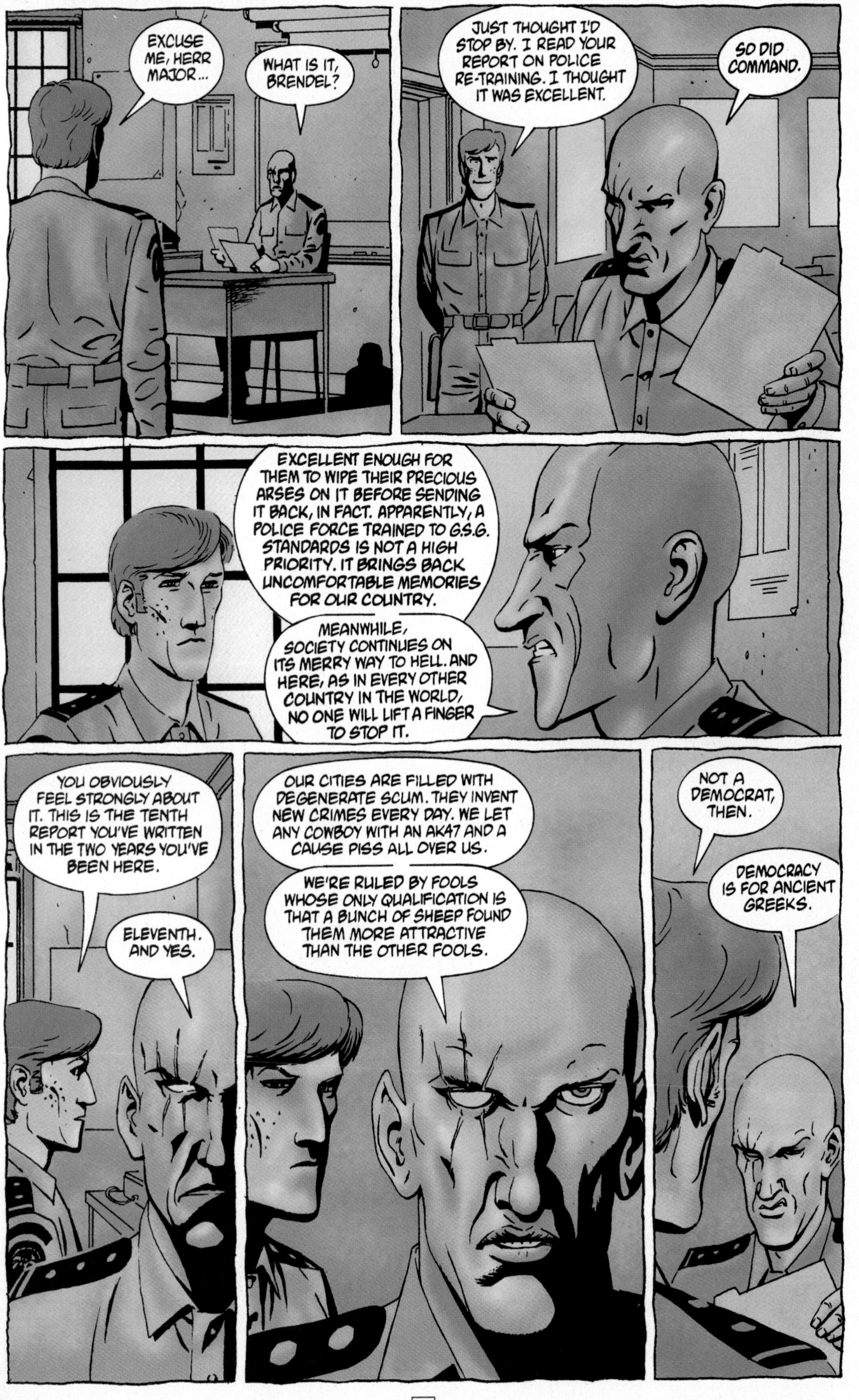
EXCUSE ME, HERR MAJOR...
WHAT IS IT, BRENDEL?
JUST THOUGHT I'D STOP BY. I READ YOUR REPORT ON POLICE RE-TRAINING. I THOUGHT IT WAS EXCELLENT.
SO DID COMMAND.
EXCELLENT ENOUGH FOR THEM TO WIPE THEIR PRECIOUS ARSES ON IT BEFORE SENDING IT BACK, IN FACT. APPARENTLY, A POLICE FORCE TRAINED TO G.S.G. STANDARDS IS NOT A HIGH PRIORITY. IT BRINGS BACK UNCOMFORTABLE MEMORIES FOR OUR COUNTRY.
MEANWHILE, SOCIETY CONTINUES ON ITS MERRY WAY TO HELL. AND HERE, AS IN EVERY OTHER COUNTRY IN THE WORLD, NO ONE WILL LIFT A FINGER TO STOP IT.
YOU OBVIOUSLY FEEL STRONGLY ABOUT IT. THIS IS THE TENTH REPORT YOU'VE WRITTEN IN THE TWO YEARS YOU'VE BEEN HERE.
ELEVENTH. AND YES.
OUR CITIES ARE FILLED WITH DEGENERATE SCUM. THEY INVENT NEW CRIMES EVERY DAY. WE LET ANY COWBOY WITH AN AK47 AND A CAUSE PISS ALL OVER US.
WE'RE RULED BY FOOLS WHOSE ONLY QUALIFICATION IS THAT A BUNCH OF SHEEP FOUND THEM MORE ATTRACTIVE THAN THE OTHER FOOLS.
NOT A DEMOCRAT, THEN.
DEMOCRACY IS FOR ANCIENT GREEKS.

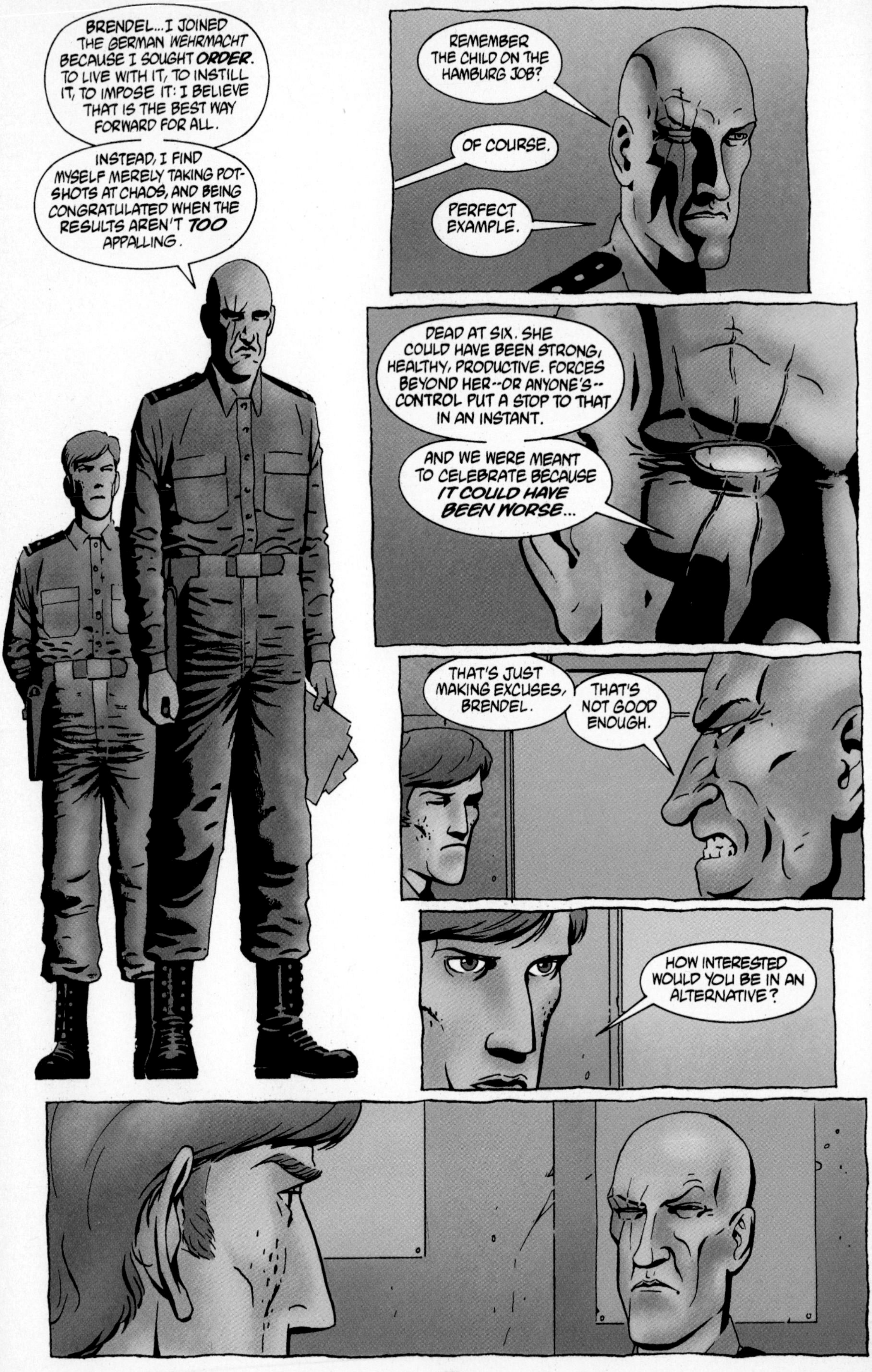
BRENDEL... I JOINED THE GERMAN WEHRMACHT BECAUSE I SOUGHT ORDER. TO LIVE WITH IT, TO INSTILL IT, TO IMPOSE IT: I BELIEVE THAT IS THE BEST WAY FORWARD FOR ALL.
INSTEAD, I FIND MYSELF MERELY TAKING POT-SHOTS AT CHAOS, AND BEING CONGRATULATED WHEN THE RESULTS AREN'T TOO APPALLING.
REMEMBER THE CHILD ON THE HAMBURG JOB?
OF COURSE.
PERFECT EXAMPLE.
DEAD AT SIX. SHE COULD HAVE BEEN STRONG, HEALTHY, PRODUCTIVE. FORCES BEYOND HER--OR ANYONE'S--CONTROL PUT A STOP TO THAT IN AN INSTANT.
AND WE WERE MEANT TO CELEBRATE BECAUSE IT COULD HAVE BEEN WORSE...
THAT'S JUST MAKING EXCUSES, BRENDEL.
THAT'S NOT GOOD ENOUGH.
HOW INTERESTED WOULD YOU BE IN AN ALTERNATIVE?

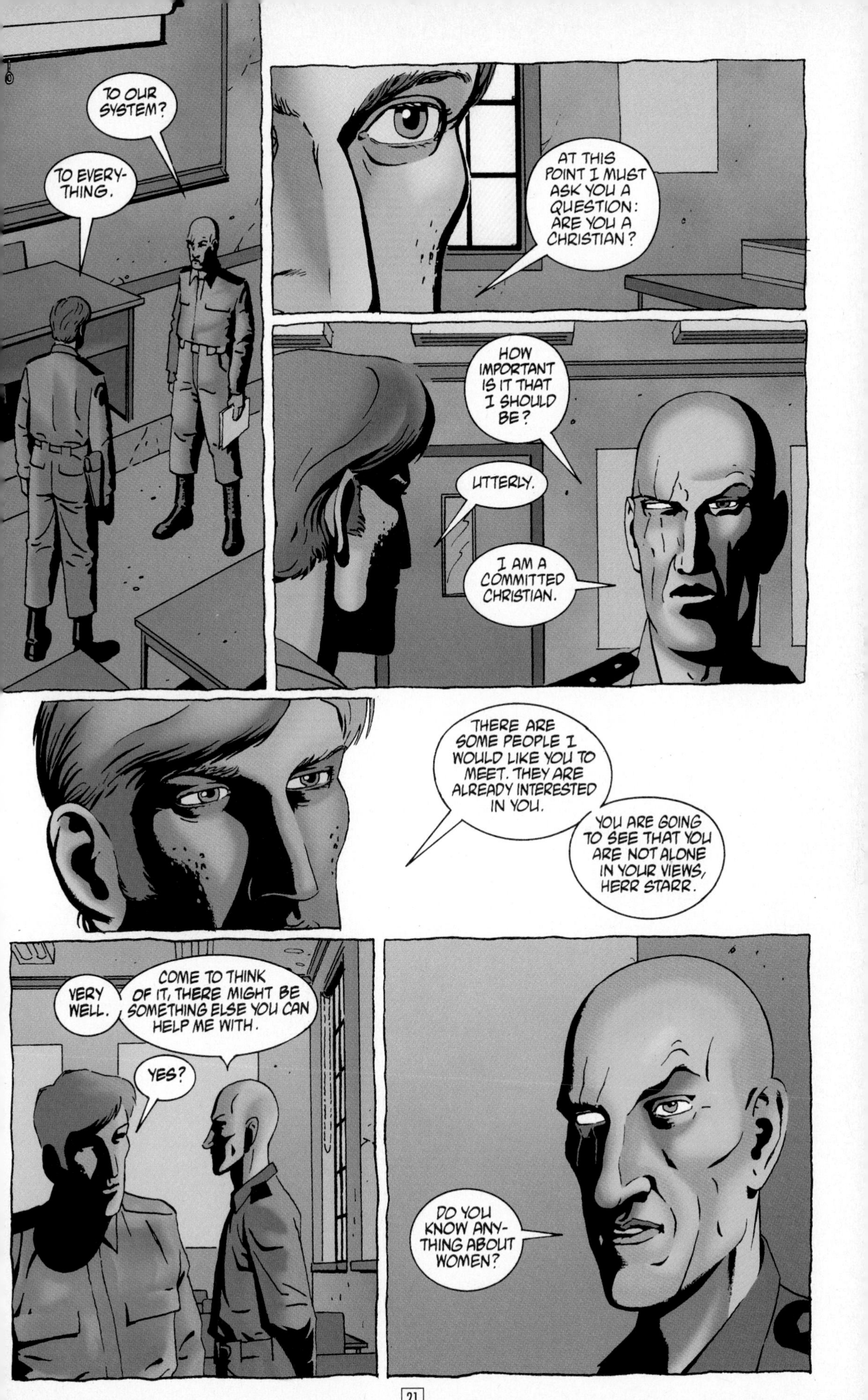
TO OUR SYSTEM?
TO EVERYTHING.
AT THIS POINT I MUST ASK YOU A QUESTION: ARE YOU A CHRISTIAN?
HOW IMPORTANT IS IT THAT I SHOULD BE?
UTTERLY.
I AM A COMMITTED CHRISTIAN.
THERE ARE SOME PEOPLE I WOULD LIKE YOU TO MEET. THEY ARE ALREADY INTERESTED IN YOU.
YOU ARE GOING TO SEE THAT YOU ARE NOT ALONE IN YOUR VIEWS, HERR STARR.
VERY WELL.
COME TO THINK OF IT, THERE MIGHT BE SOMETHING ELSE YOU CAN HELP ME WITH.
YES?
DO YOU KNOW ANYTHING ABOUT WOMEN?

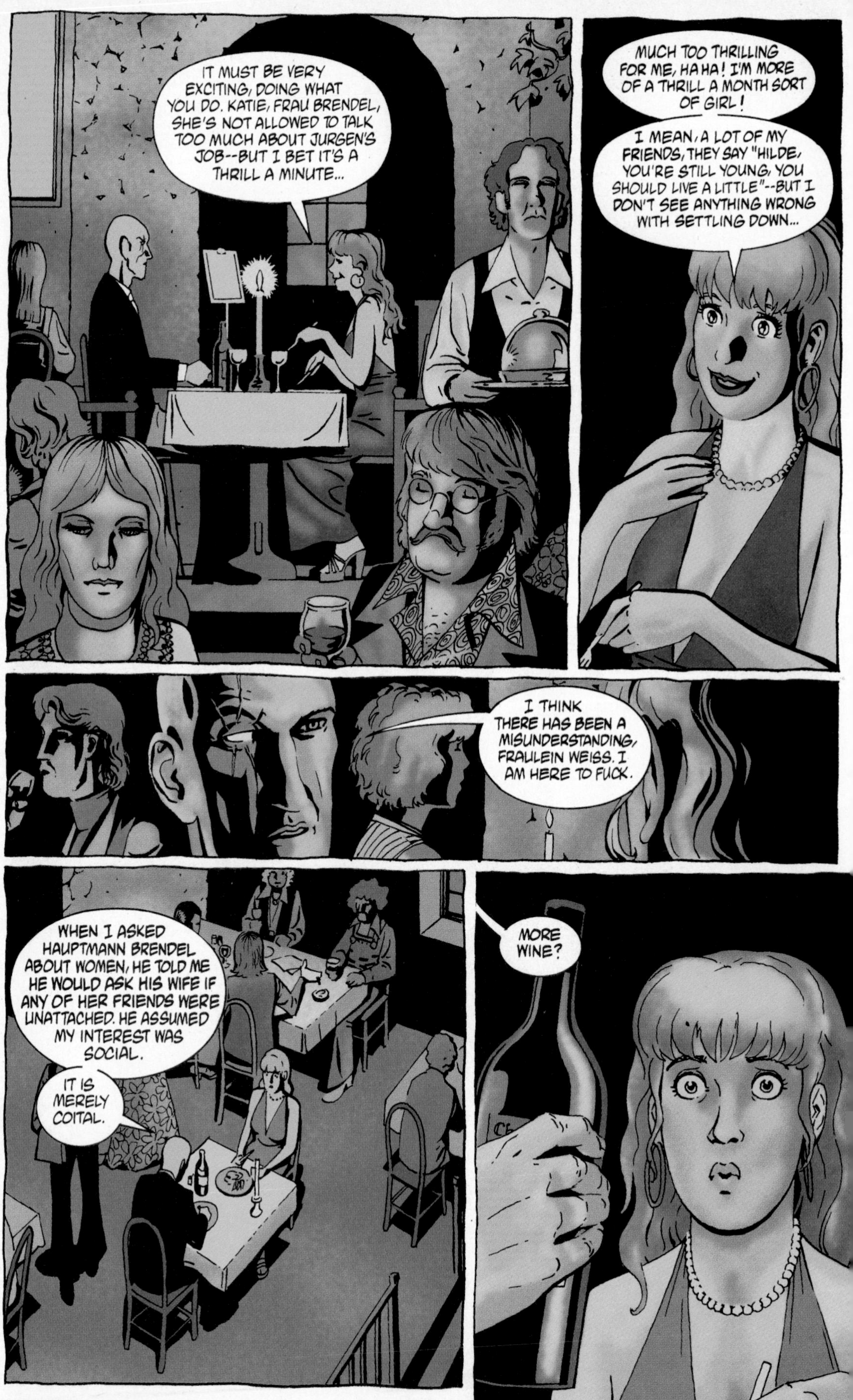
IT MUST BE VERY EXCITING, DOING WHAT YOU DO. KATIE, FRAU BRENDEL, SHE'S NOT ALLOWED TO TALK TOO MUCH ABOUT JURGEN'S JOB--BUT I BET IT'S A THRILL A MINUTE...
MUCH TOO THRILLING FOR ME, HA HA! I'M MORE OF A THRILL A MONTH SORT OF GIRL!
I MEAN, A LOT OF MY FRIENDS, THEY SAY "HILDE, YOU'RE STILL YOUNG, YOU SHOULD LIVE A LITTLE"--BUT I DON'T SEE ANYTHING WRONG WITH SETTLING DOWN...
I THINK THERE HAS BEEN A MISUNDERSTANDING, FRAULEIN WEISS. I AM HERE TO FUCK.
WHEN I ASKED HAUPTMANN BRENDEL ABOUT WOMEN, HE TOLD ME HE WOULD ASK HIS WIFE IF ANY OF HER FRIENDS WERE UNATTACHED. HE ASSUMED MY INTEREST WAS SOCIAL.
IT IS MERELY COITAL.
MORE WINE?

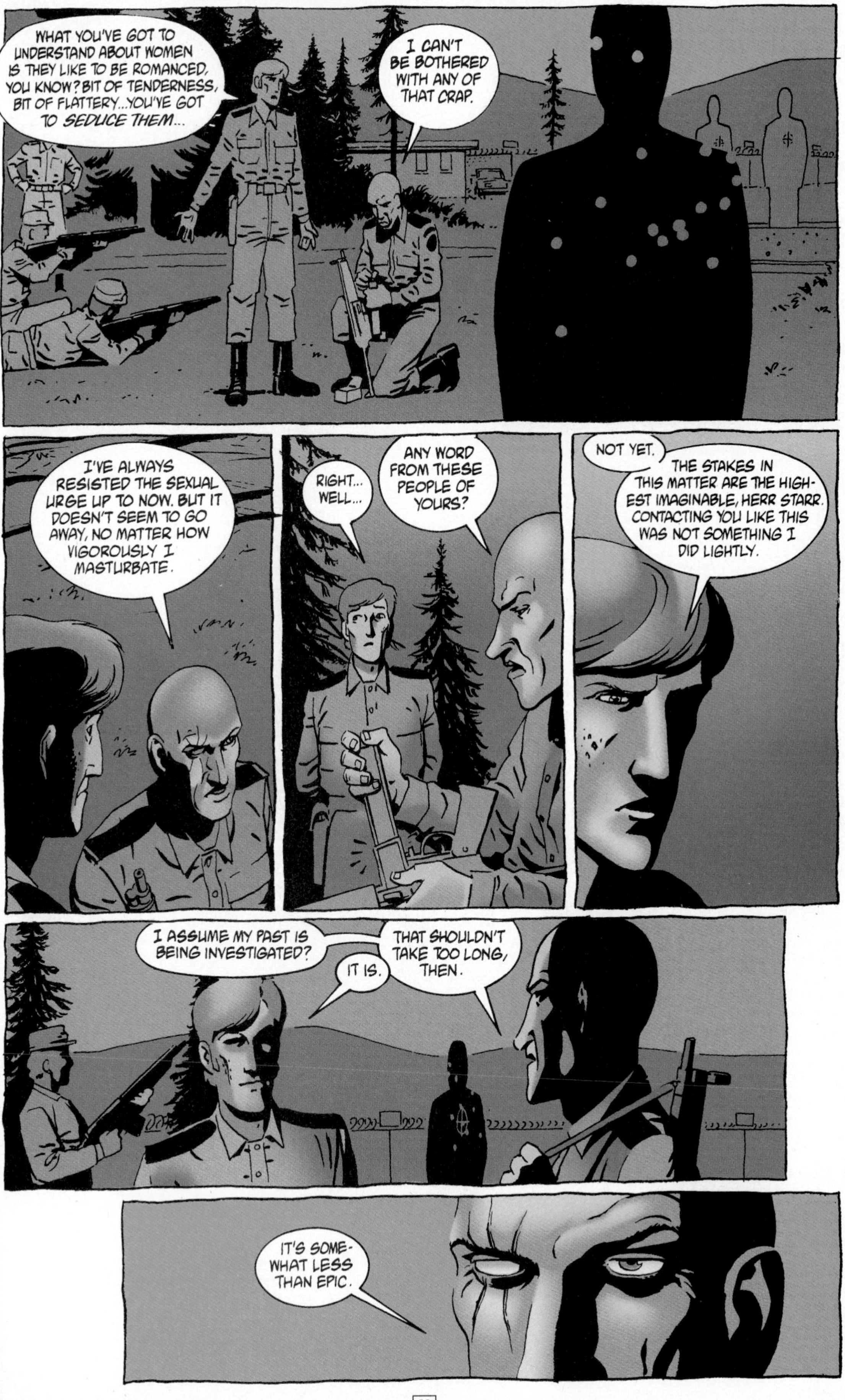
WHAT YOU'VE GOT TO UNDERSTAND ABOUT WOMEN IS THEY LIKE TO BE ROMANCED, YOU KNOW? BIT OF TENDERNESS, BIT OF FLATTERY... YOU'VE GOT TO SEDUCE THEM...
I CAN'T BE BOTHERED WITH ANY OF THAT CRAP.
I'VE ALWAYS RESISTED THE SEXUAL URGE UP TO NOW. BUT IT DOESN'T SEEM TO GO AWAY, NO MATTER HOW VIGOROUSLY I MASTURBATE.
RIGHT... WELL...
ANY WORD FROM THESE PEOPLE OF YOURS?
NOT YET.
THE STAKES IN THIS MATTER ARE THE HIGHEST IMAGINABLE, HERR STARR. CONTACTING YOU LIKE THIS WAS NOT SOMETHING I DID LIGHTLY.
I ASSUME MY PAST IS BEING INVESTIGATED?
IT IS.
THAT SHOULDN'T TAKE TOO LONG, THEN.
IT'S SOMEWHAT LESS THAN EPIC.

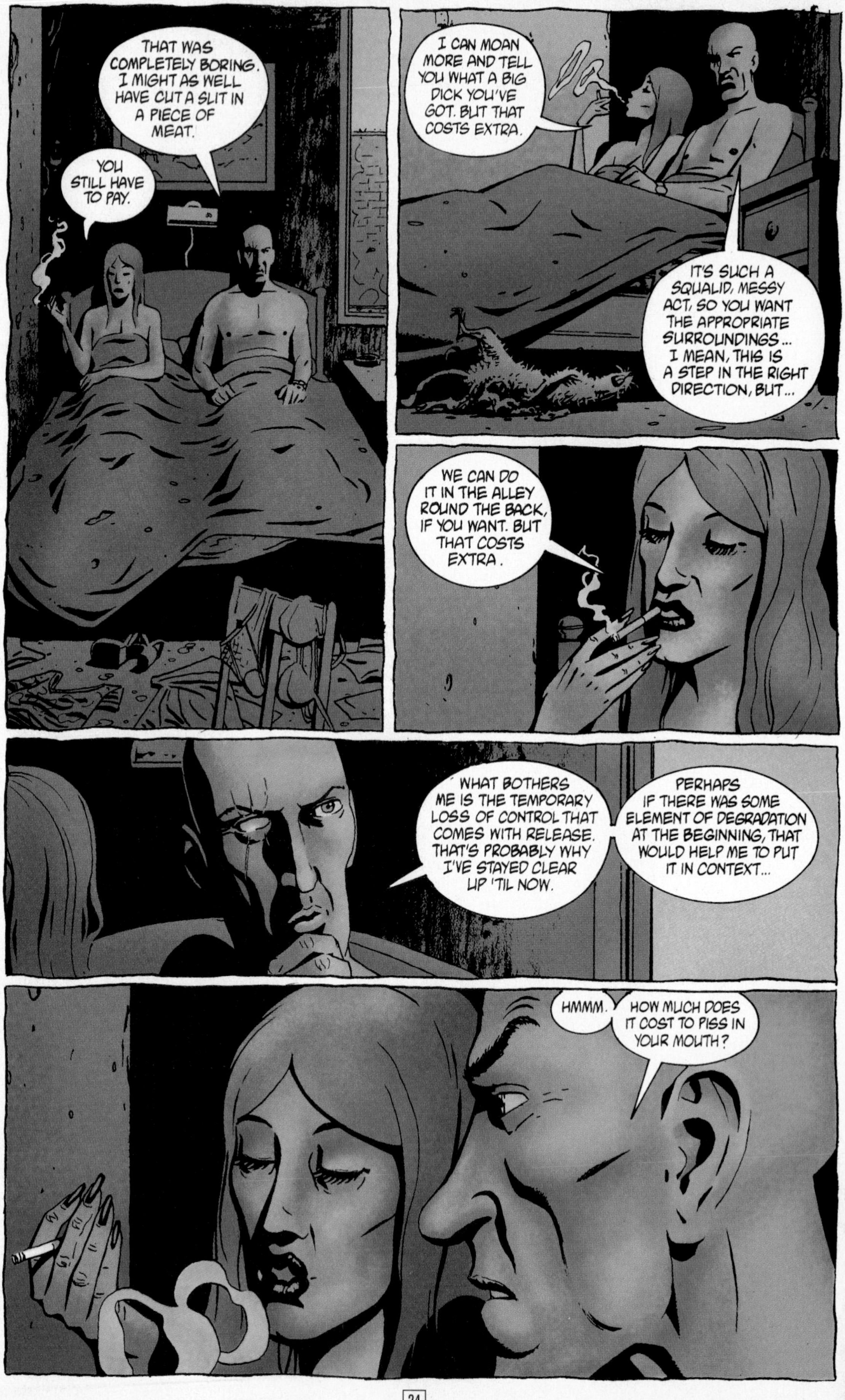
THAT WAS COMPLETELY BORING. I MIGHT AS WELL HAVE CUT A SLIT IN A PIECE OF MEAT.
YOU STILL HAVE TO PAY.
I CAN MOAN MORE AND TELL YOU WHAT A BIG DICK YOU'VE GOT. BUT THAT COSTS EXTRA.
IT'S SUCH A SQUALID, MESSY ACT, SO YOU WANT THE APPROPRIATE SURROUNDINGS... I MEAN, THIS IS A STEP IN THE RIGHT DIRECTION, BUT...
WE CAN DO IT IN THE ALLEY ROUND THE BACK, IF YOU WANT. BUT THAT COSTS EXTRA.
WHAT BOTHERS ME IS THE TEMPORARY LOSS OF CONTROL THAT COMES WITH RELEASE. THAT'S PROBABLY WHY I'VE STAYED CLEAR UP 'TIL NOW.
PERHAPS IF THERE WAS SOME ELEMENT OF DEGRADATION AT THE BEGINNING, THAT WOULD HELP ME TO PUT IT IN CONTEXT...
HMMM.
HOW MUCH DOES IT COST TO PISS IN YOUR MOUTH?

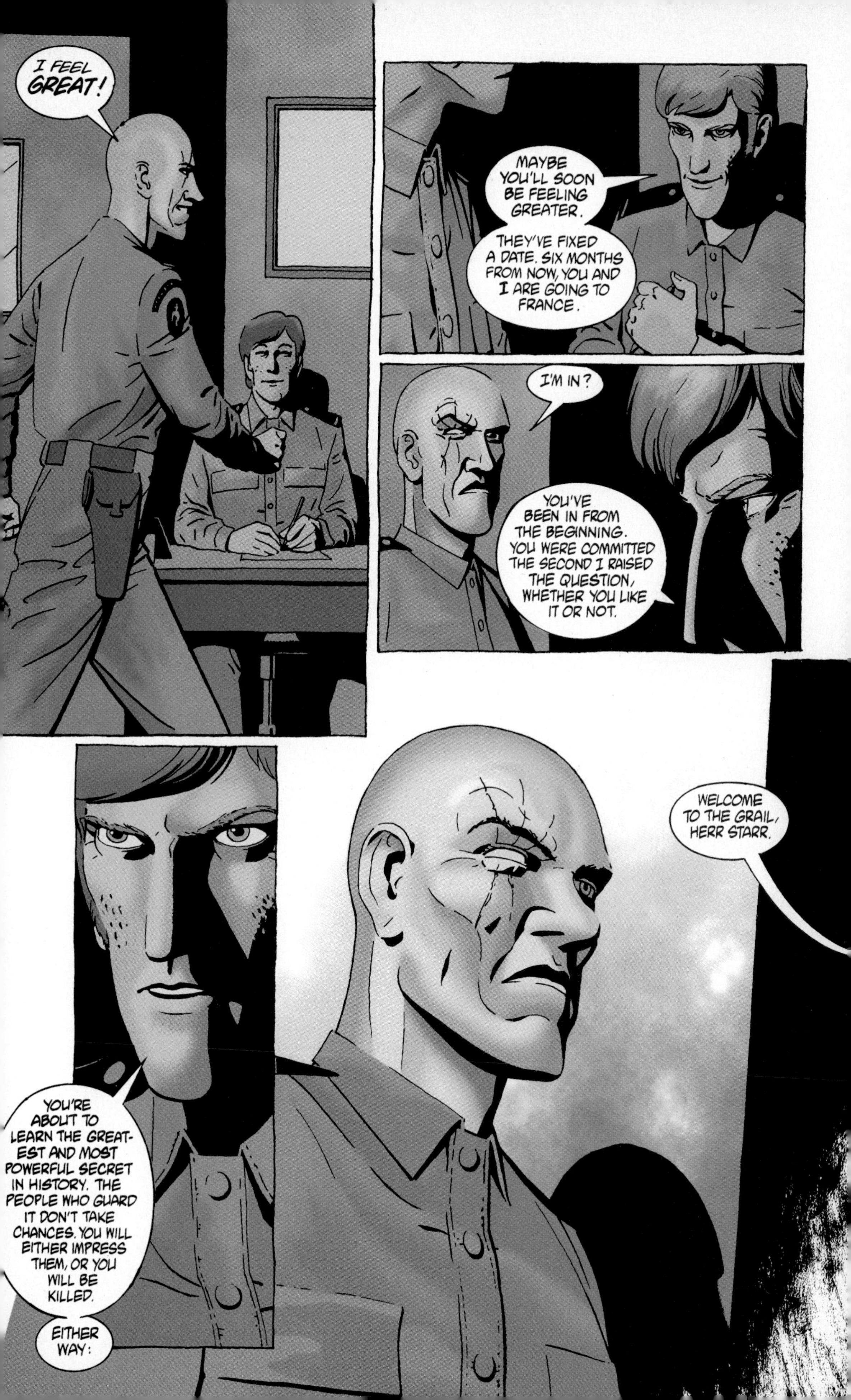

I FEEL GREAT!
MAYBE YOU'LL SOON BE FEELING GREATER.
THEY'VE FIXED A DATE. SIX MONTHS FROM NOW, YOU AND I ARE GOING TO FRANCE.
I'M IN?
YOU'VE BEEN IN FROM THE BEGINNING. YOU WERE COMMITTED THE SECOND I RAISED THE QUESTION, WHETHER YOU LIKE IT OR NOT.
YOU'RE ABOUT TO LEARN THE GREATEST AND MOST POWERFUL SECRET IN HISTORY. THE PEOPLE WHO GUARD IT DON'T TAKE CHANCES. YOU WILL EITHER IMPRESS THEM, OR YOU WILL BE KILLED.
EITHER WAY:
WELCOME TO THE GRAIL, HERR STARR.

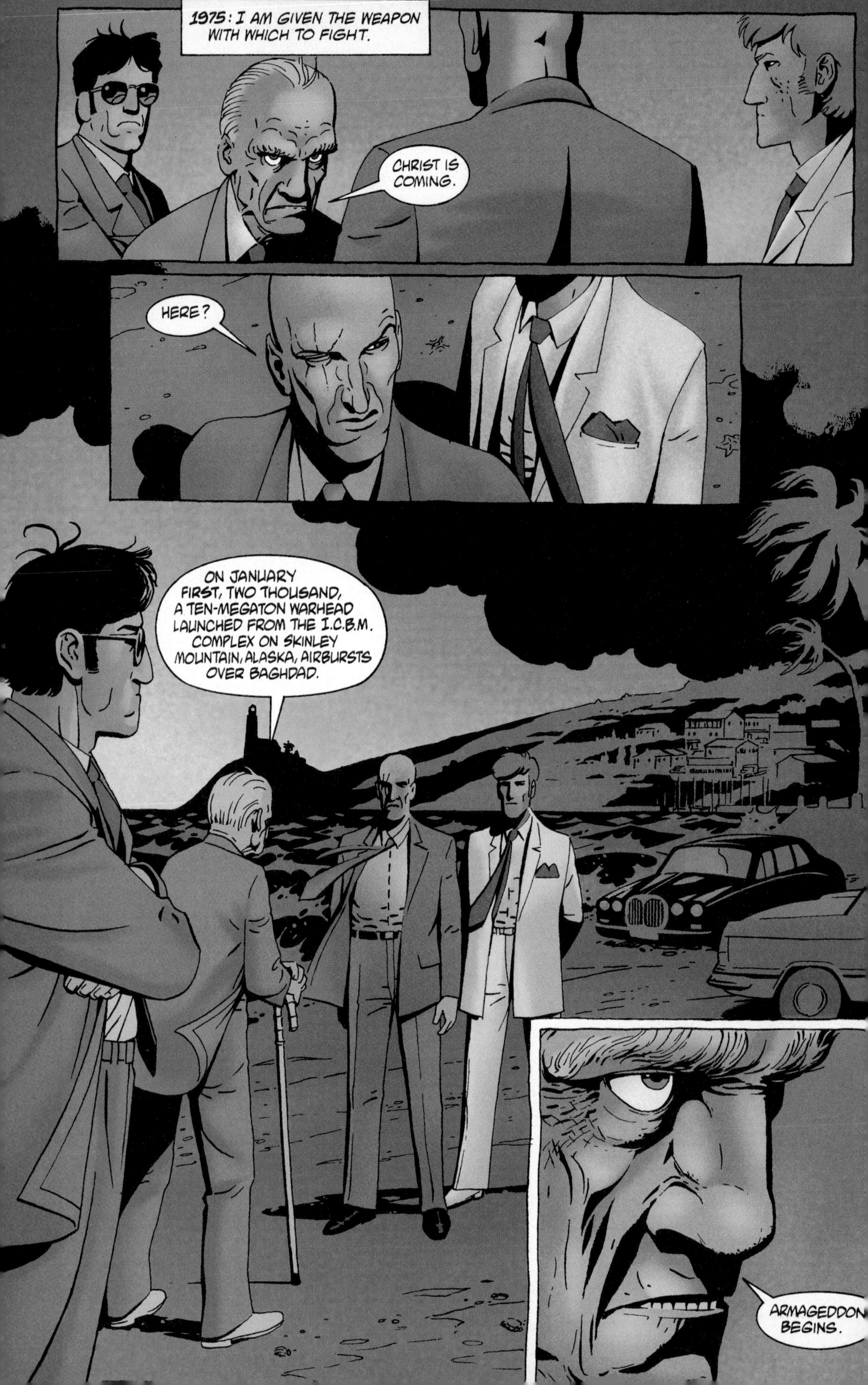
1975: I AM GIVEN THE WEAPON WITH WHICH TO FIGHT.
CHRIST IS COMING.
HERE?
ON JANUARY FIRST, TWO THOUSAND, A TEN-MEGATON WARHEAD LAUNCHED FROM THE I.C.B.M. COMPLEX ON SKINLEY MOUNTAIN, ALASKA, AIRBURSTS OVER BAGHDAD.
ARMAGEDDON BEGINS.

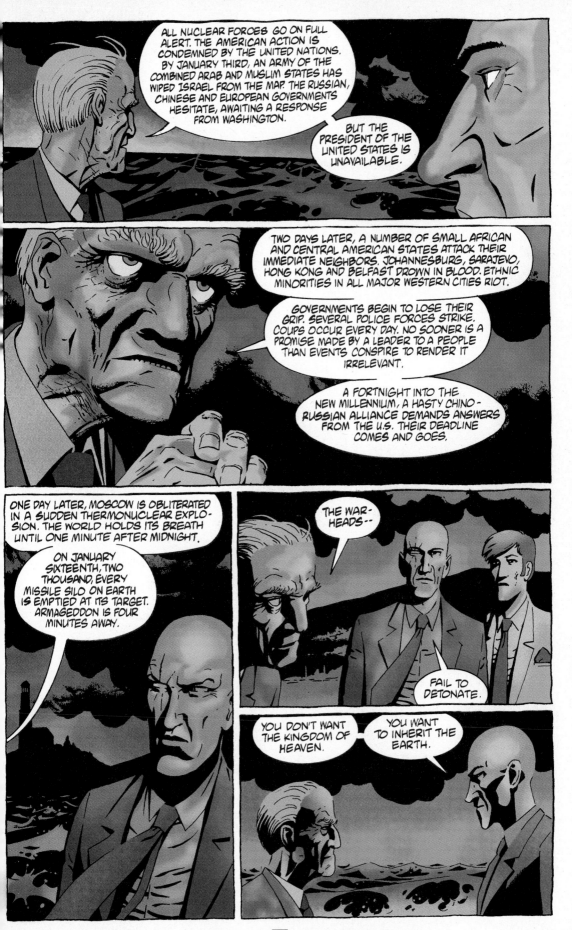

ALL NUCLEAR FORCES GO ON FULL ALERT. THE AMERICAN ACTION IS CONDEMNED BY THE UNITED NATIONS. BY JANUARY THIRD, AN ARMY OF THE COMBINED ARAB AND MUSLIM STATES HAS WIPED ISRAEL FROM THE MAP. THE RUSSIAN, CHINESE AND EUROPEAN GOVERNMENTS HESITATE, AWAITING A RESPONSE FROM WASHINGTON.

BUT THE PRESIDENT OF THE UNITED STATES IS UNAVAILABLE.

TWO DAYS LATER, A NUMBER OF SMALL AFRICAN AND CENTRAL AMERICAN STATES ATTACK THEIR IMMEDIATE NEIGHBORS. JOHANNESBURG, SARAJEVO, HONG KONG AND BELFAST DROWN IN BLOOD. ETHNIC MINORITIES IN ALL MAJOR WESTERN CITIES RIOT.

GOVERNMENTS BEGIN TO LOSE THEIR GRIP. SEVERAL POLICE FORCES STRIKE. COUPS OCCUR EVERY DAY. NO SOONER IS A PROMISE MADE BY A LEADER TO A PEOPLE THAN EVENTS CONSPIRE TO RENDER IT IRRELEVANT.

A FORTNIGHT INTO THE NEW MILLENNIUM, A HASTY CHINO-RUSSIAN ALLIANCE DEMANDS ANSWERS FROM THE U.S. THEIR DEADLINE COMES AND GOES.

ONE DAY LATER, MOSCOW IS OBLITERATED IN A SUDDEN THERMONUCLEAR EXPLOSION. THE WORLD HOLDS ITS BREATH UNTIL ONE MINUTE AFTER MIDNIGHT.

ON JANUARY SIXTEENTH, TWO THOUSAND, EVERY MISSILE SILO ON EARTH IS EMPTIED AT ITS TARGET. ARMAGEDDON IS FOUR MINUTES AWAY.

THE WAR-HEADS--

FAIL TO DETONATE.

YOU DON'T WANT THE KINGDOM OF HEAVEN.

YOU WANT TO INHERIT THE EARTH.

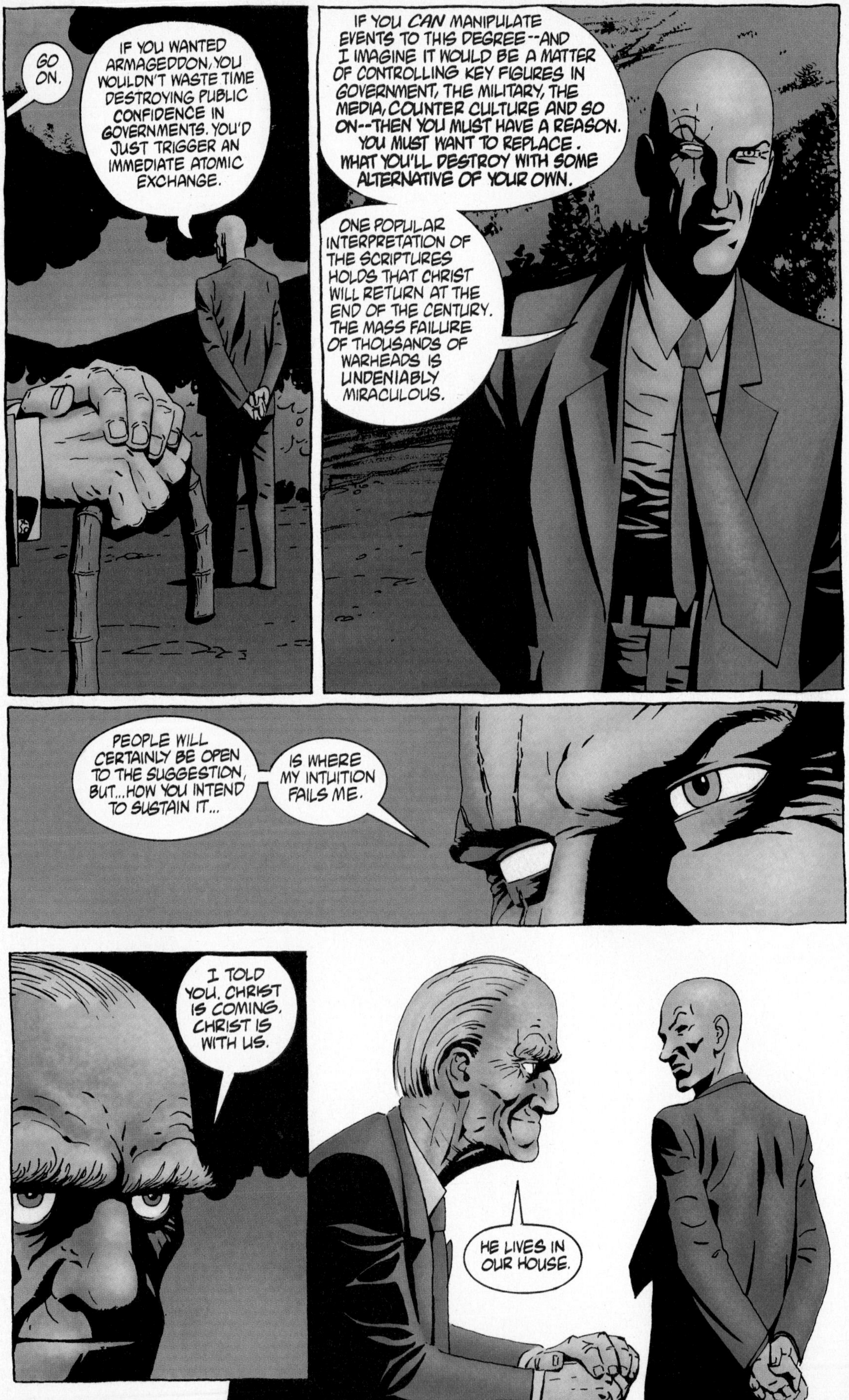
GO ON.
IF YOU WANTED ARMAGEDDON, YOU WOULDN'T WASTE TIME DESTROYING PUBLIC CONFIDENCE IN GOVERNMENTS. YOU'D JUST TRIGGER AN IMMEDIATE ATOMIC EXCHANGE.
IF YOU CAN MANIPULATE EVENTS TO THIS DEGREE--AND I IMAGINE IT WOULD BE A MATTER OF CONTROLLING KEY FIGURES IN GOVERNMENT, THE MILITARY, THE MEDIA, COUNTER CULTURE AND SO ON--THEN YOU MUST HAVE A REASON. YOU MUST WANT TO REPLACE . WHAT YOU'LL DESTROY WITH SOME ALTERNATIVE OF YOUR OWN.
ONE POPULAR INTERPRETATION OF THE SCRIPTURES HOLDS THAT CHRIST WILL RETURN AT THE END OF THE CENTURY. THE MASS FAILURE OF THOUSANDS OF WARHEADS IS UNDENIABLY MIRACULOUS.
PEOPLE WILL CERTAINLY BE OPEN TO THE SUGGESTION, BUT...HOW YOU INTEND TO SUSTAIN IT...
IS WHERE MY INTUITION FAILS ME.
I TOLD YOU. CHRIST IS COMING. CHRIST IS WITH US.
HE LIVES IN OUR HOUSE.

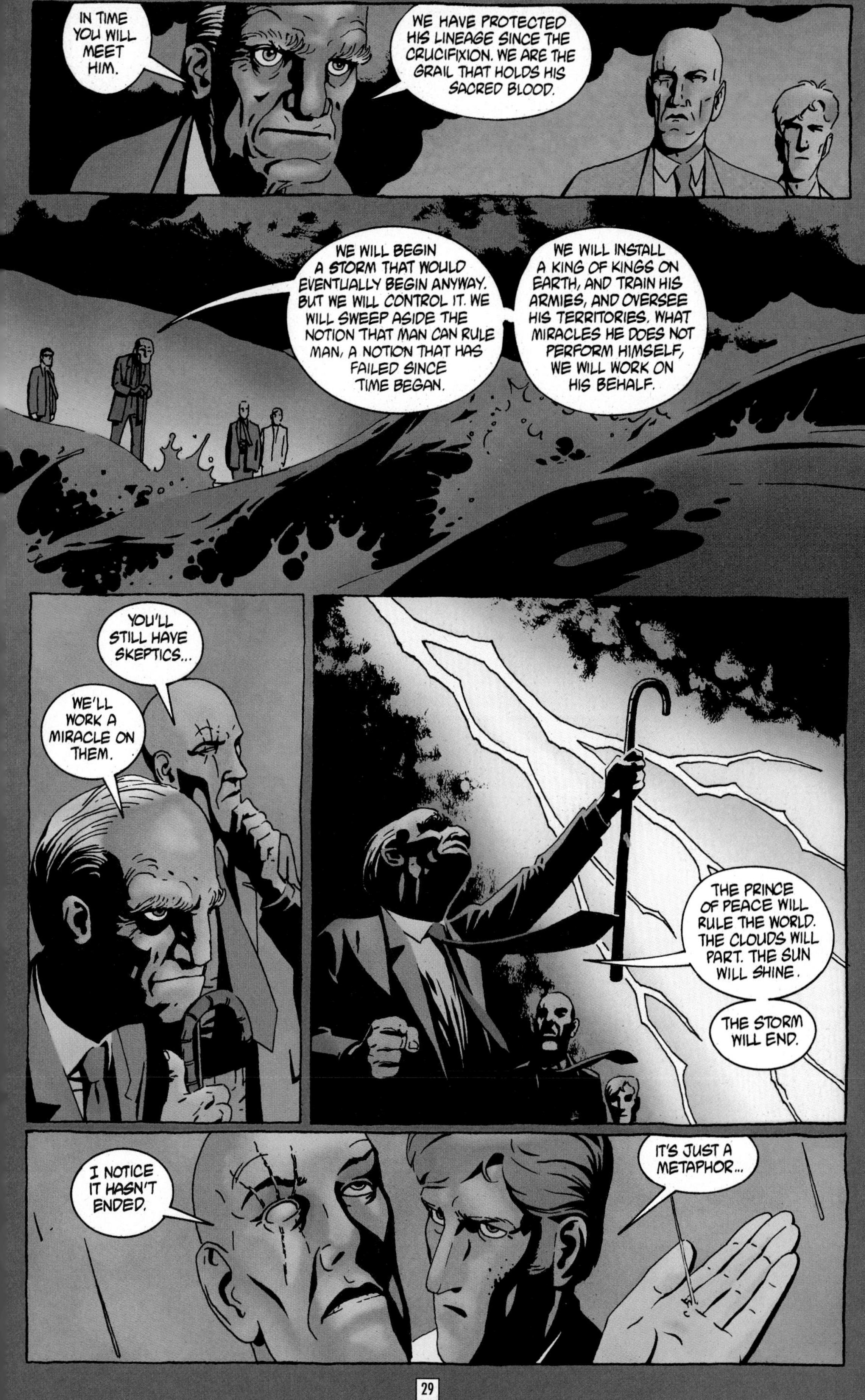
IN TIME YOU WILL MEET HIM.
WE HAVE PROTECTED HIS LINEAGE SINCE THE CRUCIFIXION. WE ARE THE GRAIL THAT HOLDS HIS SACRED BLOOD.
WE WILL BEGIN A STORM THAT WOULD EVENTUALLY BEGIN ANYWAY. BUT WE WILL CONTROL IT. WE WILL SWEEP ASIDE THE NOTION THAT MAN CAN RULE MAN, A NOTION THAT HAS FAILED SINCE TIME BEGAN.
WE WILL INSTALL A KING OF KINGS ON EARTH, AND TRAIN HIS ARMIES, AND OVERSEE HIS TERRITORIES. WHAT MIRACLES HE DOES NOT PERFORM HIMSELF, WE WILL WORK ON HIS BEHALF.
YOU'LL STILL HAVE SKEPTICS...
WE'LL WORK A MIRACLE ON THEM.
THE PRINCE OF PEACE WILL RULE THE WORLD. THE CLOUDS WILL PART. THE SUN WILL SHINE.
THE STORM WILL END.
I NOTICE IT HASN'T ENDED.
IT'S JUST A METAPHOR...

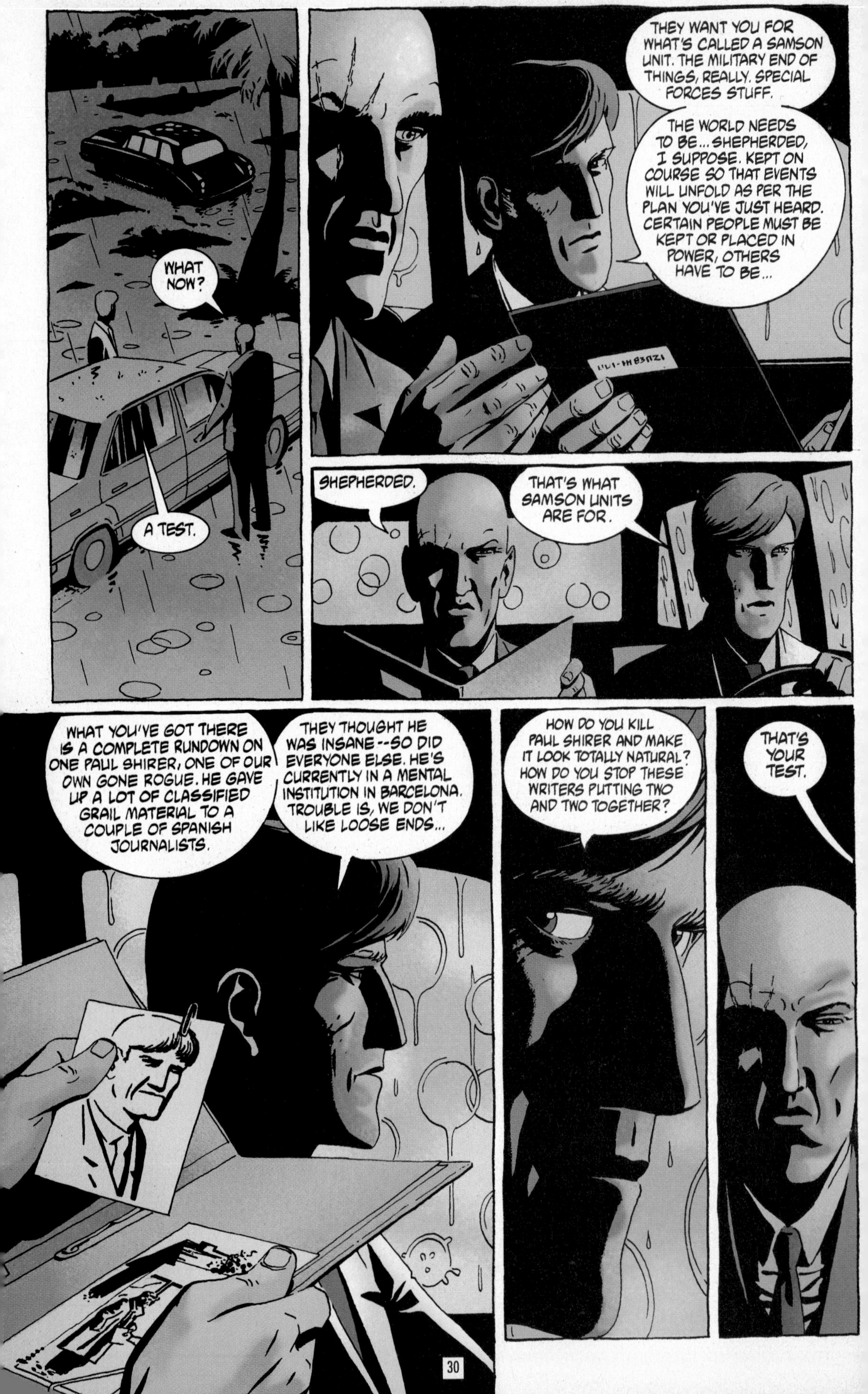

THEY WANT YOU FOR WHAT'S CALLED A SAMSON UNIT. THE MILITARY END OF THINGS, REALLY. SPECIAL FORCES STUFF.
THE WORLD NEEDS TO BE... SHEPHERDED, I SUPPOSE. KEPT ON COURSE SO THAT EVENTS WILL UNFOLD AS PER THE PLAN YOU'VE JUST HEARD. CERTAIN PEOPLE MUST BE KEPT OR PLACED IN POWER, OTHERS HAVE TO BE...
WHAT NOW?
A TEST.
SHEPHERDED.
THAT'S WHAT SAMSON UNITS ARE FOR.
WHAT YOU'VE GOT THERE IS A COMPLETE RUNDOWN ON ONE PAUL SHIRER, ONE OF OUR OWN GONE ROGUE. HE GAVE UP A LOT OF CLASSIFIED GRAIL MATERIAL TO A COUPLE OF SPANISH JOURNALISTS.
THEY THOUGHT HE WAS INSANE--SO DID EVERYONE ELSE. HE'S CURRENTLY IN A MENTAL INSTITUTION IN BARCELONA. TROUBLE IS, WE DON'T LIKE LOOSE ENDS...
HOW DO YOU KILL PAUL SHIRER AND MAKE IT LOOK TOTALLY NATURAL? HOW DO YOU STOP THESE WRITERS PUTTING TWO AND TWO TOGETHER?
THAT'S YOUR TEST.

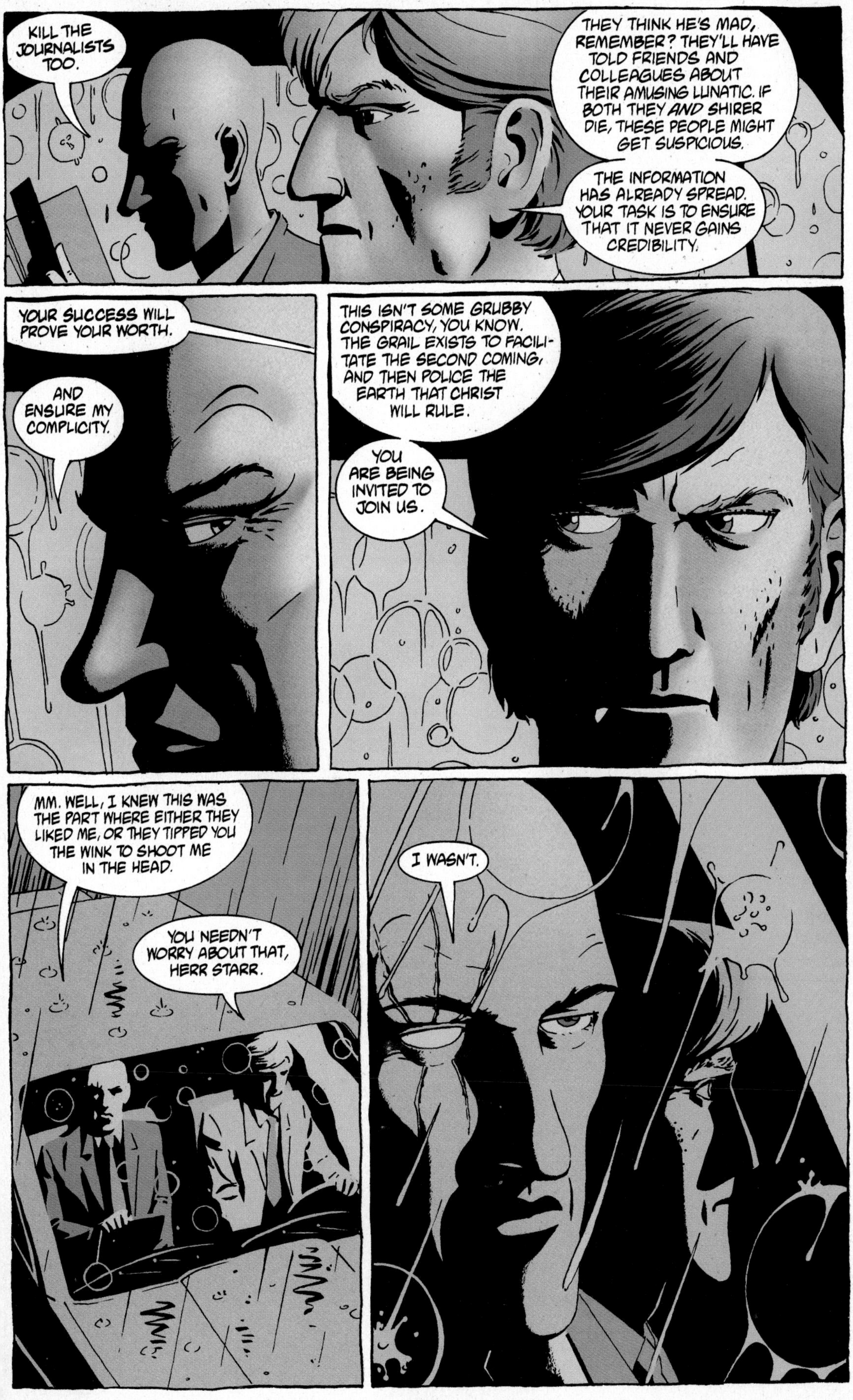
KILL THE JOURNALISTS TOO.
THEY THINK HE'S MAD, REMEMBER? THEY'LL HAVE TOLD FRIENDS AND COLLEAGUES ABOUT THEIR AMUSING LUNATIC. IF BOTH THEY *AND* SHIRER DIE, THESE PEOPLE MIGHT GET SUSPICIOUS.
THE INFORMATION HAS ALREADY SPREAD. YOUR TASK IS TO ENSURE THAT IT NEVER GAINS CREDIBILITY.
YOUR SUCCESS WILL PROVE YOUR WORTH.
AND ENSURE MY COMPLICITY.
THIS ISN'T SOME GRUBBY CONSPIRACY, YOU KNOW. THE GRAIL EXISTS TO FACILITATE THE SECOND COMING, AND THEN POLICE THE EARTH THAT CHRIST WILL RULE.
YOU ARE BEING INVITED TO JOIN US.
MM. WELL, I KNEW THIS WAS THE PART WHERE EITHER THEY LIKED ME, OR THEY TIPPED YOU THE WINK TO SHOOT ME IN THE HEAD.
YOU NEEDN'T WORRY ABOUT THAT, HERR STARR.
I WASN'T.

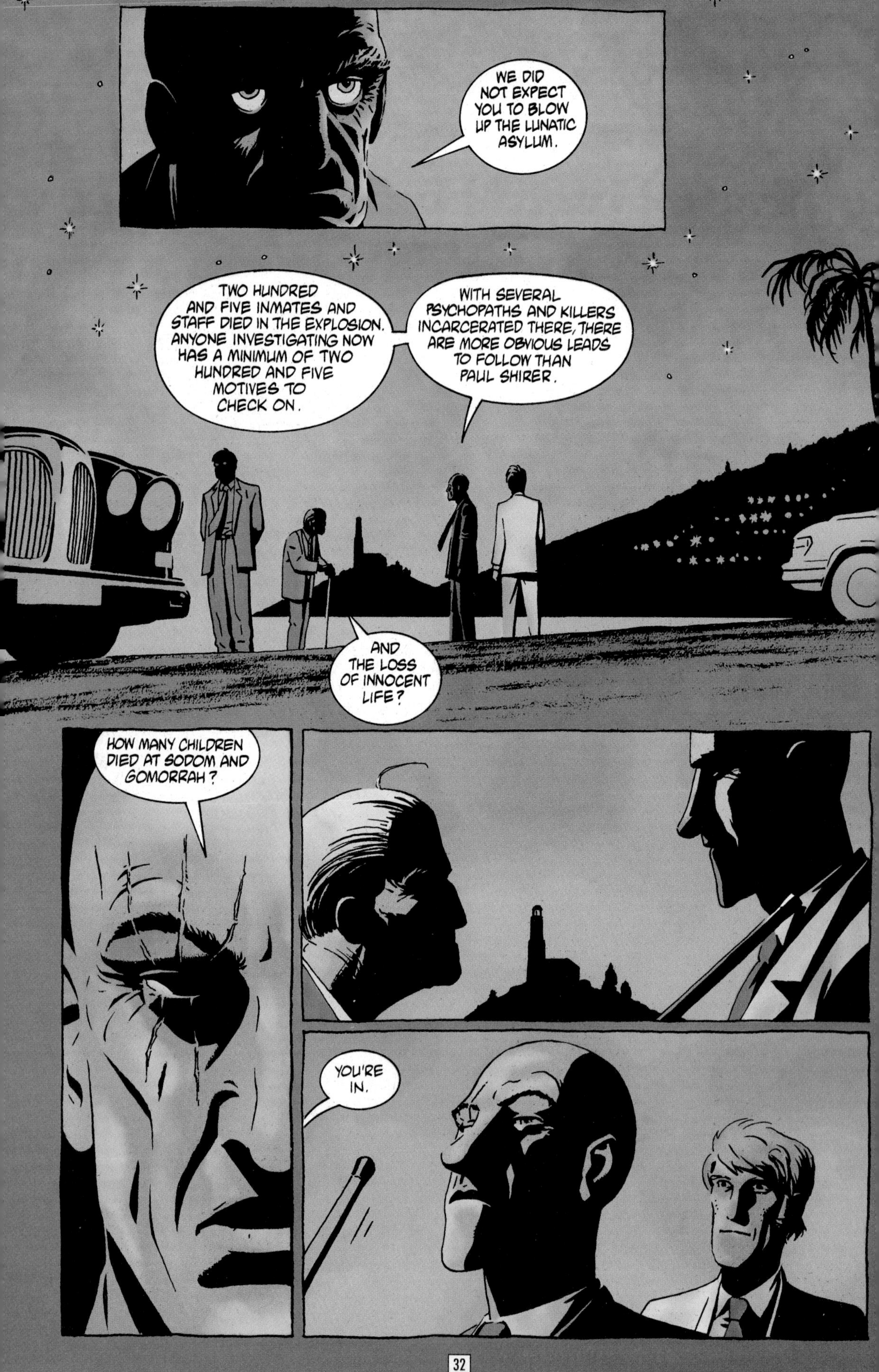
WE DID NOT EXPECT YOU TO BLOW UP THE LUNATIC ASYLUM.
TWO HUNDRED AND FIVE INMATES AND STAFF DIED IN THE EXPLOSION. ANYONE INVESTIGATING NOW HAS A MINIMUM OF TWO HUNDRED AND FIVE MOTIVES TO CHECK ON.
WITH SEVERAL PSYCHOPATHS AND KILLERS INCARCERATED THERE, THERE ARE MORE OBVIOUS LEADS TO FOLLOW THAN PAUL SHIRER.
AND THE LOSS OF INNOCENT LIFE?
HOW MANY CHILDREN DIED AT SODOM AND GOMORRAH?
YOU'RE IN.

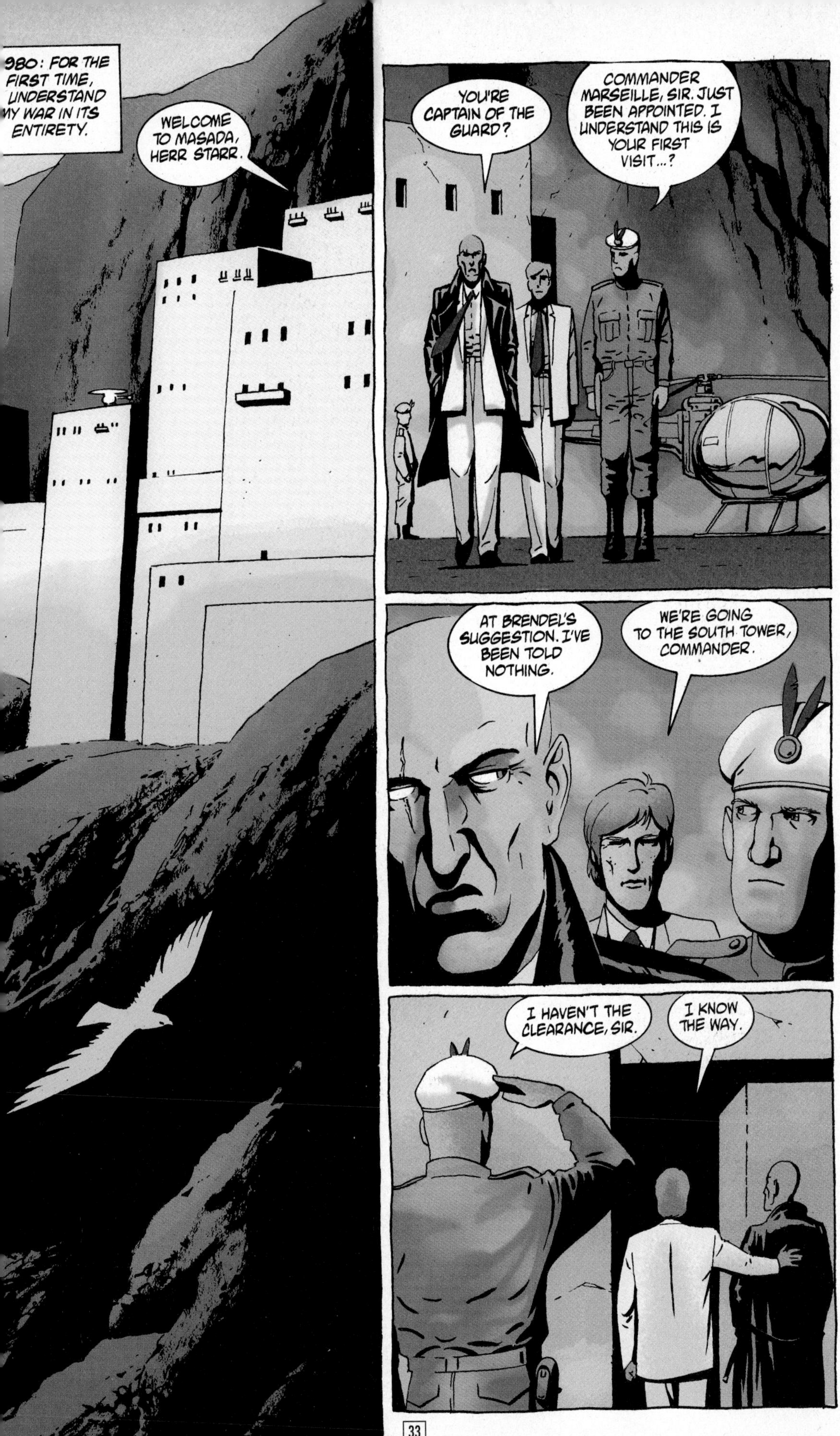
980: FOR THE FIRST TIME, UNDERSTAND MY WAR IN ITS ENTIRETY.
WELCOME TO MASADA, HERR STARR.
YOU'RE CAPTAIN OF THE GUARD?
COMMANDER MARSEILLE, SIR. JUST BEEN APPOINTED. I UNDERSTAND THIS IS YOUR FIRST VISIT...?
AT BRENDEL'S SUGGESTION. I'VE BEEN TOLD NOTHING.
WE'RE GOING TO THE SOUTH TOWER, COMMANDER.
I HAVEN'T THE CLEARANCE, SIR.
I KNOW THE WAY.

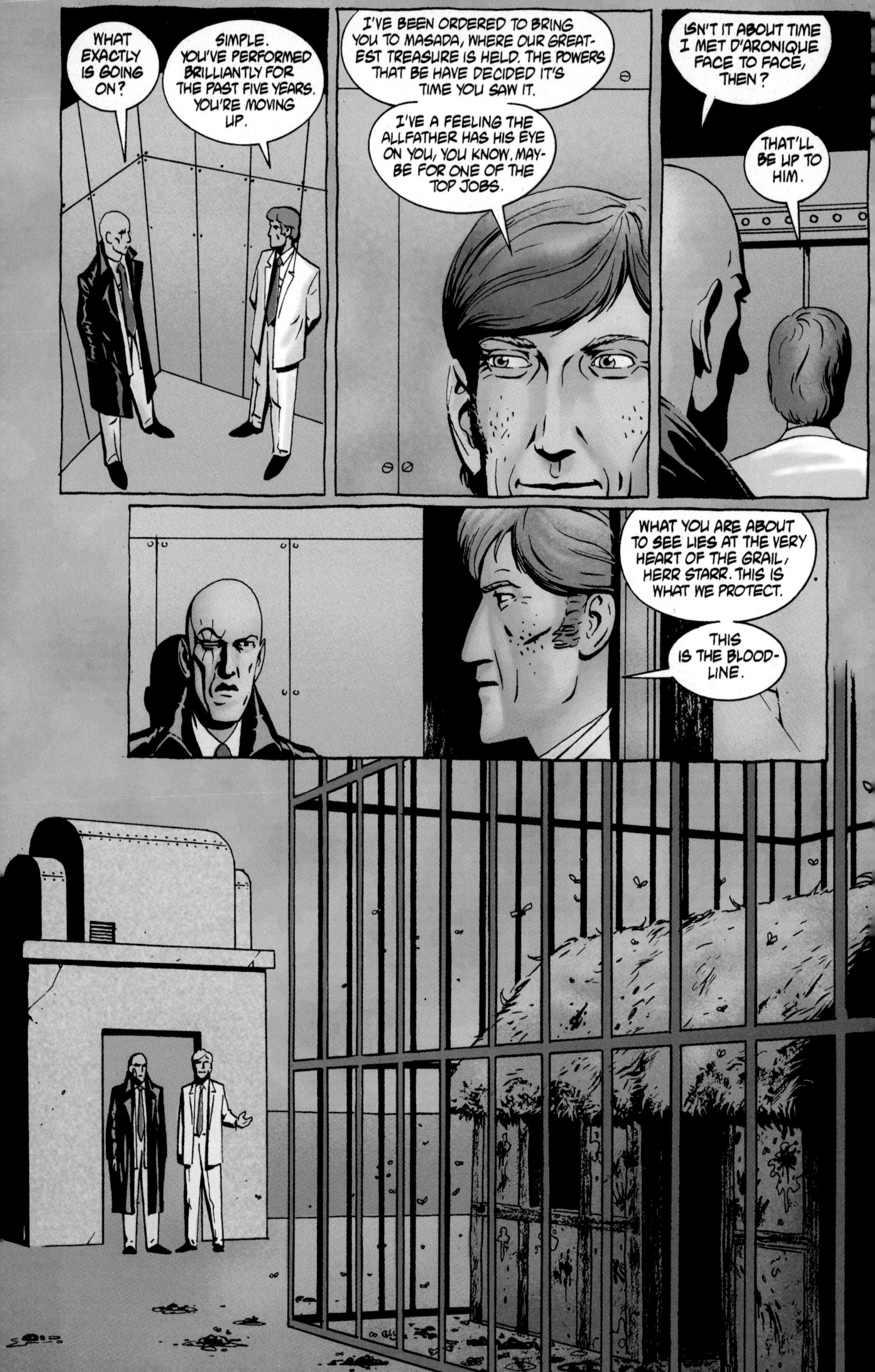

WHAT EXACTLY IS GOING ON?
SIMPLE. YOU'VE PERFORMED BRILLIANTLY FOR THE PAST FIVE YEARS. YOU'RE MOVING UP.
I'VE BEEN ORDERED TO BRING YOU TO MASADA, WHERE OUR GREATEST TREASURE IS HELD. THE POWERS THAT BE HAVE DECIDED IT'S TIME YOU SAW IT.
I'VE A FEELING THE ALLFATHER HAS HIS EYE ON YOU, YOU KNOW. MAYBE FOR ONE OF THE TOP JOBS.
ISN'T IT ABOUT TIME I MET D'ARONIQUE FACE TO FACE, THEN?
THAT'LL BE UP TO HIM.
WHAT YOU ARE ABOUT TO SEE LIES AT THE VERY HEART OF THE GRAIL, HERR STARR. THIS IS WHAT WE PROTECT.
THIS IS THE BLOODLINE.

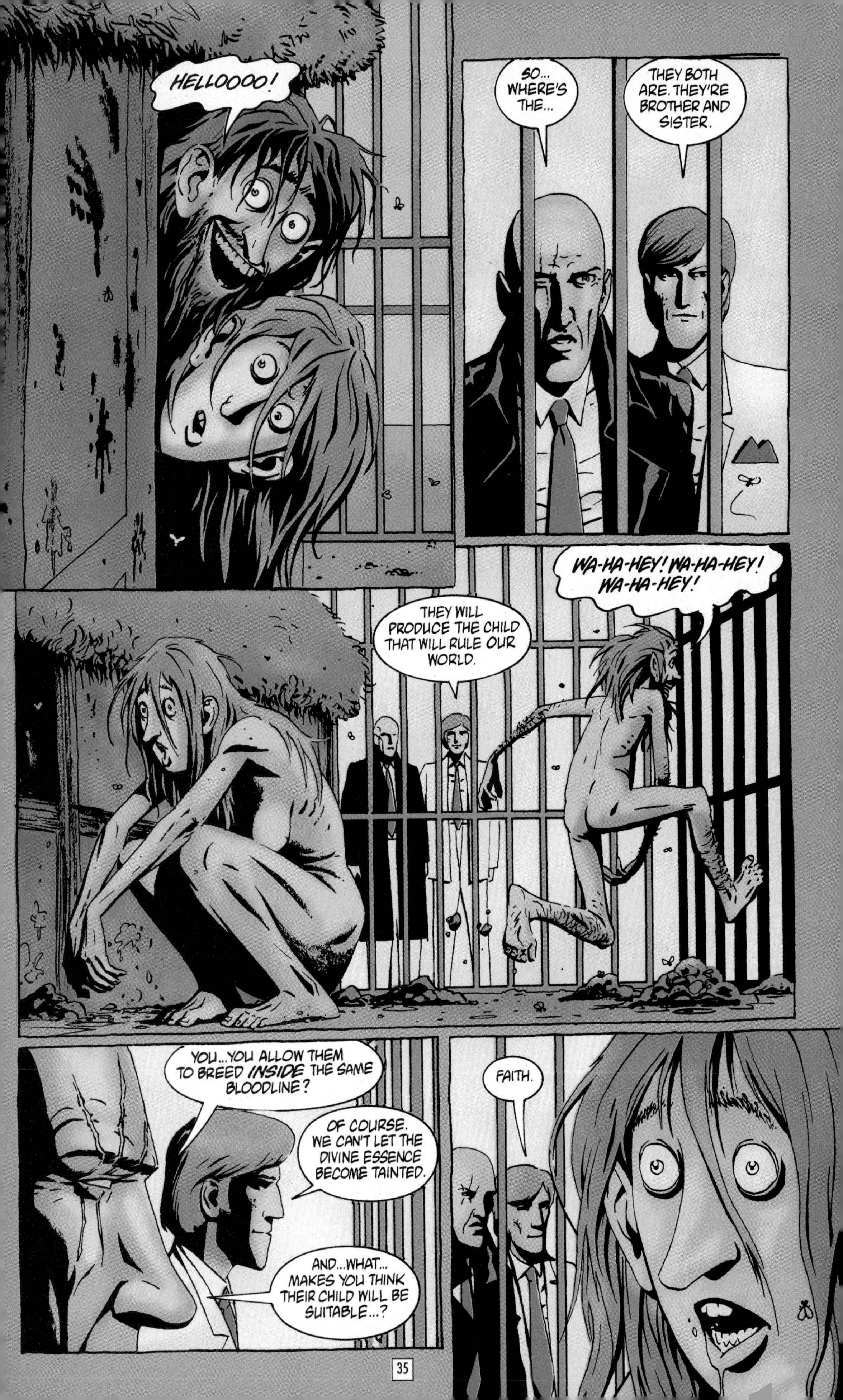
HELLOOOO!
SO... WHERE'S THE...
THEY BOTH ARE. THEY'RE BROTHER AND SISTER.
WA-HA-HEY! WA-HA-HEY! WA-HA-HEY!
THEY WILL PRODUCE THE CHILD THAT WILL RULE OUR WORLD.
YOU...YOU ALLOW THEM TO BREED *INSIDE* THE SAME BLOODLINE?
OF COURSE. WE CAN'T LET THE DIVINE ESSENCE BECOME TAINTED.
AND...WHAT... MAKES YOU THINK THEIR CHILD WILL BE SUITABLE...?
FAITH.

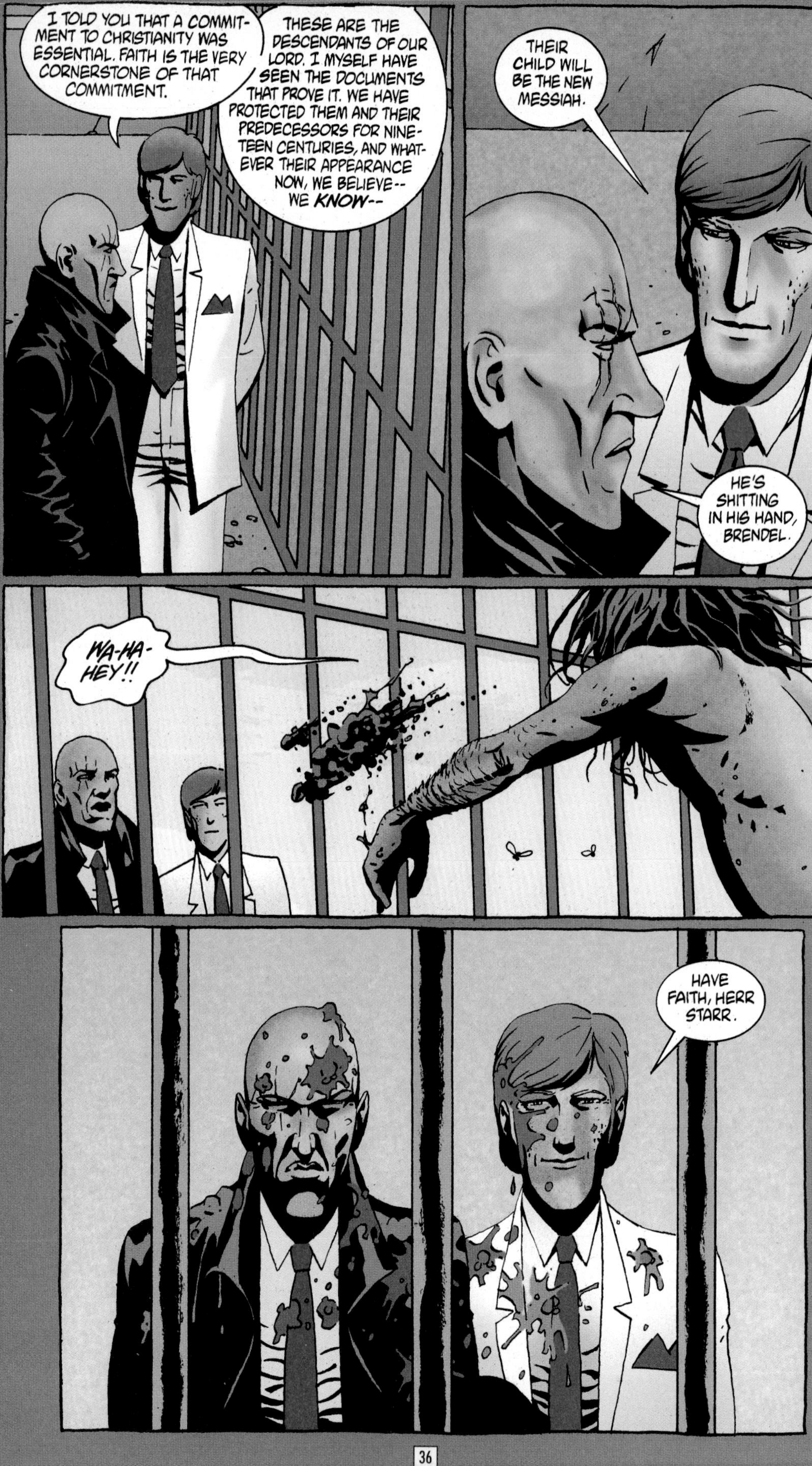
I TOLD YOU THAT A COMMITMENT TO CHRISTIANITY WAS ESSENTIAL. FAITH IS THE VERY CORNERSTONE OF THAT COMMITMENT.
THESE ARE THE DESCENDANTS OF OUR LORD. I MYSELF HAVE SEEN THE DOCUMENTS THAT PROVE IT. WE HAVE PROTECTED THEM AND THEIR PREDECESSORS FOR NINETEEN CENTURIES, AND WHATEVER THEIR APPEARANCE NOW, WE BELIEVE-- WE KNOW--
THEIR CHILD WILL BE THE NEW MESSIAH.
HE'S SHITTING IN HIS HAND, BRENDEL.
WA-HA-HEY!!
HAVE FAITH, HERR STARR.

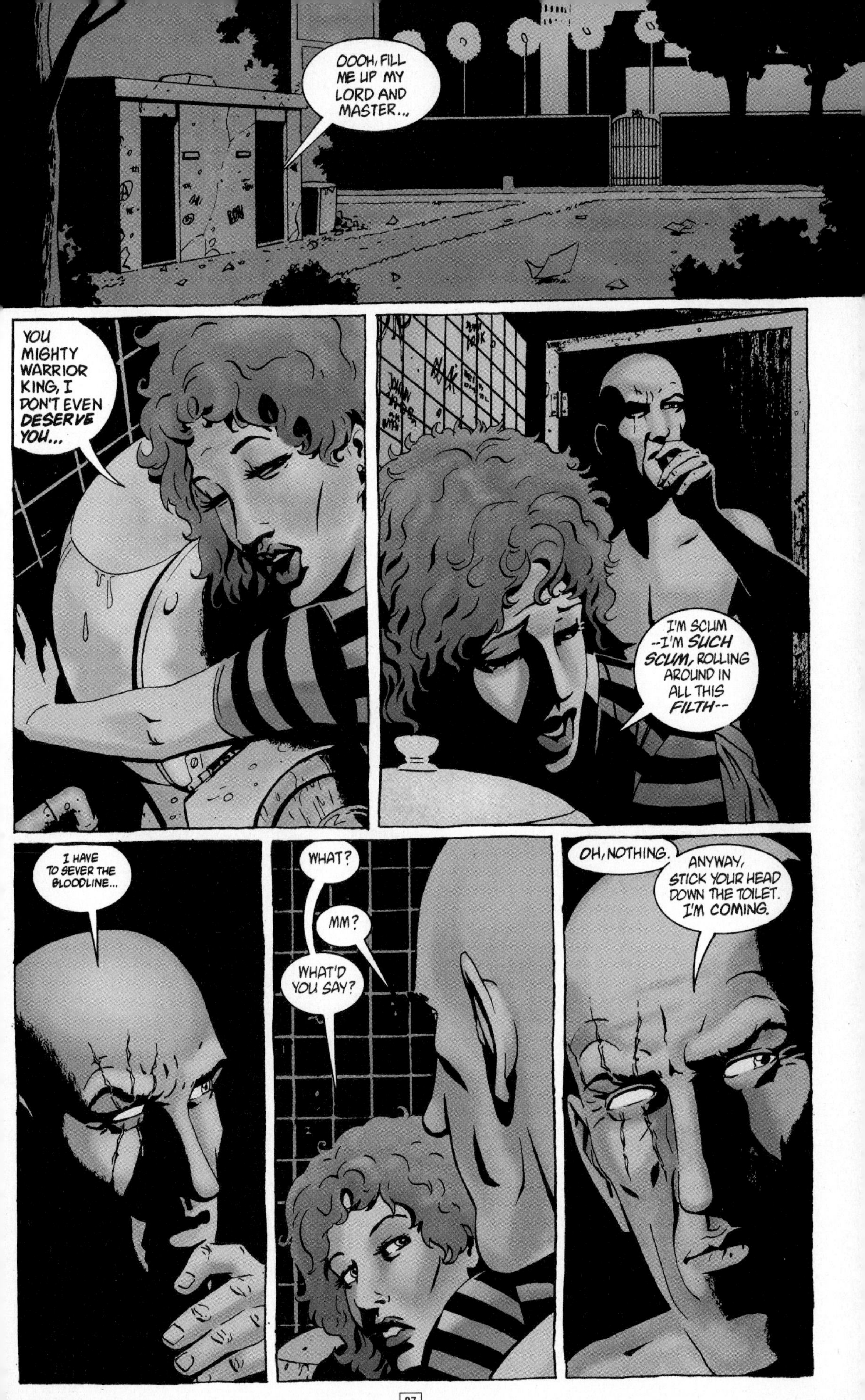

OOOH, FILL ME UP MY LORD AND MASTER...
YOU MIGHTY WARRIOR KING, I DON'T EVEN DESERVE YOU...
I'M SCUM --I'M SUCH SCUM, ROLLING AROUND IN ALL THIS FILTH--
I HAVE TO SEVER THE BLOODLINE...
WHAT?
MM?
WHAT'D YOU SAY?
OH, NOTHING.
ANYWAY, STICK YOUR HEAD DOWN THE TOILET. I'M COMING.

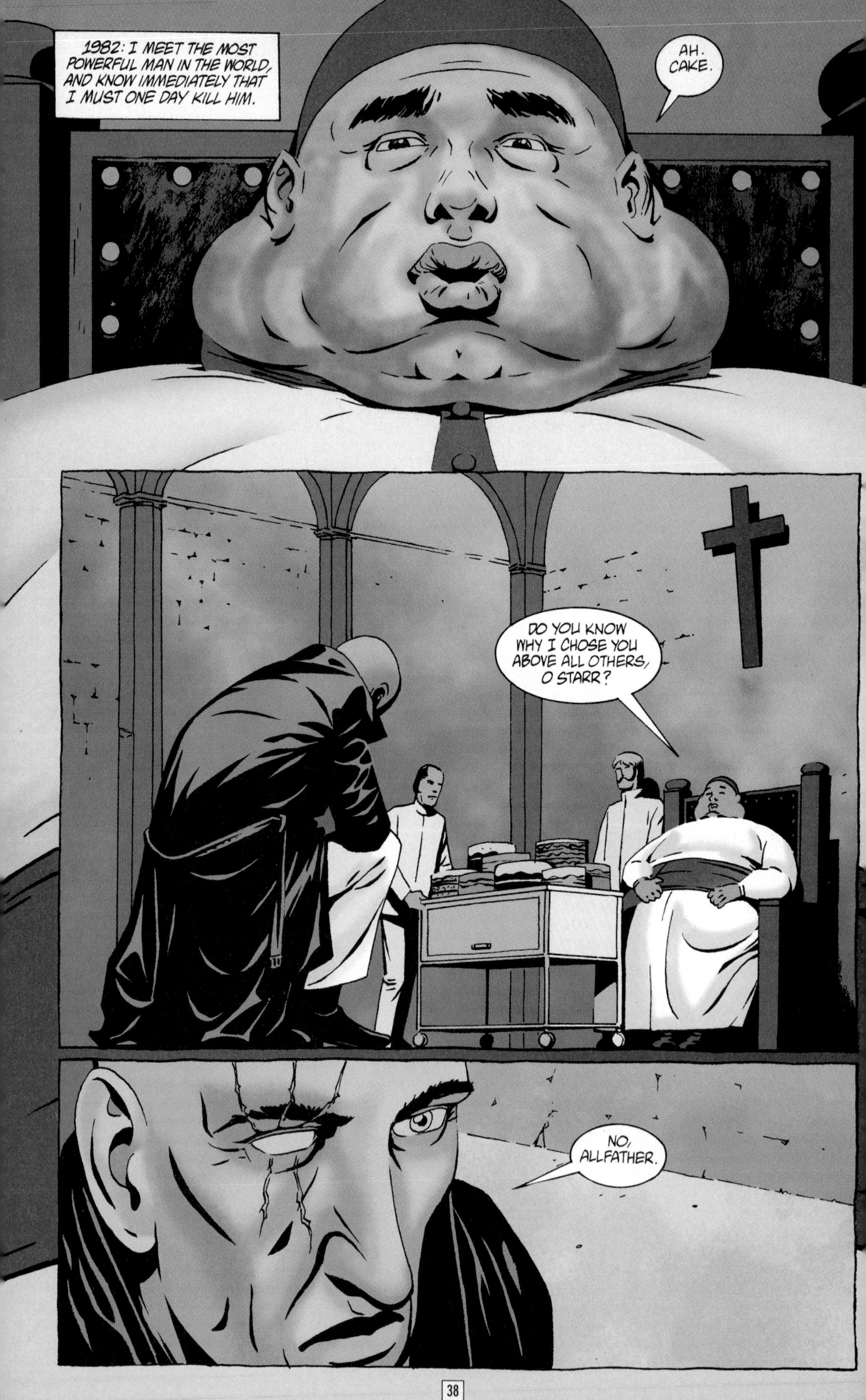
1982: I MEET THE MOST POWERFUL MAN IN THE WORLD, AND KNOW IMMEDIATELY THAT I MUST ONE DAY KILL HIM.
AH. CAKE.
DO YOU KNOW WHY I CHOSE YOU ABOVE ALL OTHERS, O STARR?
NO, ALLFATHER.

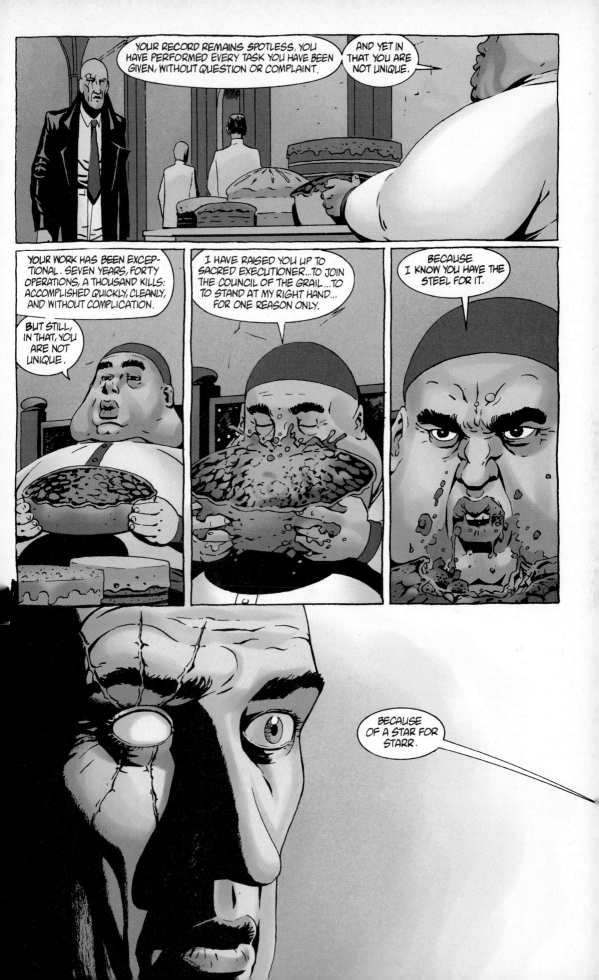

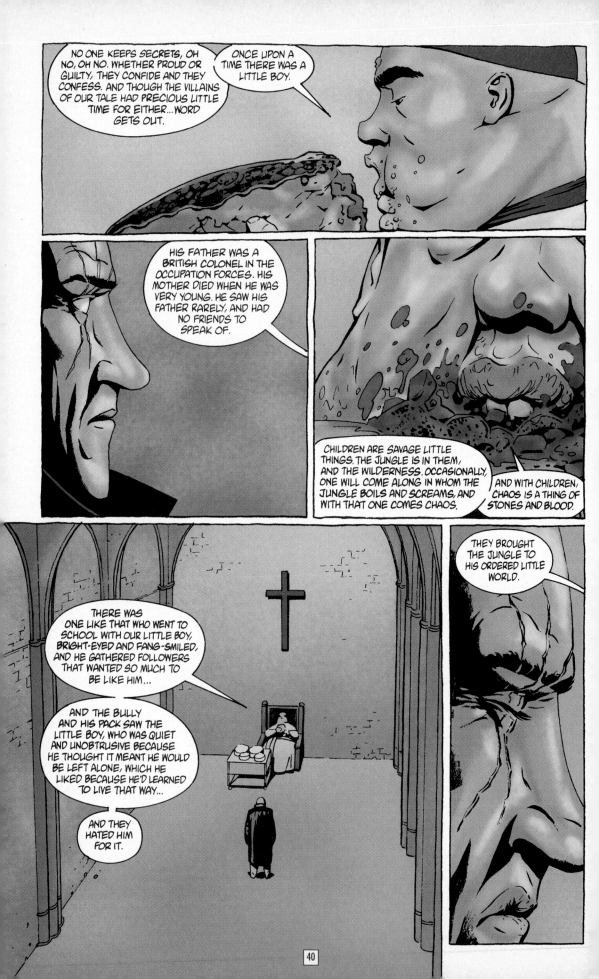

NO ONE KEEPS SECRETS, OH NO, OH NO. WHETHER PROUD OR GUILTY, THEY CONFIDE AND THEY CONFESS. AND THOUGH THE VILLAINS OF OUR TALE HAD PRECIOUS LITTLE TIME FOR EITHER...WORD GETS OUT.

ONCE UPON A TIME THERE WAS A LITTLE BOY.

HIS FATHER WAS A BRITISH COLONEL IN THE OCCUPATION FORCES. HIS MOTHER DIED WHEN HE WAS VERY YOUNG. HE SAW HIS FATHER RARELY, AND HAD NO FRIENDS TO SPEAK OF.

CHILDREN ARE SAVAGE LITTLE THINGS. THE JUNGLE IS IN THEM, AND THE WILDERNESS. OCCASIONALLY, ONE WILL COME ALONG IN WHOM THE JUNGLE BOILS AND SCREAMS, AND WITH THAT ONE COMES CHAOS.

AND WITH CHILDREN, CHAOS IS A THING OF STONES AND BLOOD.

THEY BROUGHT THE JUNGLE TO HIS ORDERED LITTLE WORLD.

THERE WAS ONE LIKE THAT WHO WENT TO SCHOOL WITH OUR LITTLE BOY, BRIGHT-EYED AND FANG-SMILED, AND HE GATHERED FOLLOWERS THAT WANTED SO MUCH TO BE LIKE HIM...

AND THE BULLY AND HIS PACK SAW THE LITTLE BOY, WHO WAS QUIET AND UNOBTRUSIVE BECAUSE HE THOUGHT IT MEANT HE WOULD BE LEFT ALONE, WHICH HE LIKED BECAUSE HE'D LEARNED TO LIVE THAT WAY...

AND THEY HATED HIM FOR IT.

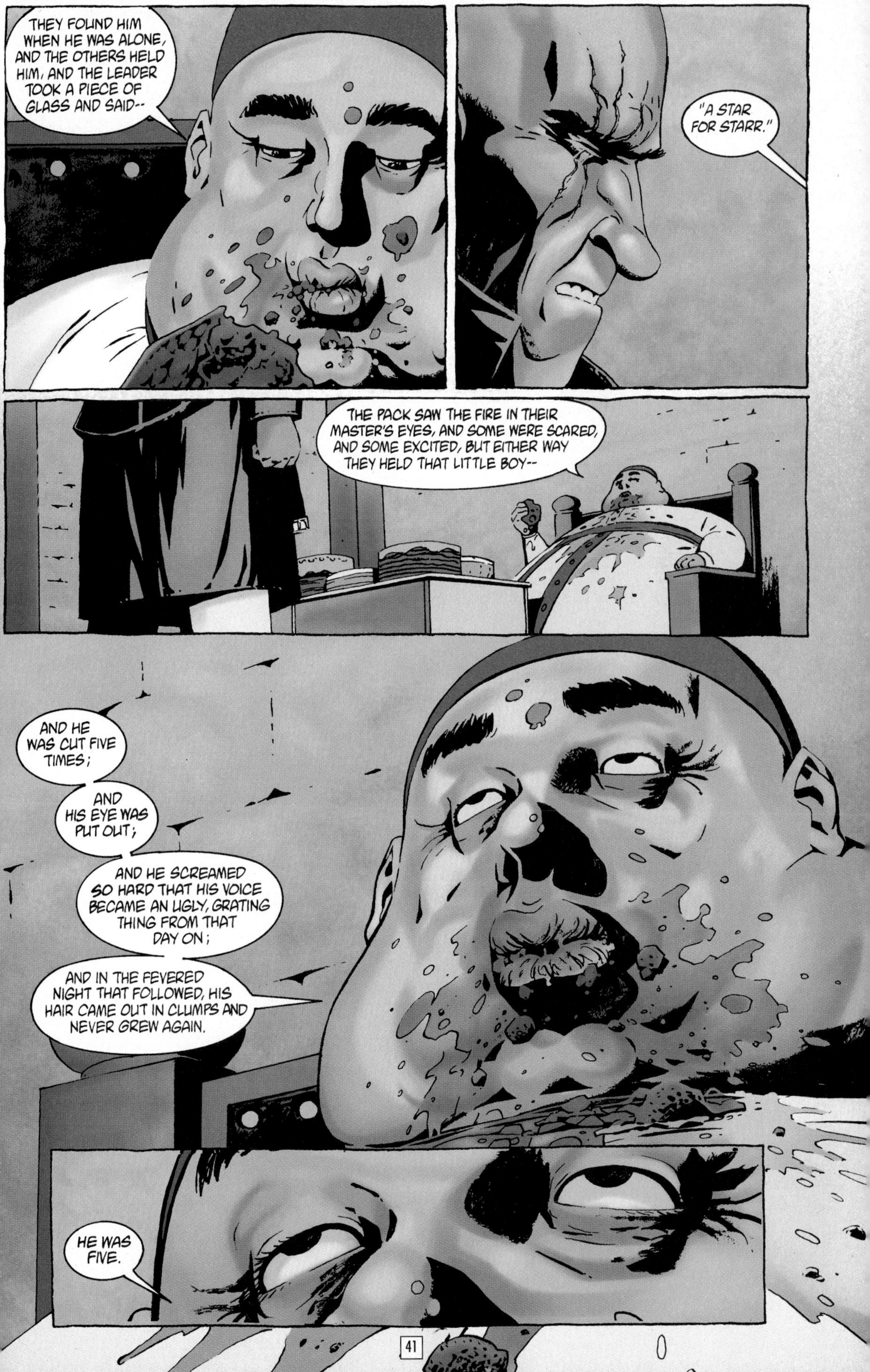

THEY FOUND HIM WHEN HE WAS ALONE, AND THE OTHERS HELD HIM, AND THE LEADER TOOK A PIECE OF GLASS AND SAID--
"A STAR FOR STARR."
THE PACK SAW THE FIRE IN THEIR MASTER'S EYES, AND SOME WERE SCARED, AND SOME EXCITED, BUT EITHER WAY THEY HELD THAT LITTLE BOY--
AND HE WAS CUT FIVE TIMES;
AND HIS EYE WAS PUT OUT;
AND HE SCREAMED SO HARD THAT HIS VOICE BECAME AN UGLY, GRATING THING FROM THAT DAY ON;
AND IN THE FEVERED NIGHT THAT FOLLOWED, HIS HAIR CAME OUT IN CLUMPS AND NEVER GREW AGAIN.
HE WAS FIVE.

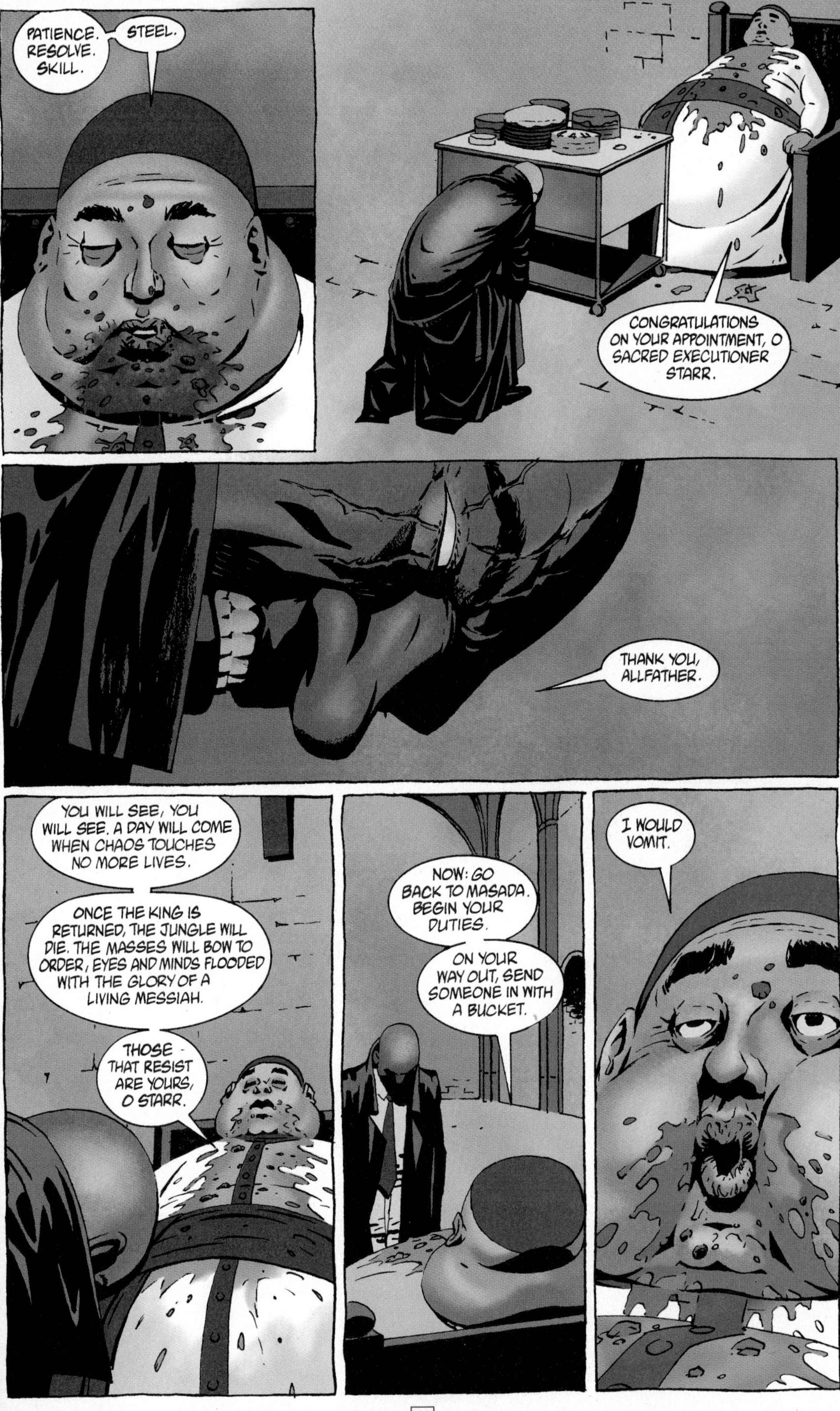
PATIENCE. RESOLVE. SKILL.
STEEL.
CONGRATULATIONS ON YOUR APPOINTMENT, O SACRED EXECUTIONER STARR.
THANK YOU, ALLFATHER.
YOU WILL SEE, YOU WILL SEE. A DAY WILL COME WHEN CHAOS TOUCHES NO MORE LIVES.
ONCE THE KING IS RETURNED, THE JUNGLE WILL DIE. THE MASSES WILL BOW TO ORDER, EYES AND MINDS FLOODED WITH THE GLORY OF A LIVING MESSIAH.
THOSE THAT RESIST ARE YOURS, O STARR.
NOW: GO BACK TO MASADA. BEGIN YOUR DUTIES.
ON YOUR WAY OUT, SEND SOMEONE IN WITH A BUCKET.
I WOULD VOMIT.

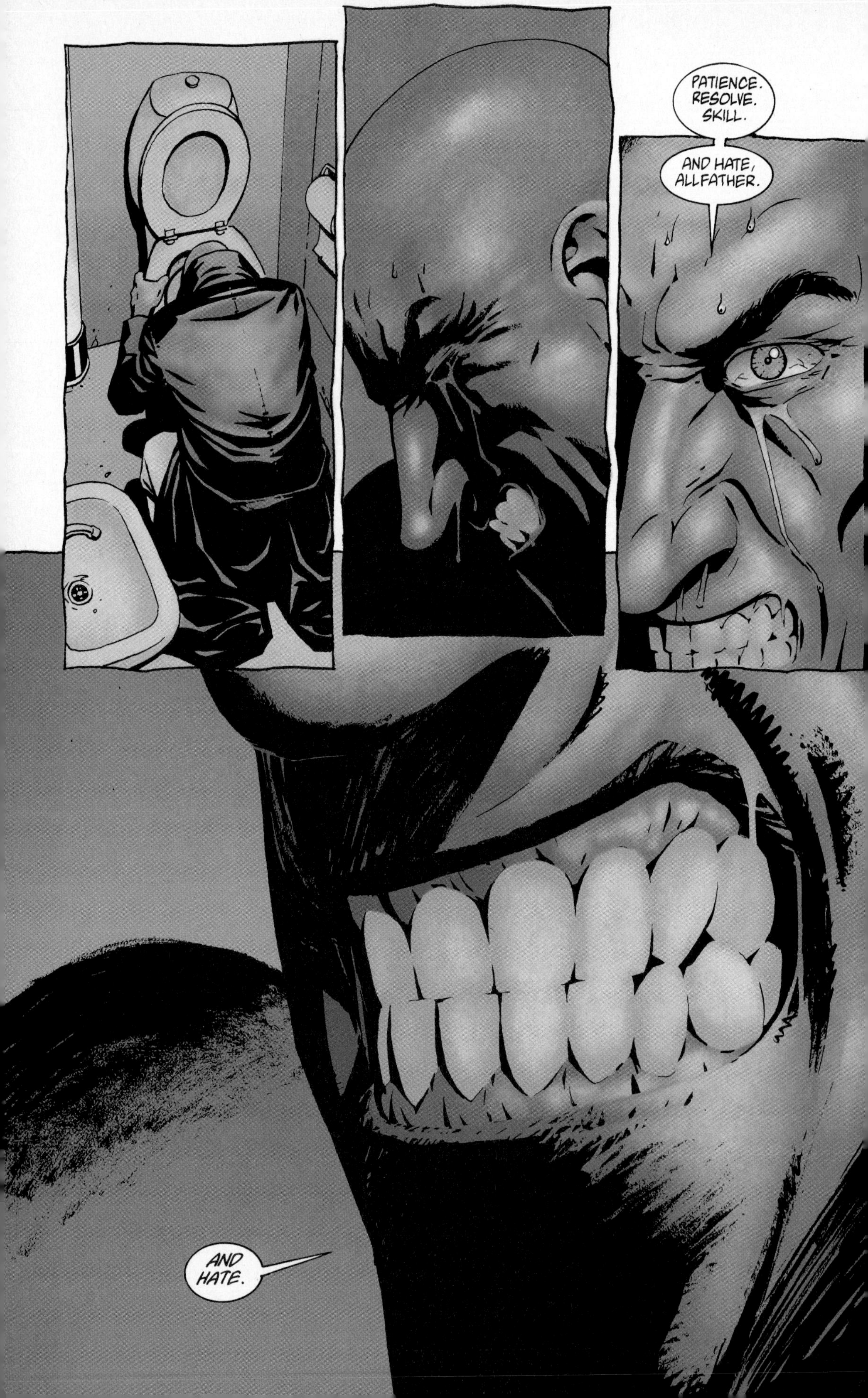
PATIENCE. RESOLVE. SKILL.
AND HATE, ALLFATHER.
AND HATE.

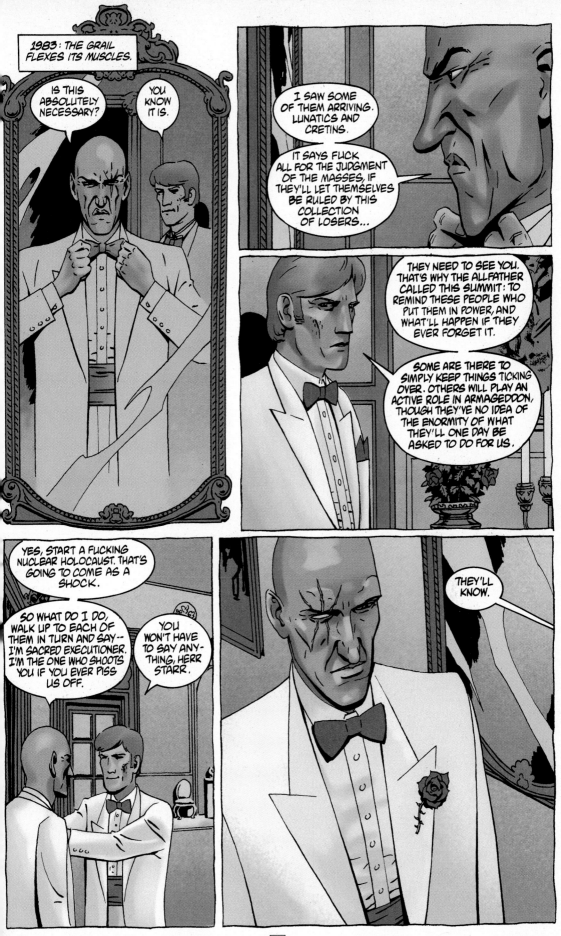

1983: THE GRAIL FLEXES ITS MUSCLES.

IS THIS ABSOLUTELY NECESSARY?

YOU KNOW IT IS.

I SAW SOME OF THEM ARRIVING. LUNATICS AND CRETINS.

IT SAYS FUCK ALL FOR THE JUDGMENT OF THE MASSES, IF THEY'LL LET THEMSELVES BE RULED BY THIS COLLECTION OF LOSERS...

THEY NEED TO SEE YOU. THAT'S WHY THE ALLFATHER CALLED THIS SUMMIT: TO REMIND THESE PEOPLE WHO PUT THEM IN POWER, AND WHAT'LL HAPPEN IF THEY EVER FORGET IT.

SOME ARE THERE TO SIMPLY KEEP THINGS TICKING OVER. OTHERS WILL PLAY AN ACTIVE ROLE IN ARMAGEDDON, THOUGH THEY'VE NO IDEA OF THE ENORMITY OF WHAT THEY'LL ONE DAY BE ASKED TO DO FOR US.

YES, START A FUCKING NUCLEAR HOLOCAUST. THAT'S GOING TO COME AS A SHOCK.

SO WHAT DO I DO, WALK UP TO EACH OF THEM IN TURN AND SAY-- I'M SACRED EXECUTIONER. I'M THE ONE WHO SHOOTS YOU IF YOU EVER PISS US OFF.

YOU WON'T HAVE TO SAY ANY-THING, HERR STARR.

THEY'LL KNOW.

45

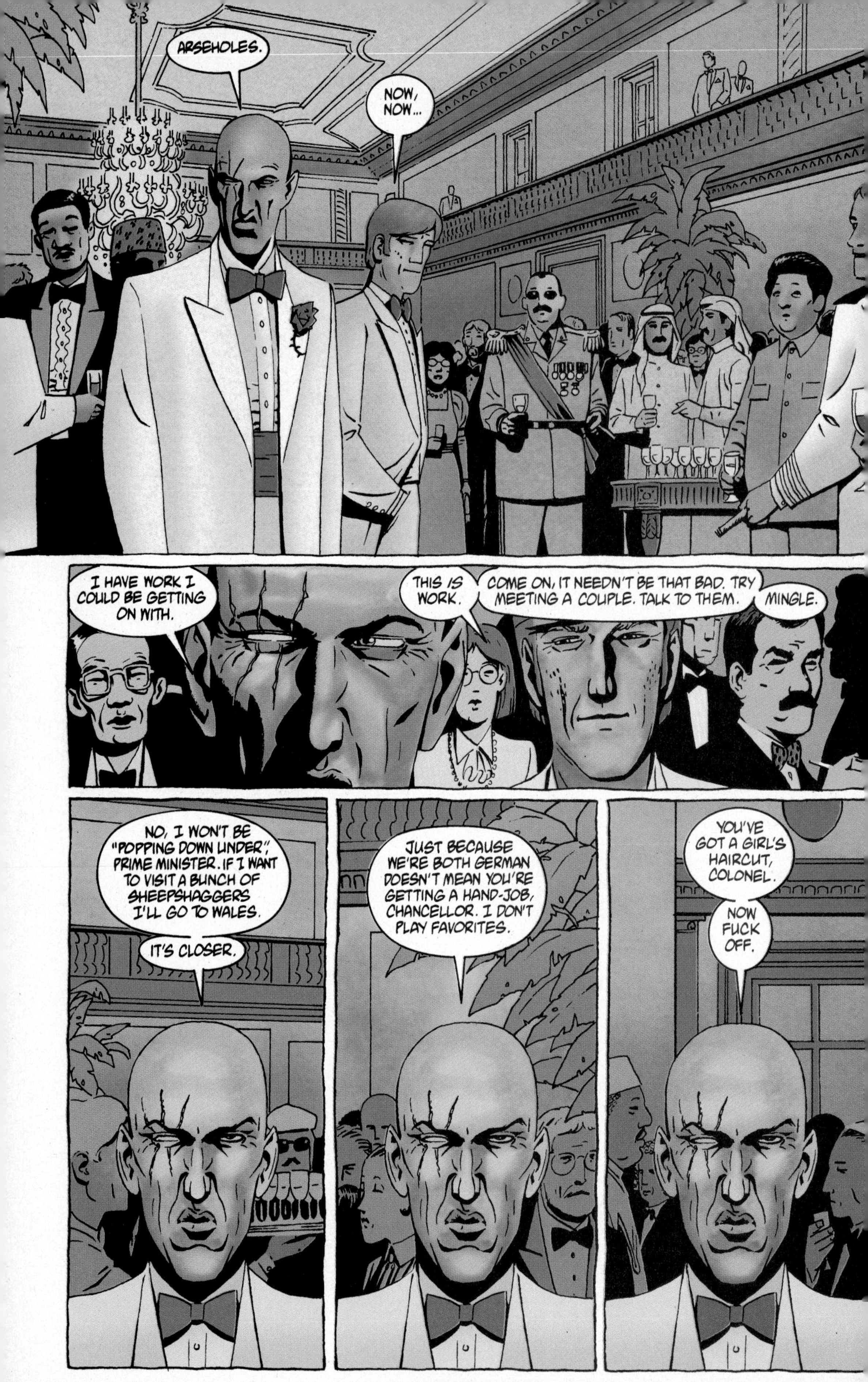
ARSEHOLES.
NOW, NOW...
I HAVE WORK I COULD BE GETTING ON WITH.
THIS IS WORK.
COME ON, IT NEEDN'T BE THAT BAD. TRY MEETING A COUPLE. TALK TO THEM.
MINGLE.
NO, I WON'T BE "POPPING DOWN UNDER", PRIME MINISTER. IF I WANT TO VISIT A BUNCH OF SHEEPSHAGGERS I'LL GO TO WALES.
IT'S CLOSER.
JUST BECAUSE WE'RE BOTH GERMAN DOESN'T MEAN YOU'RE GETTING A HAND-JOB, CHANCELLOR. I DON'T PLAY FAVORITES.
YOU'VE GOT A GIRL'S HAIRCUT, COLONEL.
NOW FUCK OFF.

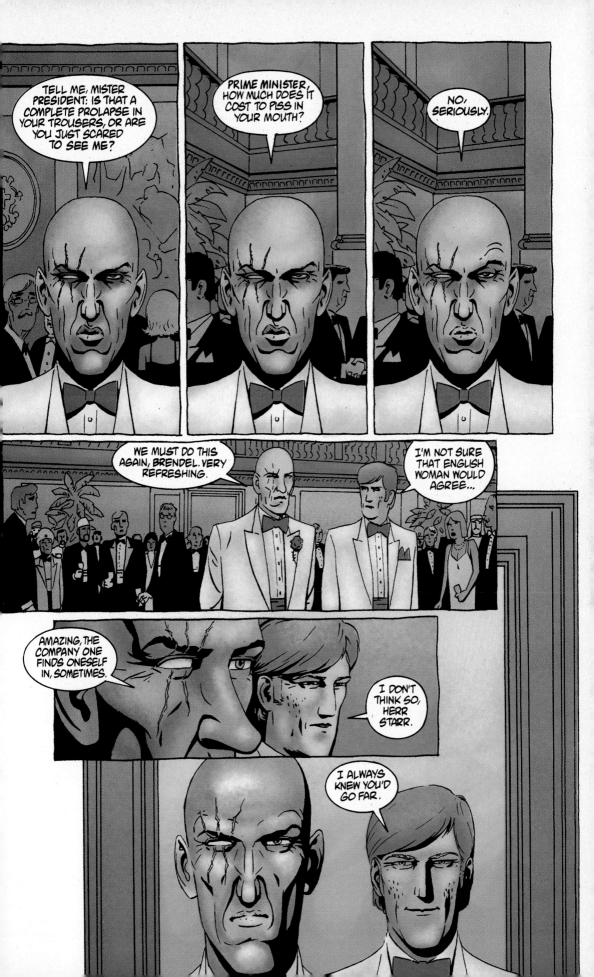

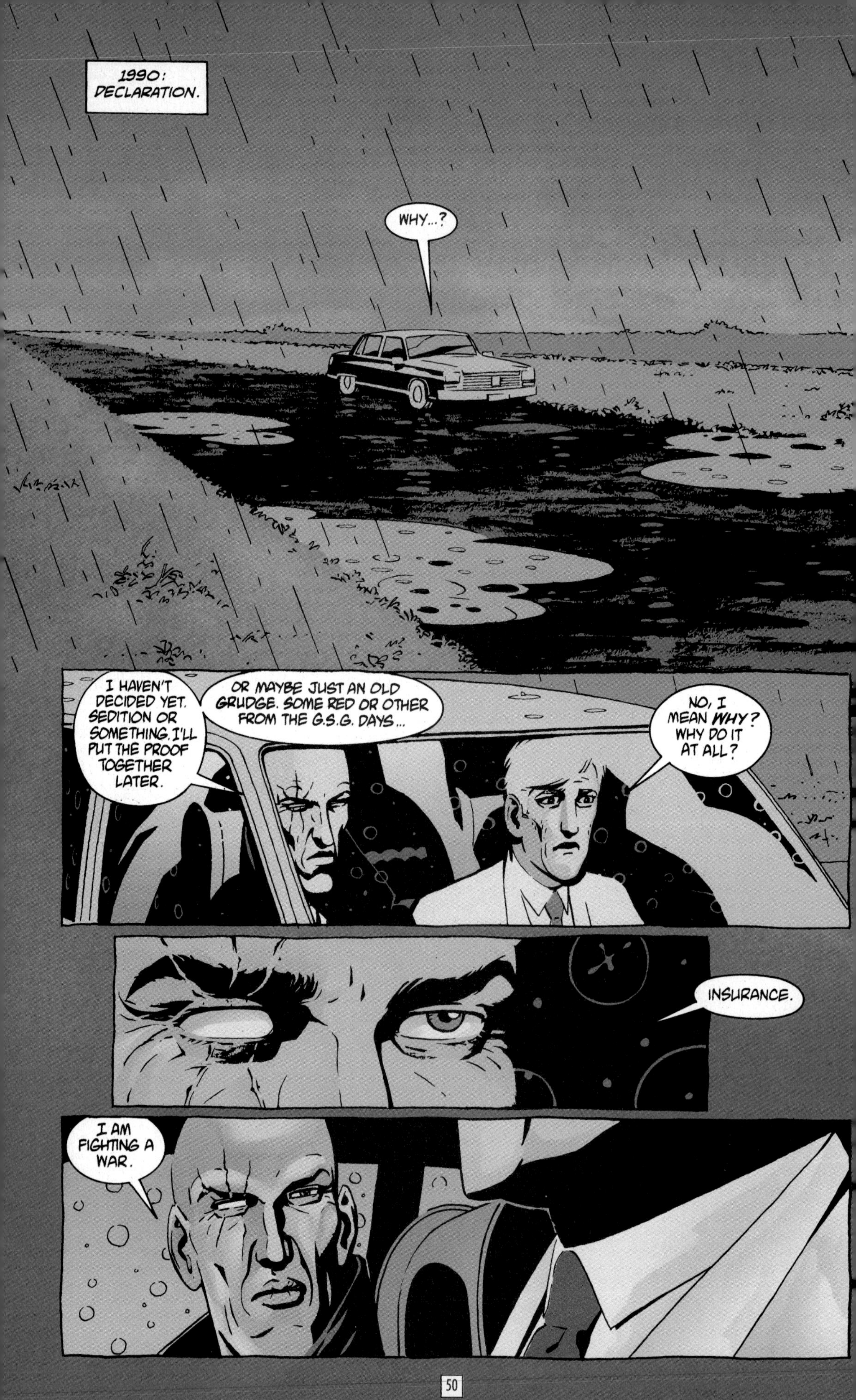
1990: DECLARATION.
WHY...?
I HAVEN'T DECIDED YET. SEDITION OR SOMETHING. I'LL PUT THE PROOF TOGETHER LATER.
OR MAYBE JUST AN OLD GRUDGE. SOME RED OR OTHER FROM THE G.S.G. DAYS...
NO, I MEAN WHY? WHY DO IT AT ALL?
INSURANCE.
I AM FIGHTING A WAR.

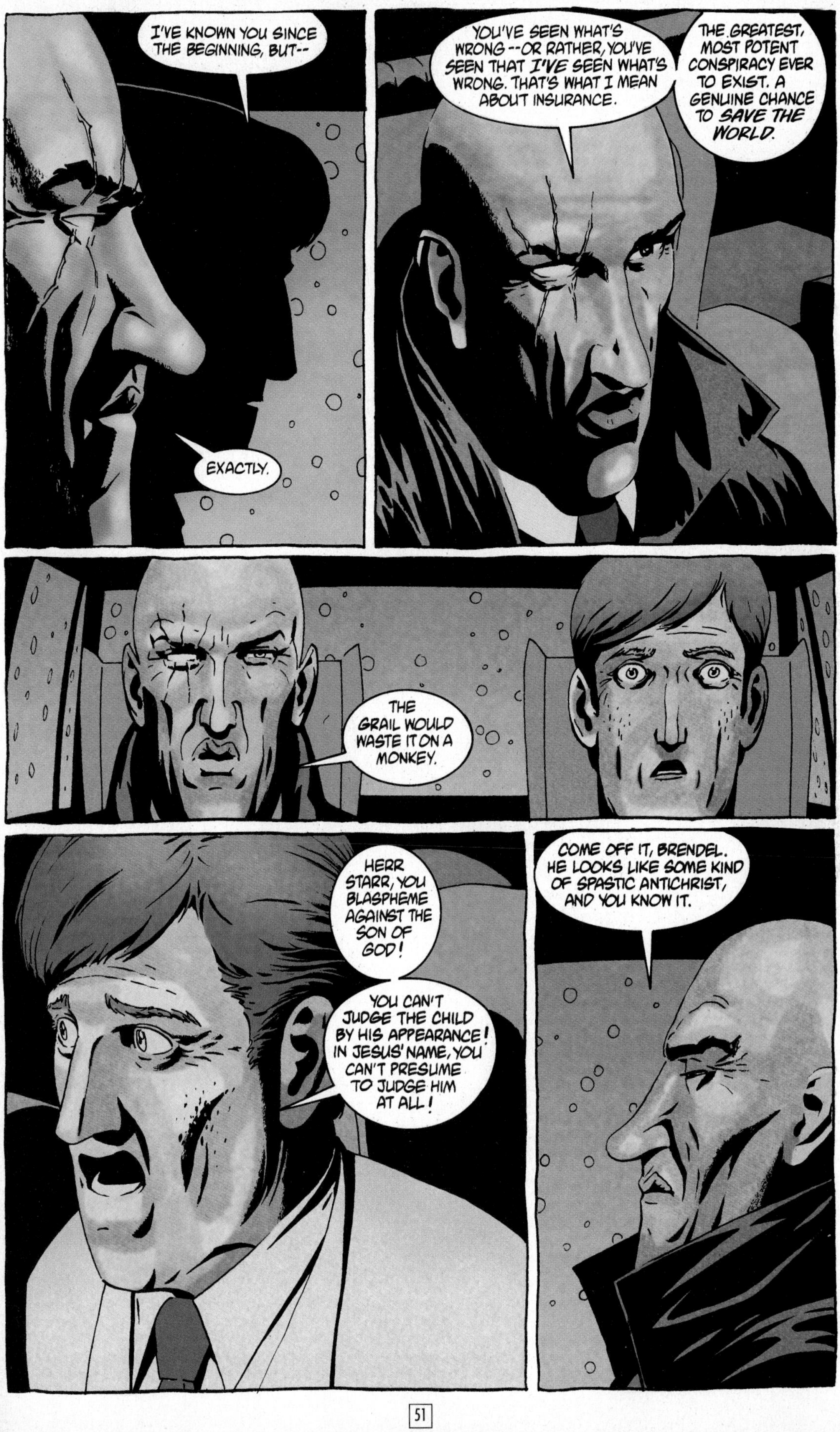
I'VE KNOWN YOU SINCE THE BEGINNING, BUT--
EXACTLY.
YOU'VE SEEN WHAT'S WRONG --OR RATHER, YOU'VE SEEN THAT I'VE SEEN WHAT'S WRONG. THAT'S WHAT I MEAN ABOUT INSURANCE.
THE GREATEST, MOST POTENT CONSPIRACY EVER TO EXIST. A GENUINE CHANCE TO SAVE THE WORLD.
THE GRAIL WOULD WASTE IT ON A MONKEY.
HERR STARR, YOU BLASPHEME AGAINST THE SON OF GOD!
YOU CAN'T JUDGE THE CHILD BY HIS APPEARANCE! IN JESUS' NAME, YOU CAN'T PRESUME TO JUDGE HIM AT ALL!
COME OFF IT, BRENDEL. HE LOOKS LIKE SOME KIND OF SPASTIC ANTICHRIST, AND YOU KNOW IT.

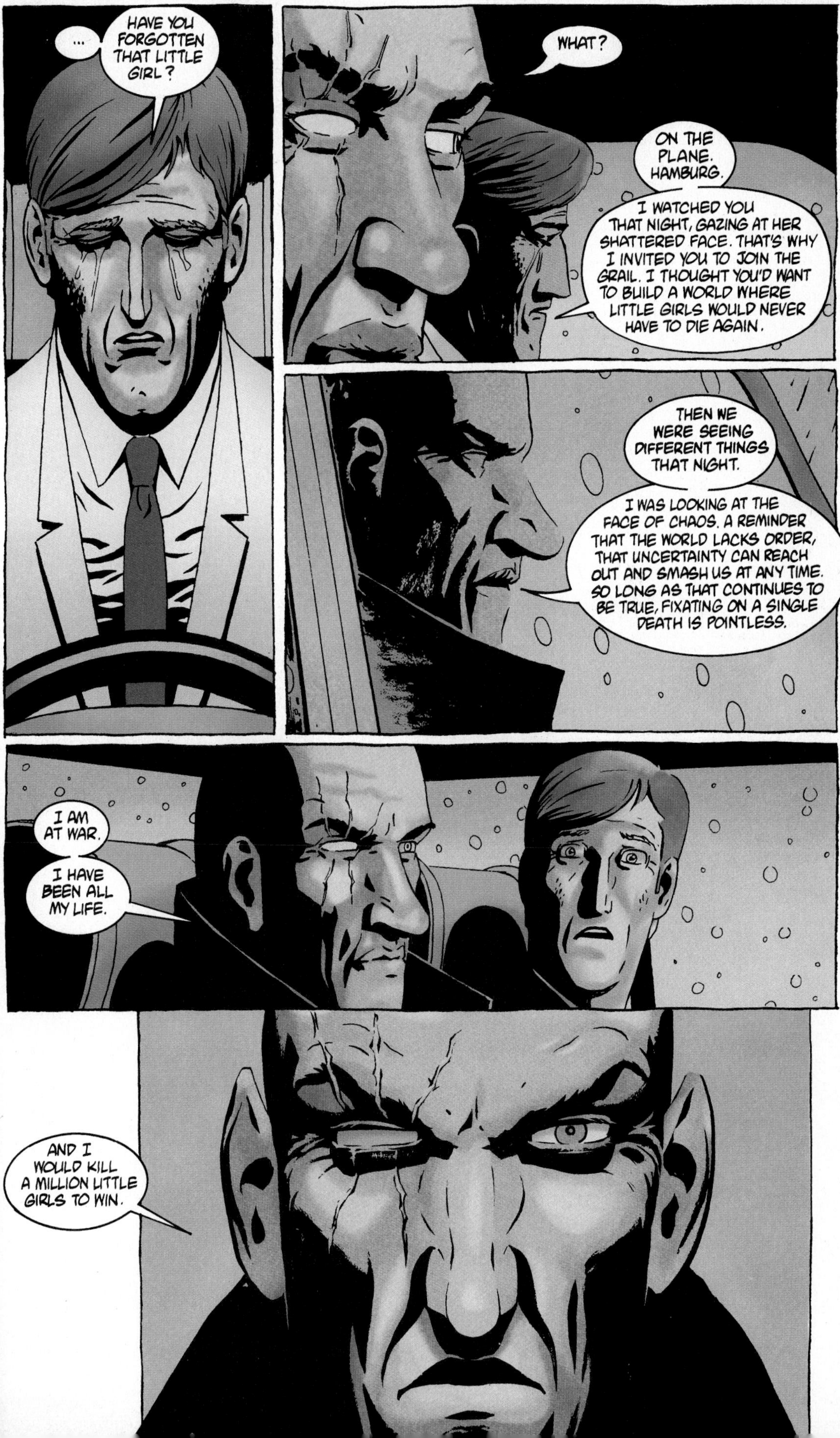
...
HAVE YOU FORGOTTEN THAT LITTLE GIRL?
WHAT?
ON THE PLANE. HAMBURG.
I WATCHED YOU THAT NIGHT, GAZING AT HER SHATTERED FACE. THAT'S WHY I INVITED YOU TO JOIN THE GRAIL. I THOUGHT YOU'D WANT TO BUILD A WORLD WHERE LITTLE GIRLS WOULD NEVER HAVE TO DIE AGAIN.
THEN WE WERE SEEING DIFFERENT THINGS THAT NIGHT.
I WAS LOOKING AT THE FACE OF CHAOS. A REMINDER THAT THE WORLD LACKS ORDER, THAT UNCERTAINTY CAN REACH OUT AND SMASH US AT ANY TIME. SO LONG AS THAT CONTINUES TO BE TRUE, FIXATING ON A SINGLE DEATH IS POINTLESS.
I AM AT WAR.
I HAVE BEEN ALL MY LIFE.
AND I WOULD KILL A MILLION LITTLE GIRLS TO WIN.

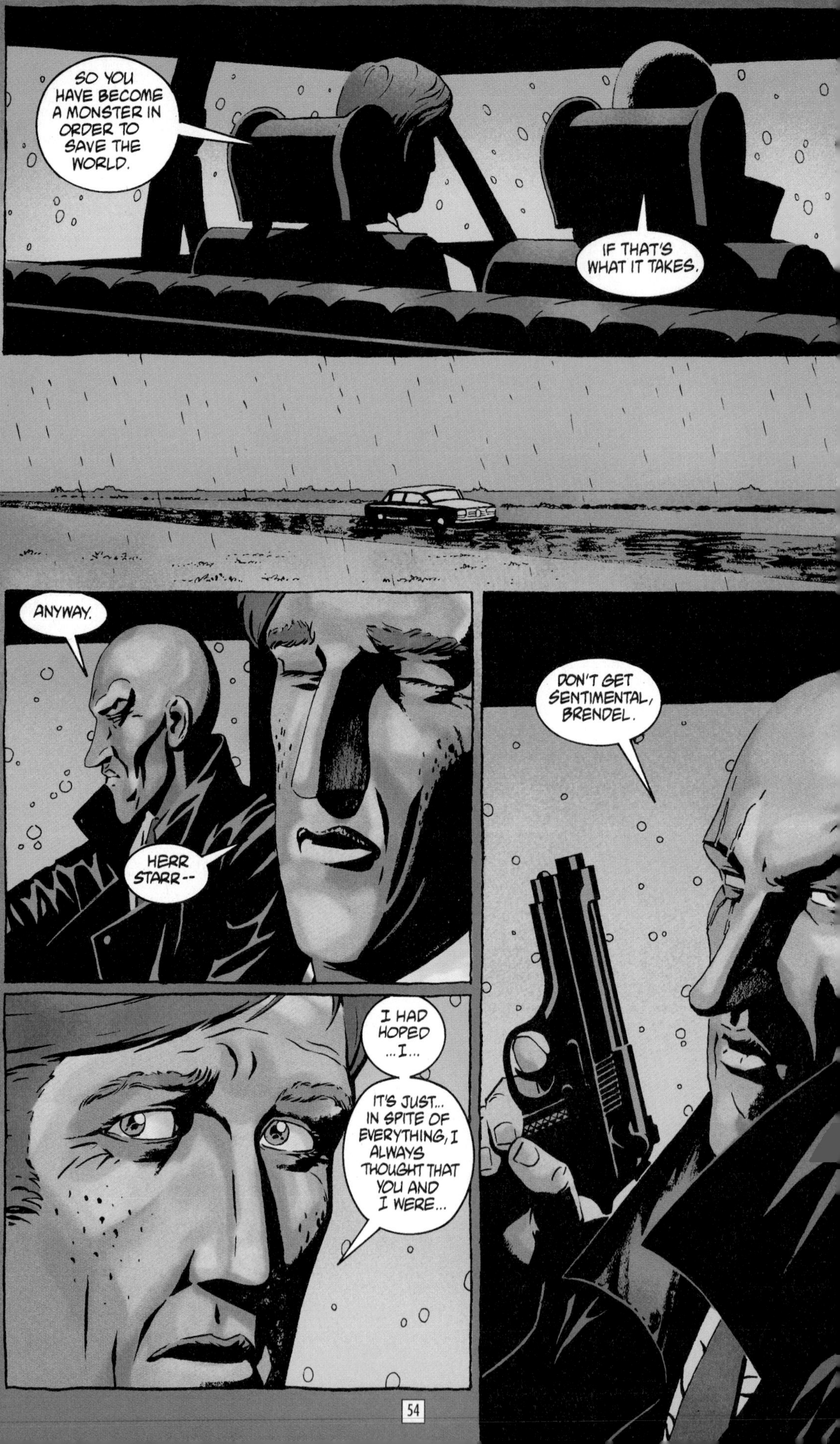
SO YOU HAVE BECOME A MONSTER IN ORDER TO SAVE THE WORLD.
IF THAT'S WHAT IT TAKES.
ANYWAY.
HERR STARR--
DON'T GET SENTIMENTAL, BRENDEL.
I HAD HOPED ...I...
IT'S JUST... IN SPITE OF EVERYTHING, I ALWAYS THOUGHT THAT YOU AND I WERE...

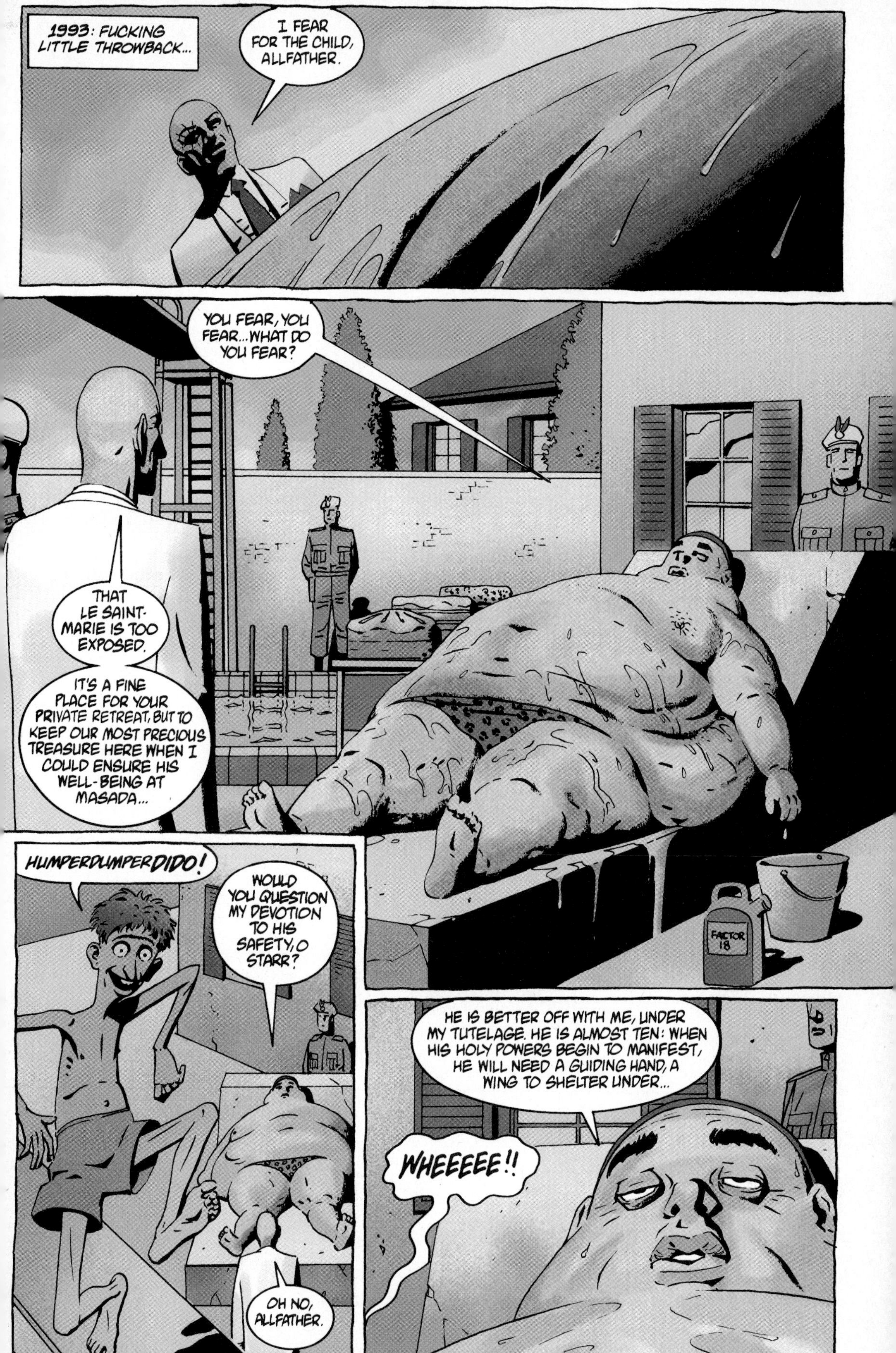
1993: FUCKING LITTLE THROWBACK...
I FEAR FOR THE CHILD, ALLFATHER.
YOU FEAR, YOU FEAR...WHAT DO YOU FEAR?
THAT LE SAINT-MARIE IS TOO EXPOSED.
IT'S A FINE PLACE FOR YOUR PRIVATE RETREAT, BUT TO KEEP OUR MOST PRECIOUS TREASURE HERE WHEN I COULD ENSURE HIS WELL-BEING AT MASADA...
FACTOR 18
HUMPERDUMPERDIDO!
WOULD YOU QUESTION MY DEVOTION TO HIS SAFETY, O STARR?
OH NO, ALLFATHER.
HE IS BETTER OFF WITH ME, UNDER MY TUTELAGE. HE IS ALMOST TEN: WHEN HIS HOLY POWERS BEGIN TO MANIFEST, HE WILL NEED A GUIDING HAND, A WING TO SHELTER UNDER...
WHEEEEE!!

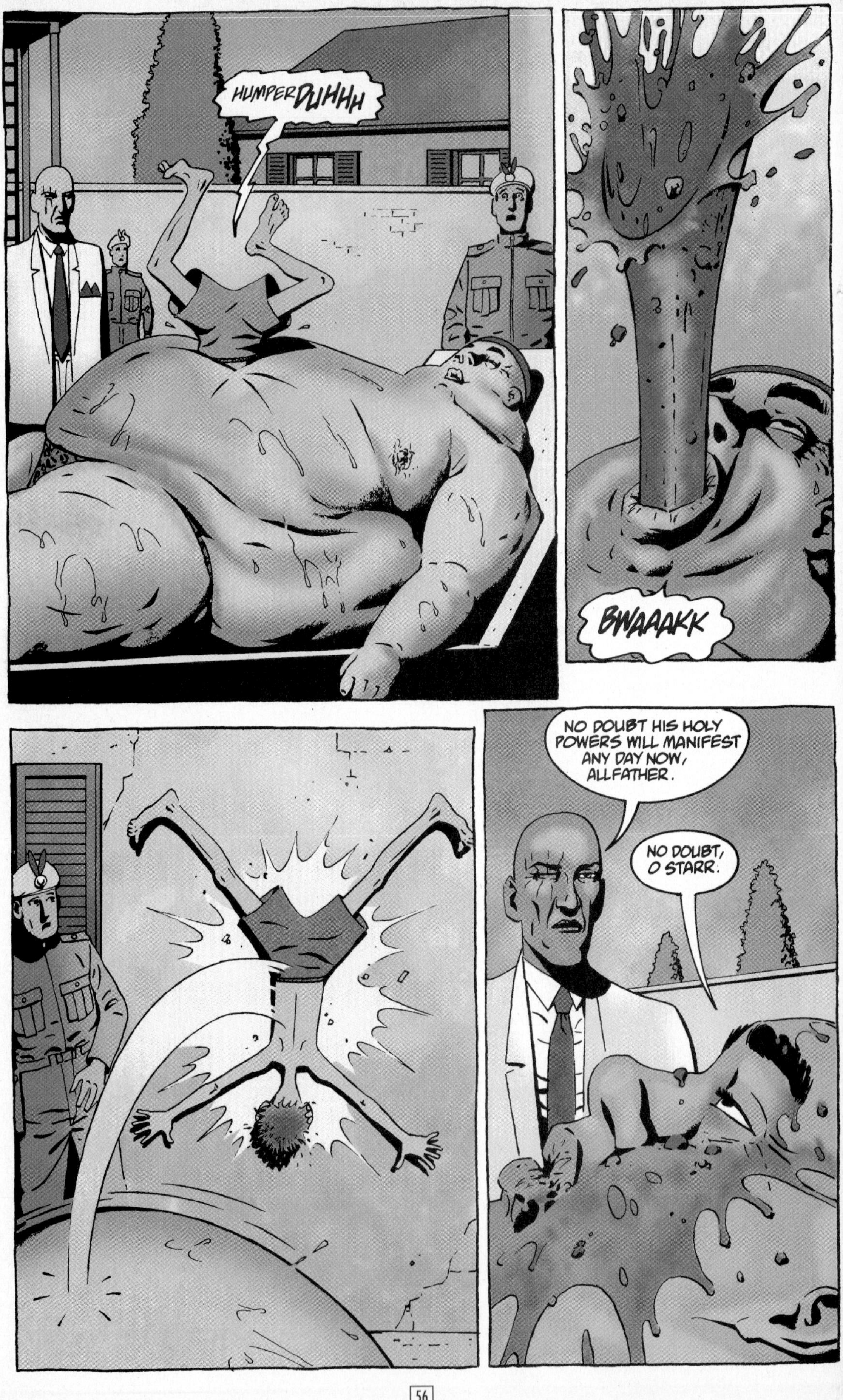
HUMPERDUHHH
BWAAAKK
NO DOUBT HIS HOLY POWERS WILL MANIFEST ANY DAY NOW, ALLFATHER.
NO DOUBT, O STARR.

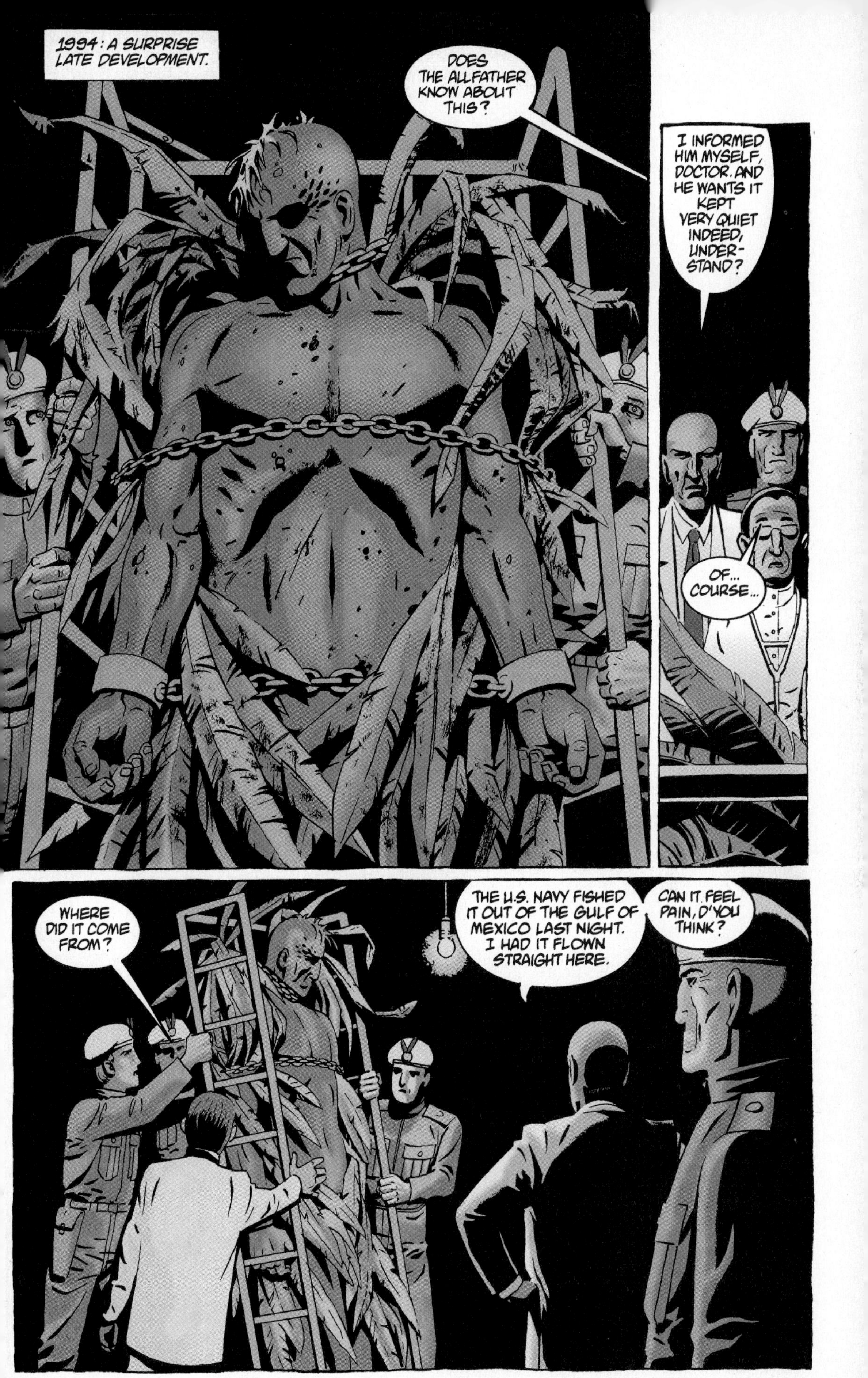
1994: A SURPRISE LATE DEVELOPMENT.
DOES THE ALLFATHER KNOW ABOUT THIS?
I INFORMED HIM MYSELF, DOCTOR. AND HE WANTS IT KEPT VERY QUIET INDEED, UNDER-STAND?
OF... COURSE...
WHERE DID IT COME FROM?
THE U.S. NAVY FISHED IT OUT OF THE GULF OF MEXICO LAST NIGHT. I HAD IT FLOWN STRAIGHT HERE.
CAN IT FEEL PAIN, D'YOU THINK?

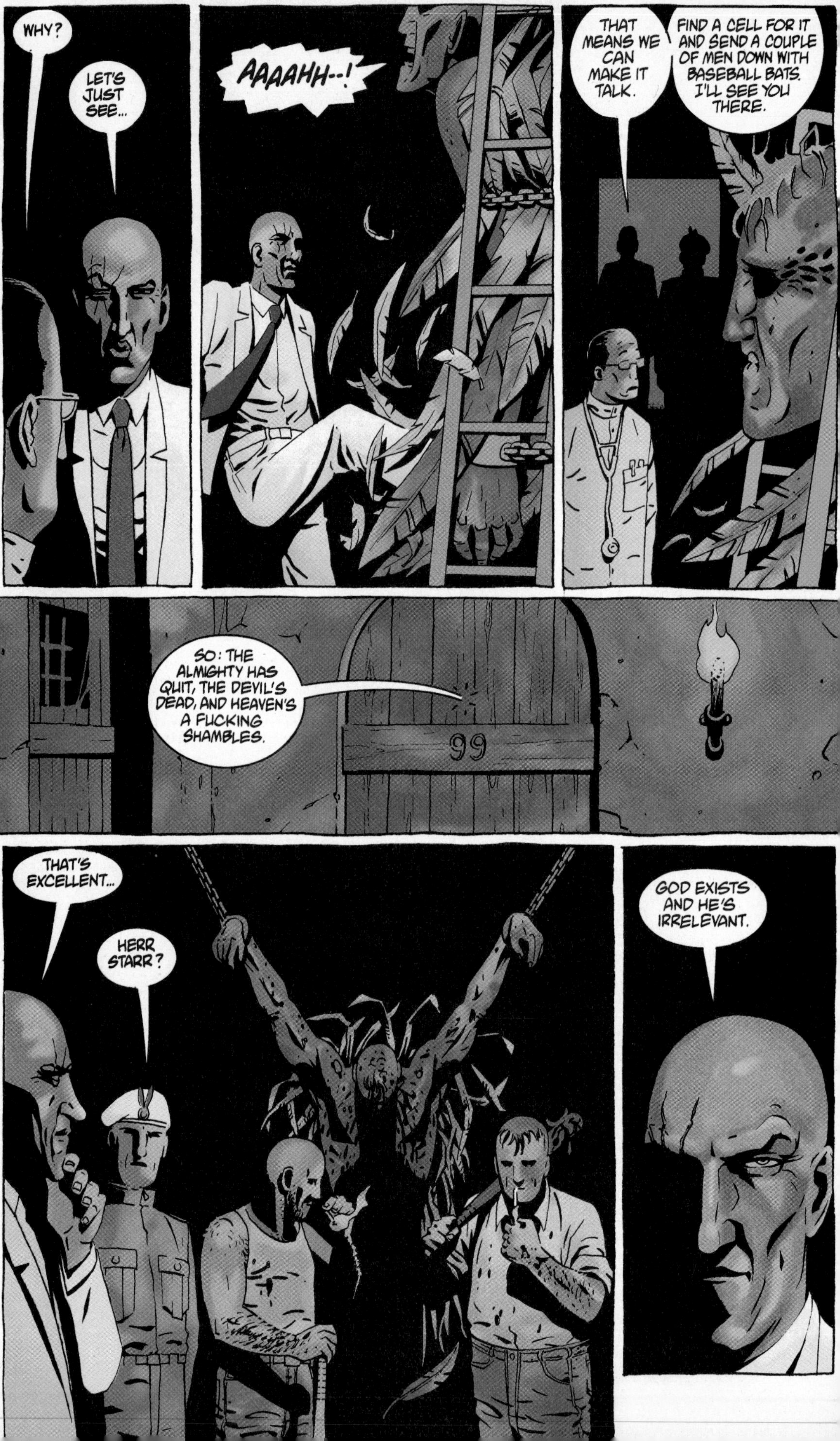
WHY?
LET'S JUST SEE...
AAAAHH--!
THAT MEANS WE CAN MAKE IT TALK.
FIND A CELL FOR IT AND SEND A COUPLE OF MEN DOWN WITH BASEBALL BATS. I'LL SEE YOU THERE.
SO: THE ALMIGHTY HAS QUIT, THE DEVIL'S DEAD, AND HEAVEN'S A FUCKING SHAMBLES.
99
THAT'S EXCELLENT...
HERR STARR?
GOD EXISTS AND HE'S IRRELEVANT.

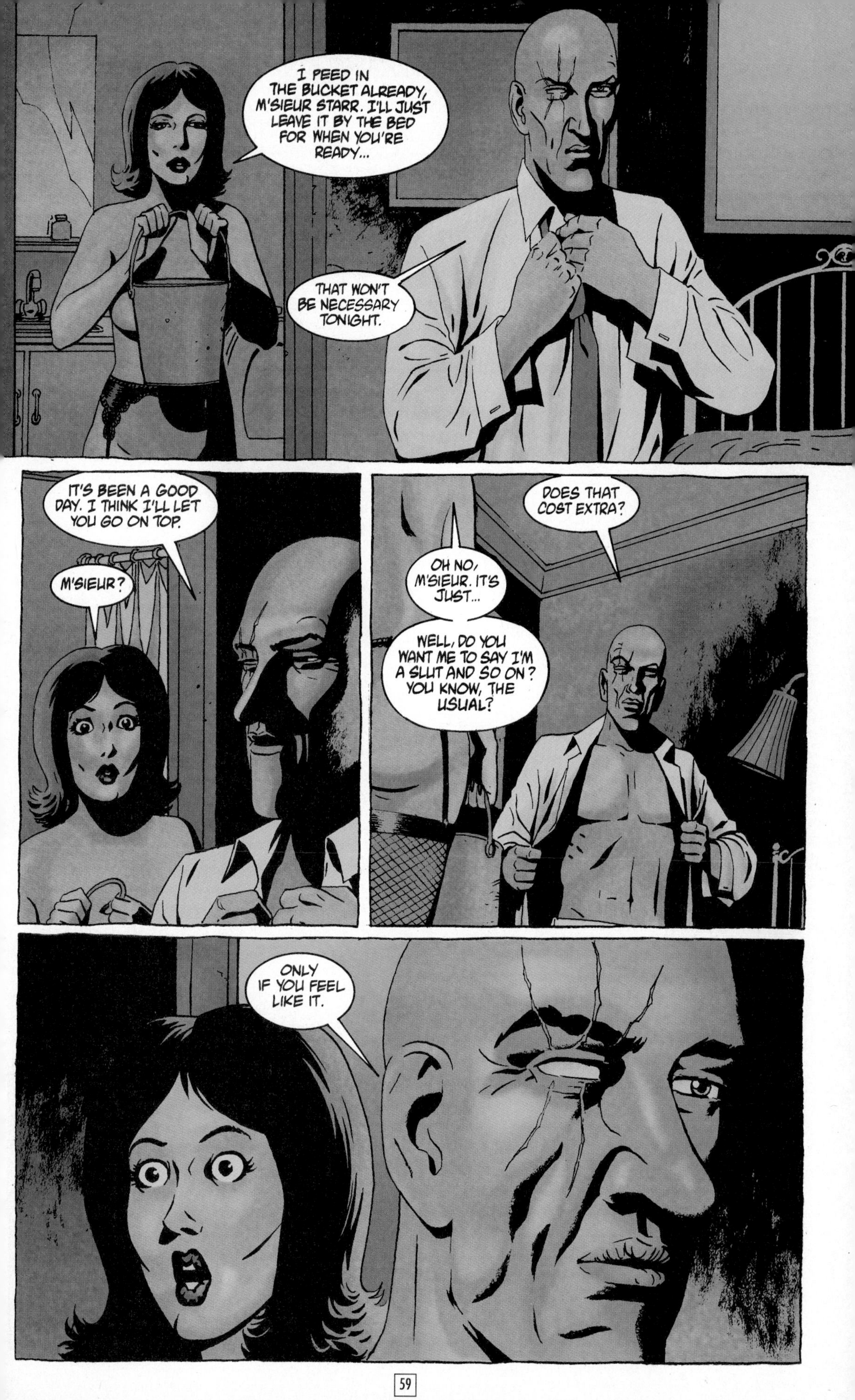

I PEED IN THE BUCKET ALREADY, M'SIEUR STARR. I'LL JUST LEAVE IT BY THE BED FOR WHEN YOU'RE READY...
THAT WON'T BE NECESSARY TONIGHT.
IT'S BEEN A GOOD DAY. I THINK I'LL LET YOU GO ON TOP.
M'SIEUR?
DOES THAT COST EXTRA?
OH NO, M'SIEUR. IT'S JUST...
WELL, DO YOU WANT ME TO SAY I'M A SLUT AND SO ON? YOU KNOW, THE USUAL?
ONLY IF YOU FEEL LIKE IT.

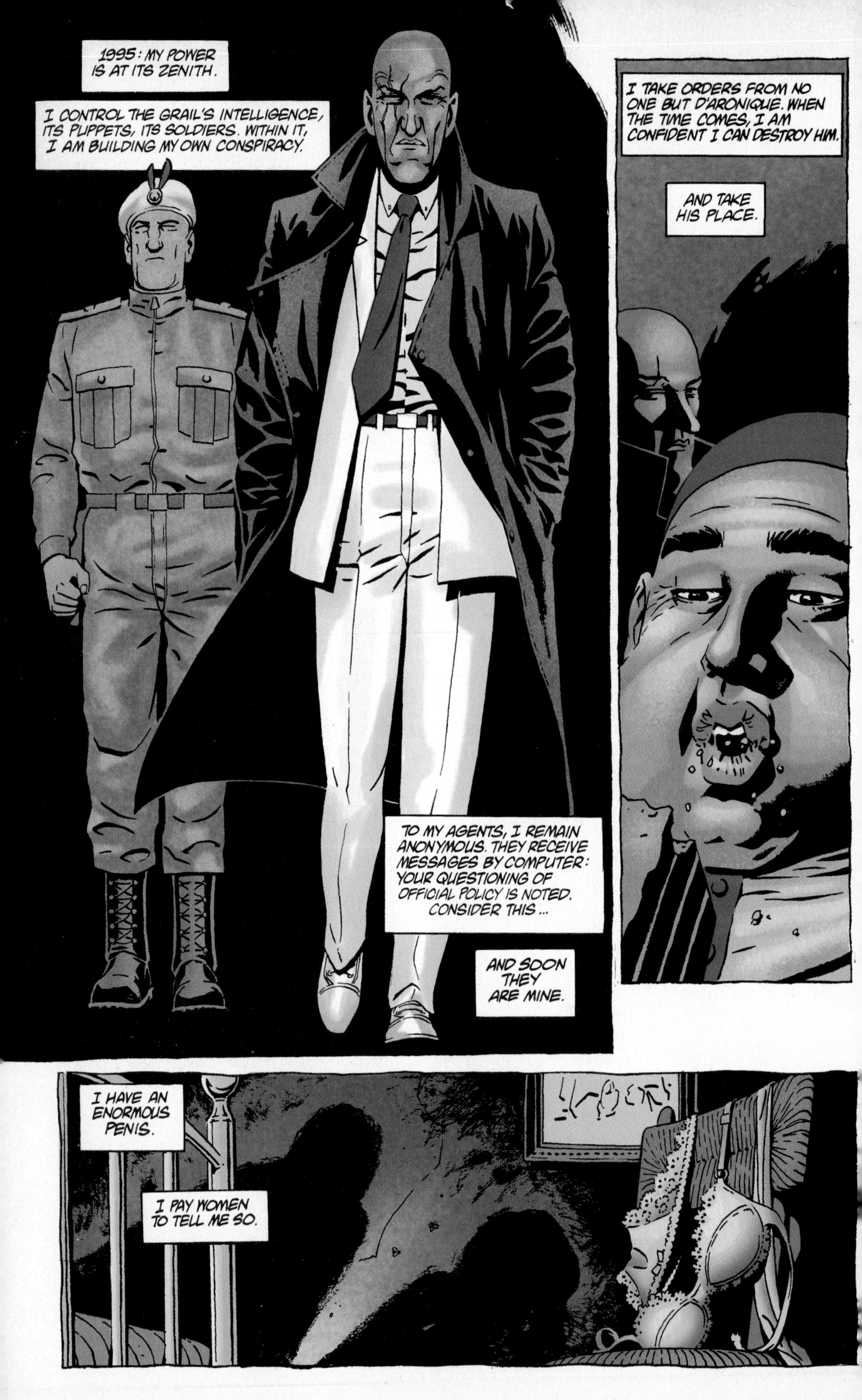
1995: MY POWER IS AT ITS ZENITH.
I CONTROL THE GRAIL'S INTELLIGENCE, ITS PUPPETS, ITS SOLDIERS. WITHIN IT, I AM BUILDING MY OWN CONSPIRACY.
TO MY AGENTS, I REMAIN ANONYMOUS. THEY RECEIVE MESSAGES BY COMPUTER: YOUR QUESTIONING OF OFFICIAL POLICY IS NOTED. CONSIDER THIS ...
AND SOON THEY ARE MINE.
I TAKE ORDERS FROM NO ONE BUT D'ARONIQUE. WHEN THE TIME COMES, I AM CONFIDENT I CAN DESTROY HIM.
AND TAKE HIS PLACE.
I HAVE AN ENORMOUS PENIS.
I PAY WOMEN TO TELL ME SO.

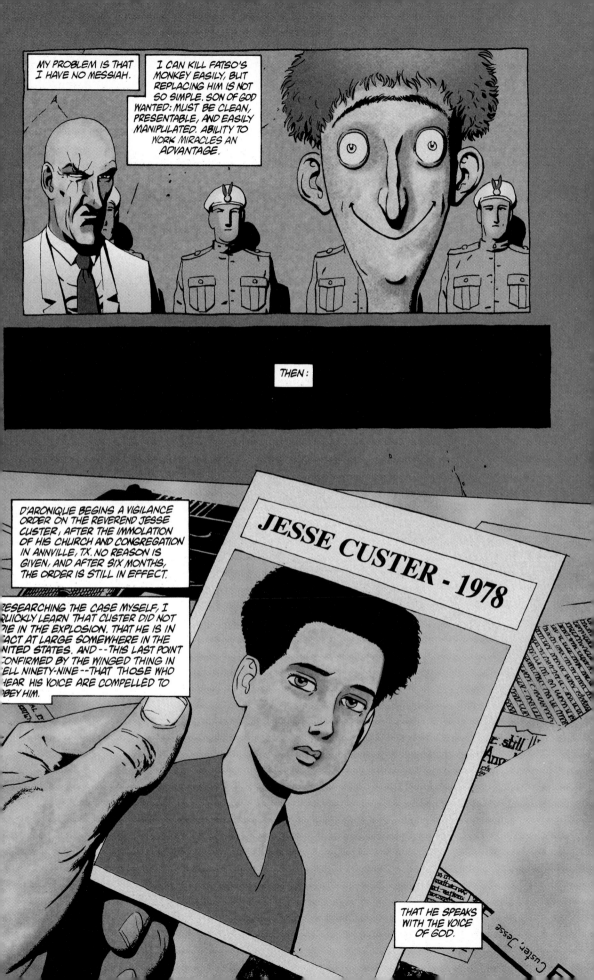

MY PROBLEM IS THAT I HAVE NO MESSIAH.

I CAN KILL FATSO'S MONKEY EASILY, BUT REPLACING HIM IS NOT SO SIMPLE. SON OF GOD WANTED: MUST BE CLEAN, PRESENTABLE, AND EASILY MANIPULATED. ABILITY TO WORK MIRACLES AN ADVANTAGE.

THEN :

D'ARONIQUE BEGINS A VIGILANCE ORDER ON THE REVEREND JESSE CUSTER, AFTER THE IMMOLATION OF HIS CHURCH AND CONGREGATION IN ANNVILLE, TX. NO REASON IS GIVEN, AND AFTER SIX MONTHS, THE ORDER IS STILL IN EFFECT.

RESEARCHING THE CASE MYSELF, I QUICKLY LEARN THAT CUSTER DID NOT DIE IN THE EXPLOSION. THAT HE IS IN FACT AT LARGE SOMEWHERE IN THE UNITED STATES. AND -- THIS LAST POINT CONFIRMED BY THE WINGED THING IN CELL NINETY-NINE -- THAT THOSE WHO HEAR HIS VOICE ARE COMPELLED TO OBEY HIM.

JESSE CUSTER - 1978

THAT HE SPEAKS WITH THE VOICE OF GOD.

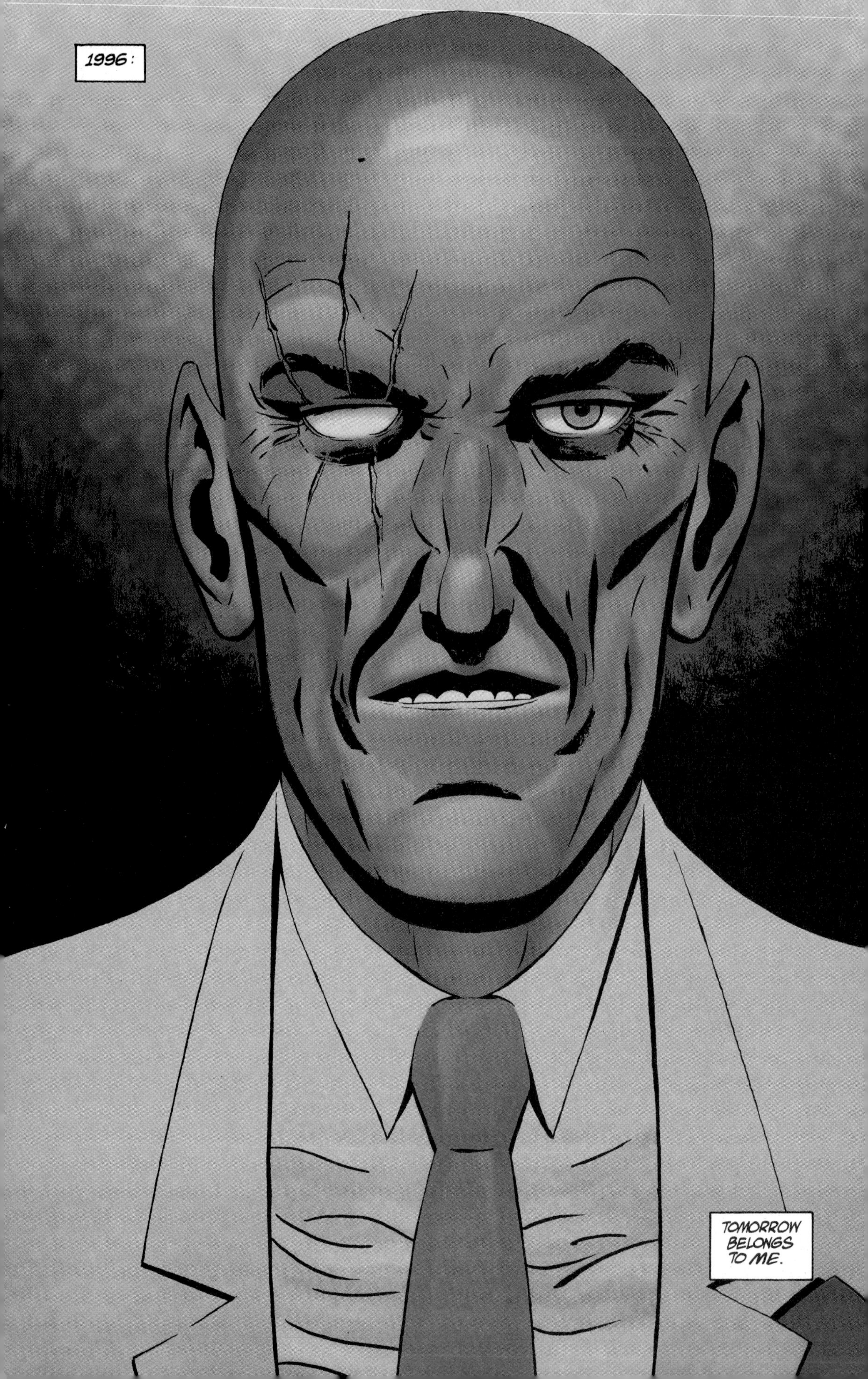
1996:
TOMORROW BELONGS TO ME.

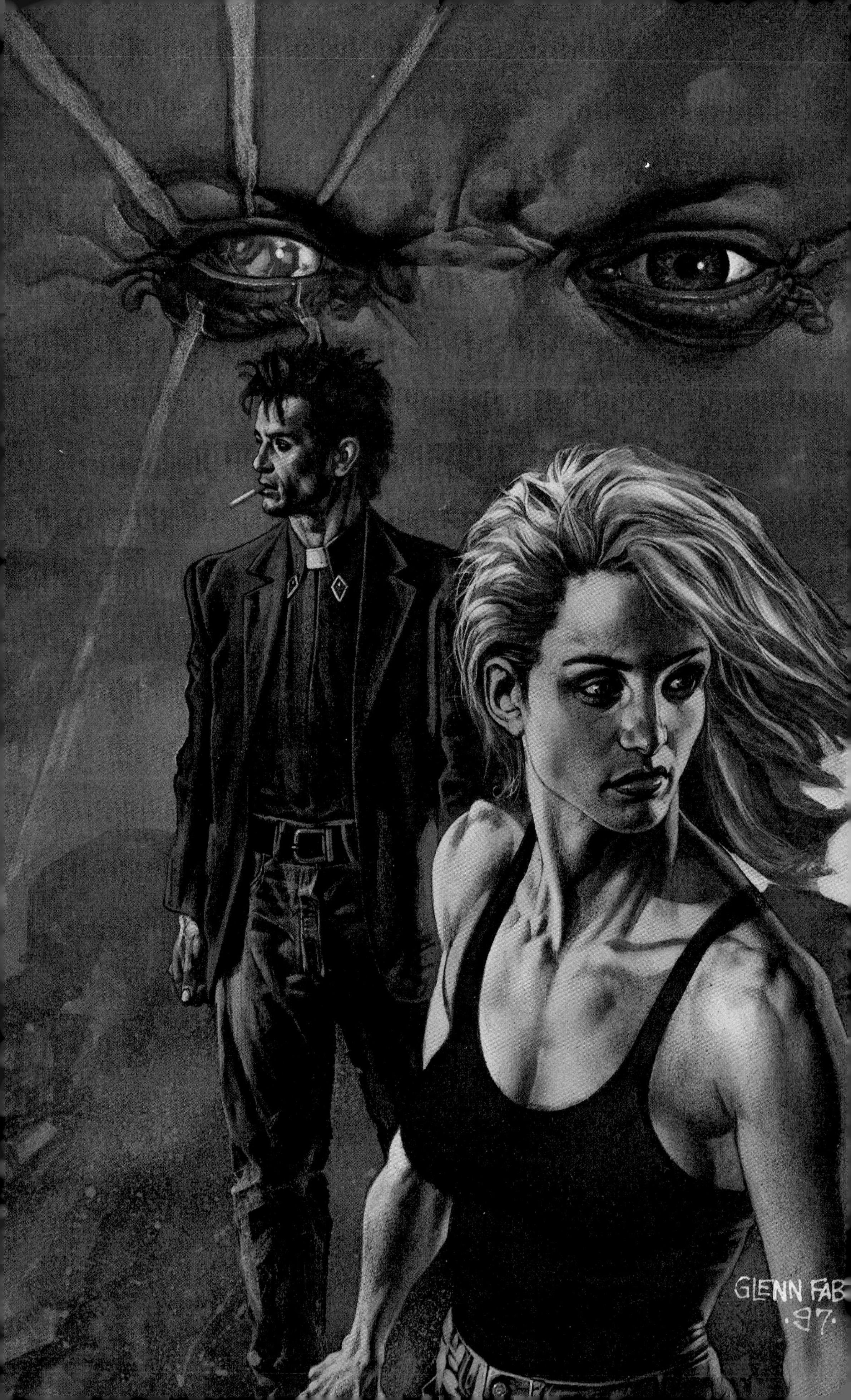
GLENN FAB
·97·

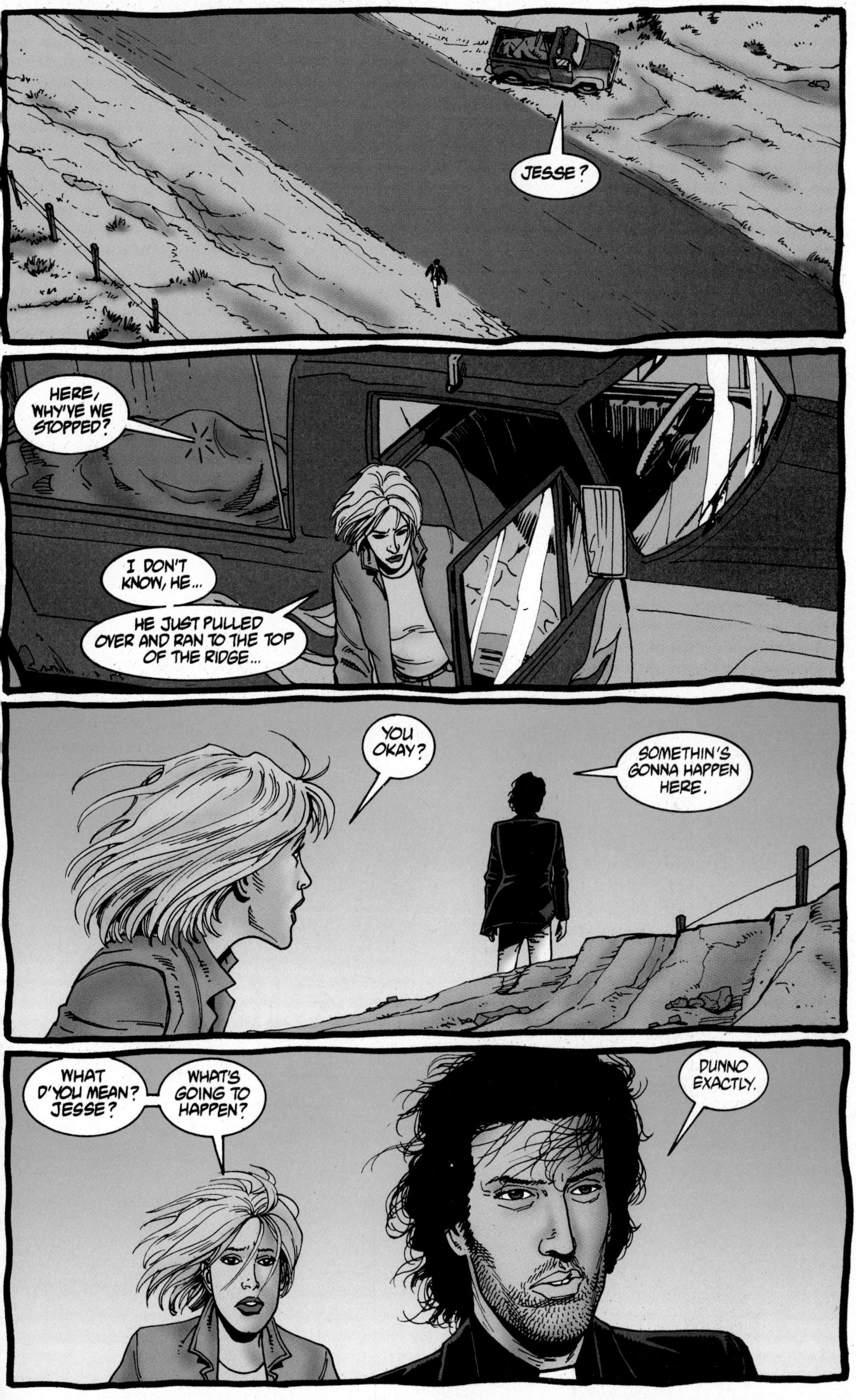
JESSE?
HERE, WHY'VE WE STOPPED?
I DON'T KNOW, HE...
HE JUST PULLED OVER AND RAN TO THE TOP OF THE RIDGE...
YOU OKAY?
SOMETHIN'S GONNA HAPPEN HERE.
WHAT D'YOU MEAN? JESSE?
WHAT'S GOING TO HAPPEN?
DUNNO EXACTLY.

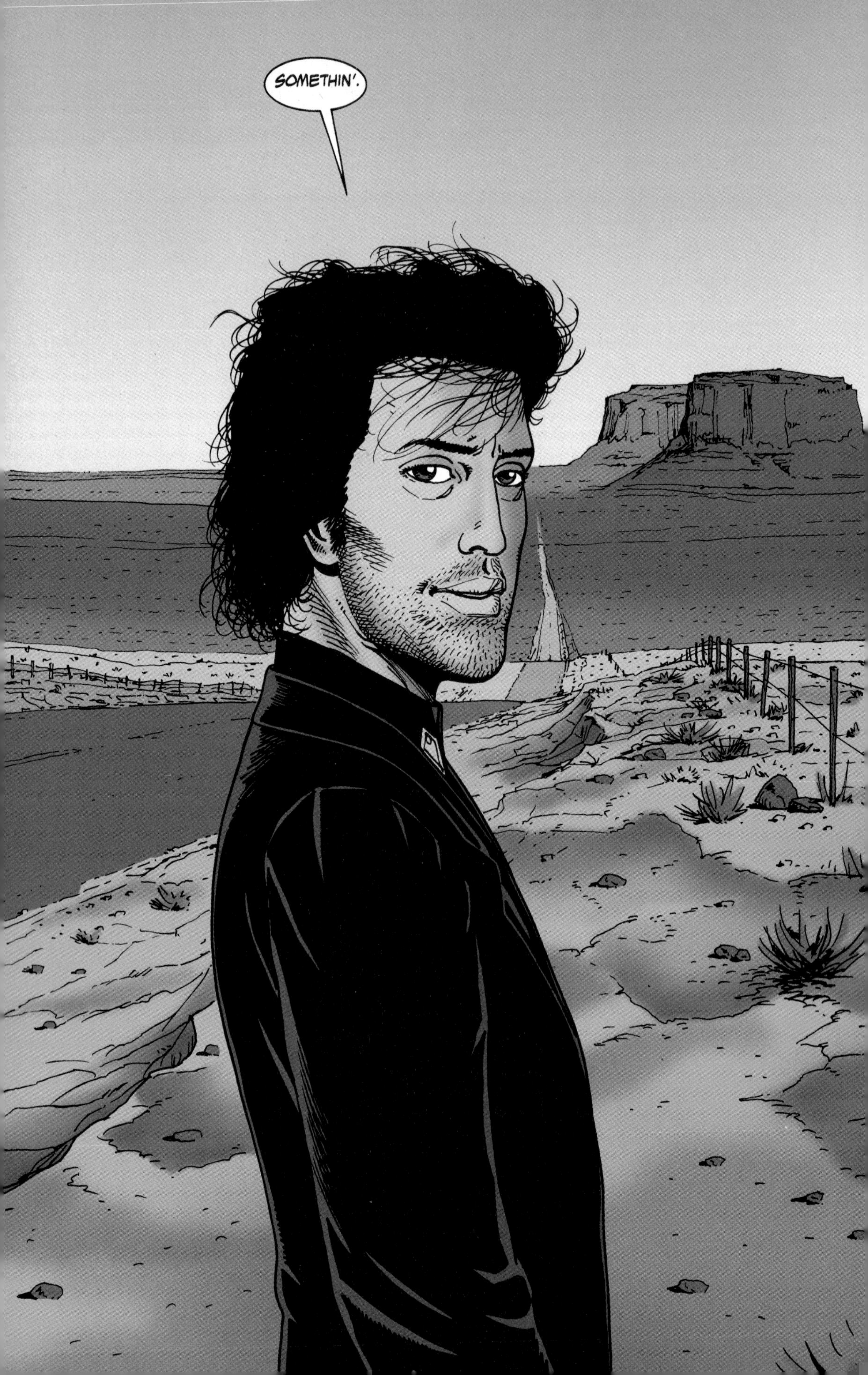
SOMETHIN'.

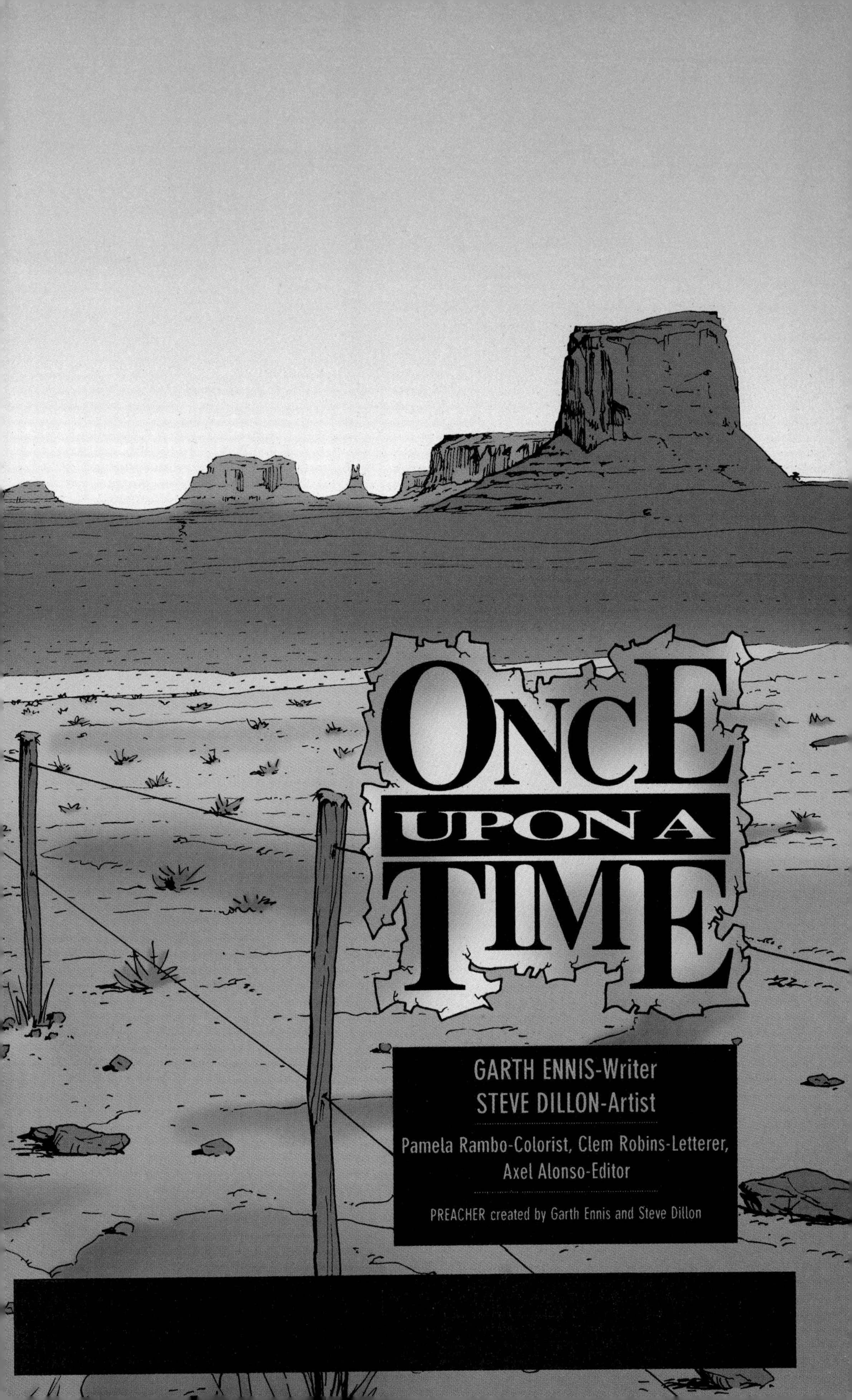
ONCE
UPON A
TIME
GARTH ENNIS-Writer
STEVE DILLON-Artist
Pamela Rambo-Colorist, Clem Robins-Letterer,
Axel Alonso-Editor
PREACHER created by Garth Ennis and Steve Dillon

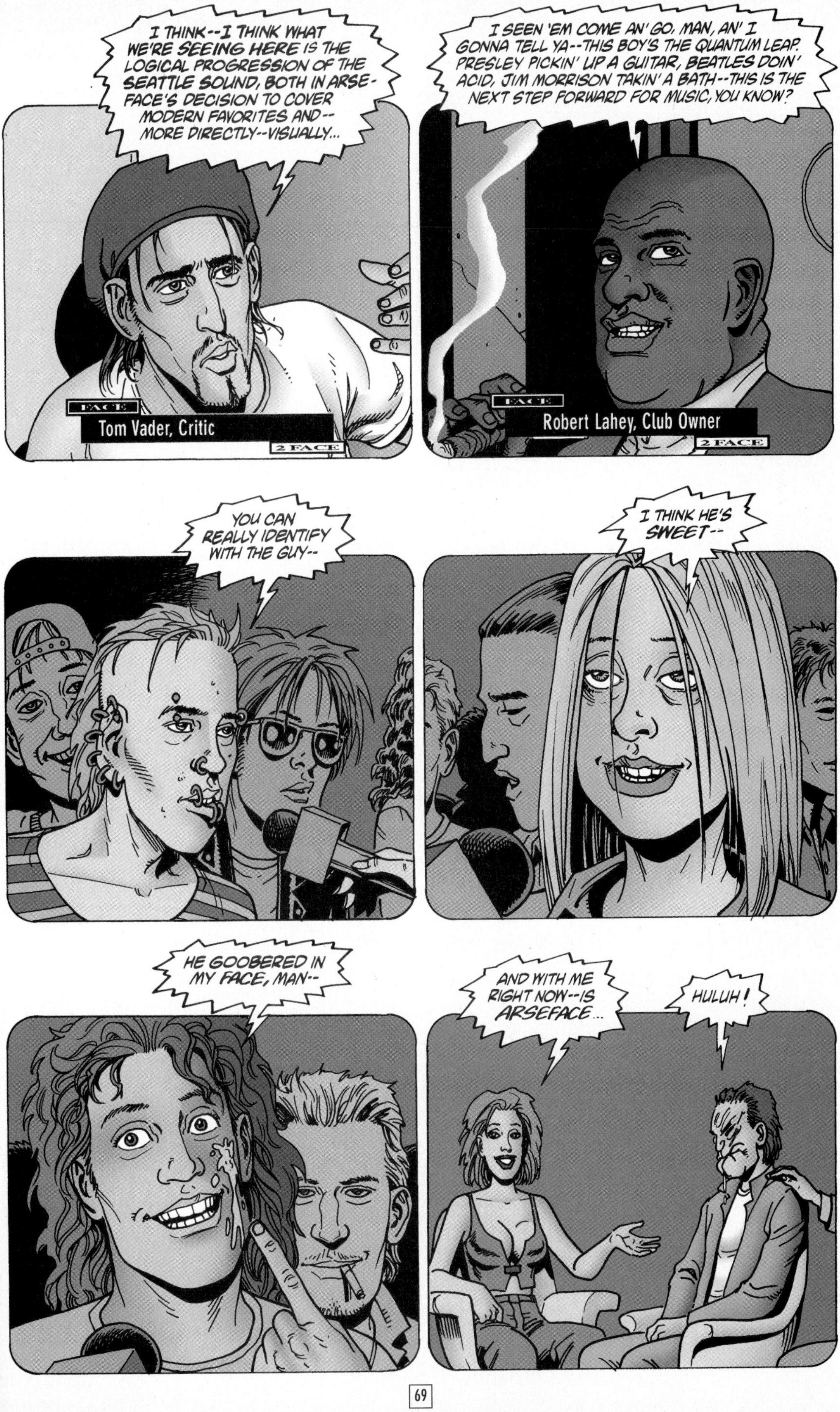

I THINK--I THINK WHAT WE'RE SEEING HERE IS THE LOGICAL PROGRESSION OF THE SEATTLE SOUND, BOTH IN ARSE-FACE'S DECISION TO COVER MODERN FAVORITES AND--MORE DIRECTLY--VISUALLY...
FACE
Tom Vader, Critic
2 FACE
I SEEN 'EM COME AN' GO, MAN, AN' I GONNA TELL YA--THIS BOY'S THE QUANTUM LEAP. PRESLEY PICKIN' UP A GUITAR, BEATLES DOIN' ACID, JIM MORRISON TAKIN' A BATH--THIS IS THE NEXT STEP FORWARD FOR MUSIC, YOU KNOW?
FACE
Robert Lahey, Club Owner
2 FACE
YOU CAN REALLY IDENTIFY WITH THE GUY--
I THINK HE'S SWEET--
HE GOOBERED IN MY FACE, MAN--
AND WITH ME RIGHT NOW--IS ARSEFACE...
HULUH!

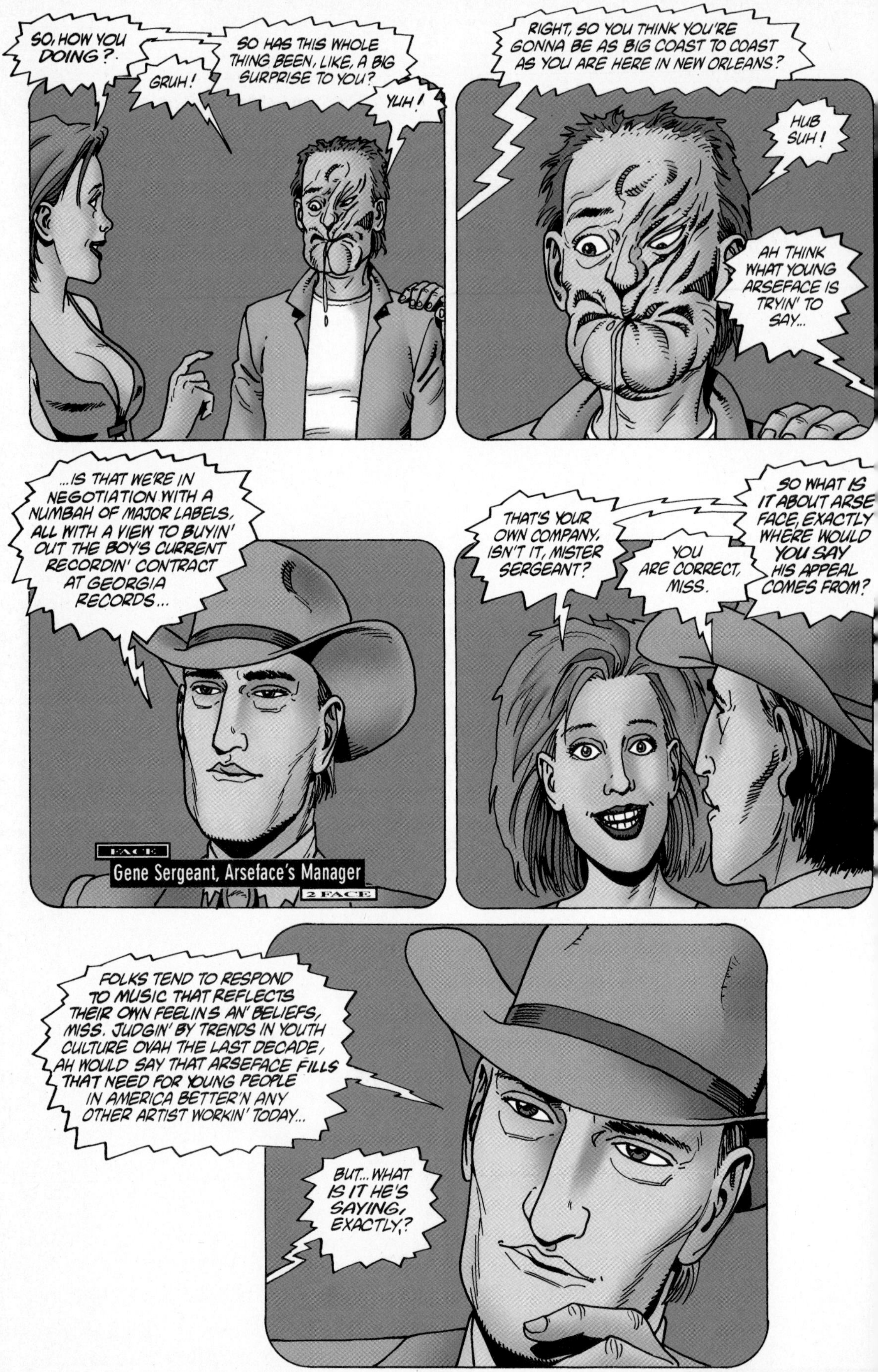
SO, HOW YOU DOING?
GRUH!
SO HAS THIS WHOLE THING BEEN, LIKE, A BIG SURPRISE TO YOU?
YUH!
RIGHT, SO YOU THINK YOU'RE GONNA BE AS BIG COAST TO COAST AS YOU ARE HERE IN NEW ORLEANS?
HUB SUH!
AH THINK WHAT YOUNG ARSEFACE IS TRYIN' TO SAY...
...IS THAT WE'RE IN NEGOTIATION WITH A NUMBAH OF MAJOR LABELS, ALL WITH A VIEW TO BUYIN' OUT THE BOY'S CURRENT RECORDIN' CONTRACT AT GEORGIA RECORDS...
FACE
Gene Sergeant, Arseface's Manager
2 FACE
THAT'S YOUR OWN COMPANY, ISN'T IT, MISTER SERGEANT?
YOU ARE CORRECT, MISS.
SO WHAT IS IT ABOUT ARSE FACE, EXACTLY WHERE WOULD YOU SAY HIS APPEAL COMES FROM?
FOLKS TEND TO RESPOND TO MUSIC THAT REFLECTS THEIR OWN FEELIN'S AN' BELIEFS, MISS. JUDGIN' BY TRENDS IN YOUTH CULTURE OVAH THE LAST DECADE, AH WOULD SAY THAT ARSEFACE FILLS THAT NEED FOR YOUNG PEOPLE IN AMERICA BETTER'N ANY OTHER ARTIST WORKIN' TODAY...
BUT...WHAT IS IT HE'S SAYING, EXACTLY?

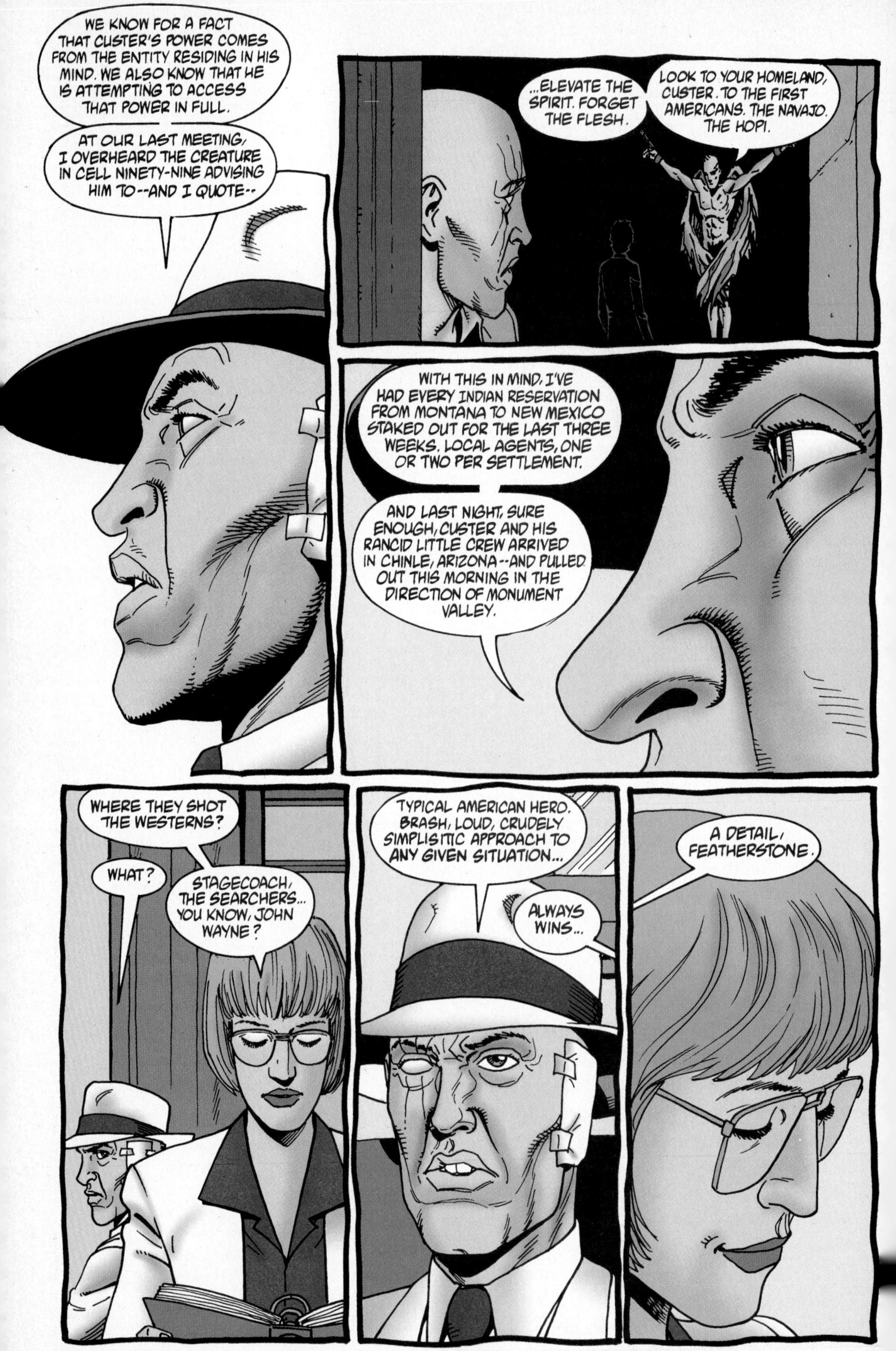
WE KNOW FOR A FACT THAT CUSTER'S POWER COMES FROM THE ENTITY RESIDING IN HIS MIND. WE ALSO KNOW THAT HE IS ATTEMPTING TO ACCESS THAT POWER IN FULL.
AT OUR LAST MEETING, I OVERHEARD THE CREATURE IN CELL NINETY-NINE ADVISING HIM TO--AND I QUOTE--
...ELEVATE THE SPIRIT. FORGET THE FLESH.
LOOK TO YOUR HOMELAND, CUSTER. TO THE FIRST AMERICANS. THE NAVAJO. THE HOPI.
WITH THIS IN MIND, I'VE HAD EVERY INDIAN RESERVATION FROM MONTANA TO NEW MEXICO STAKED OUT FOR THE LAST THREE WEEKS. LOCAL AGENTS, ONE OR TWO PER SETTLEMENT.
AND LAST NIGHT, SURE ENOUGH, CUSTER AND HIS RANCID LITTLE CREW ARRIVED IN CHINLE, ARIZONA--AND PULLED OUT THIS MORNING IN THE DIRECTION OF MONUMENT VALLEY.
WHERE THEY SHOT THE WESTERNS?
WHAT?
STAGECOACH, THE SEARCHERS... YOU KNOW, JOHN WAYNE?
TYPICAL AMERICAN HERO. BRASH, LOUD, CRUDELY SIMPLISITIC APPROACH TO ANY GIVEN SITUATION...
ALWAYS WINS...
A DETAIL, FEATHERSTONE.

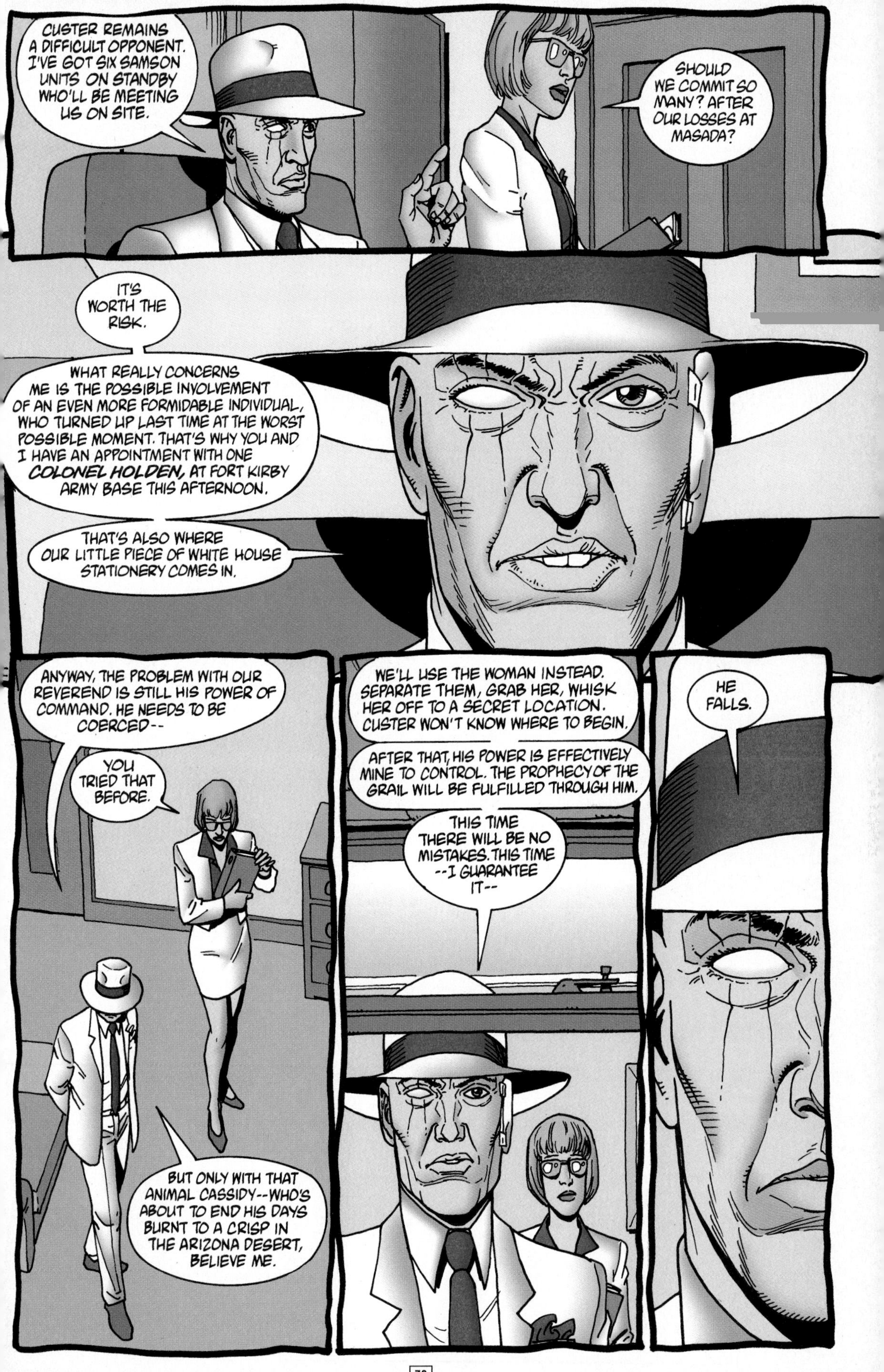
CUSTER REMAINS A DIFFICULT OPPONENT. I'VE GOT SIX SAMSON UNITS ON STANDBY WHO'LL BE MEETING US ON SITE.
SHOULD WE COMMIT SO MANY? AFTER OUR LOSSES AT MASADA?
IT'S WORTH THE RISK.
WHAT REALLY CONCERNS ME IS THE POSSIBLE INVOLVEMENT OF AN EVEN MORE FORMIDABLE INDIVIDUAL, WHO TURNED UP LAST TIME AT THE WORST POSSIBLE MOMENT. THAT'S WHY YOU AND I HAVE AN APPOINTMENT WITH ONE ***COLONEL HOLDEN,*** AT FORT KIRBY ARMY BASE THIS AFTERNOON.
THAT'S ALSO WHERE OUR LITTLE PIECE OF WHITE HOUSE STATIONERY COMES IN.
ANYWAY, THE PROBLEM WITH OUR REVEREND IS STILL HIS POWER OF COMMAND. HE NEEDS TO BE COERCED--
YOU TRIED THAT BEFORE.
BUT ONLY WITH THAT ANIMAL CASSIDY--WHO'S ABOUT TO END HIS DAYS BURNT TO A CRISP IN THE ARIZONA DESERT, BELIEVE ME.
WE'LL USE THE WOMAN INSTEAD. SEPARATE THEM, GRAB HER, WHISK HER OFF TO A SECRET LOCATION. CUSTER WON'T KNOW WHERE TO BEGIN.
AFTER THAT, HIS POWER IS EFFECTIVELY MINE TO CONTROL. THE PROPHECY OF THE GRAIL WILL BE FULFILLED THROUGH HIM.
THIS TIME THERE WILL BE NO MISTAKES. THIS TIME --I GUARANTEE IT--
HE FALLS.

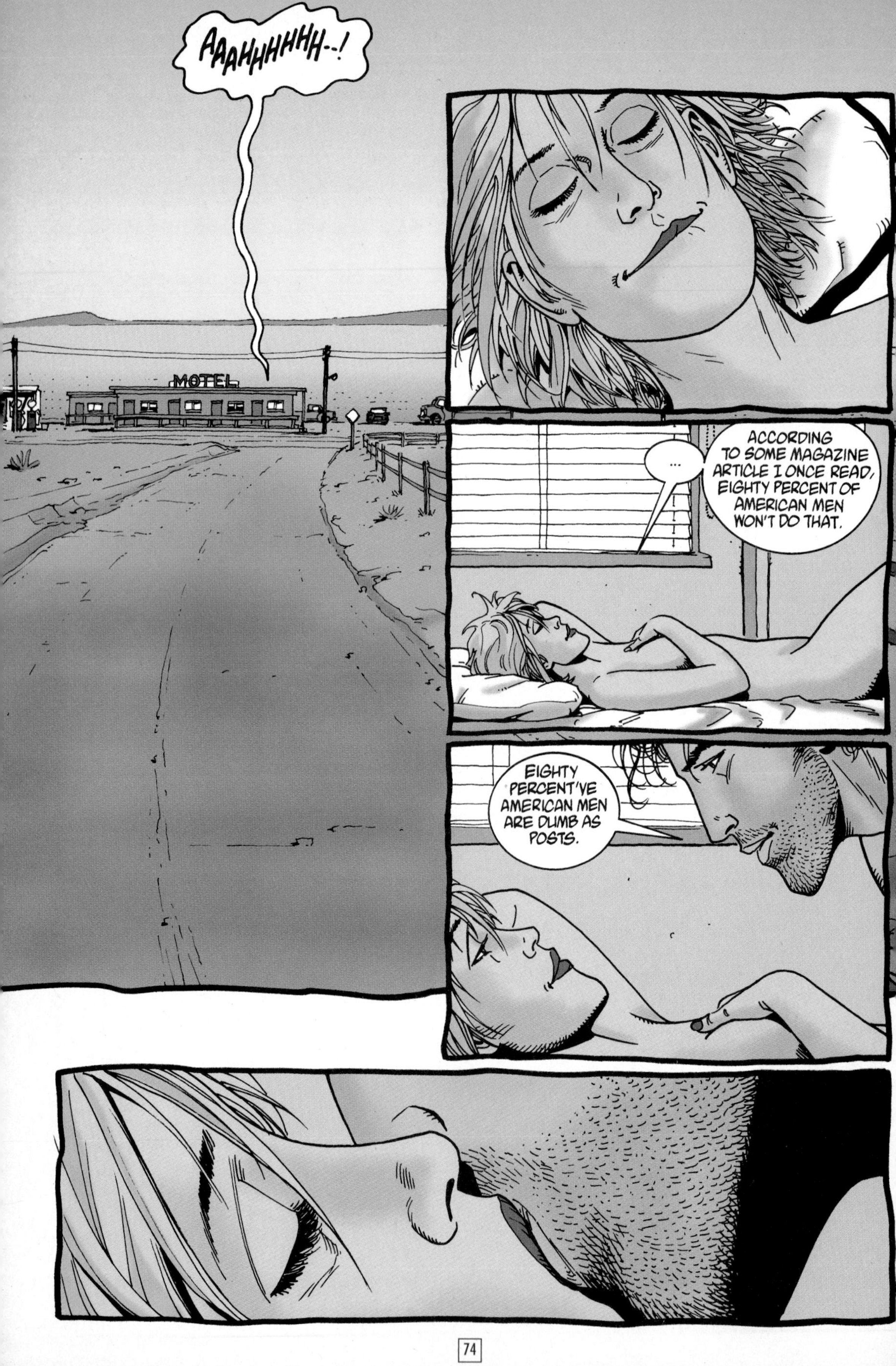
AAAHHHHHH--!
MOTEL
...
ACCORDING TO SOME MAGAZINE ARTICLE I ONCE READ, EIGHTY PERCENT OF AMERICAN MEN WON'T DO THAT.
EIGHTY PERCENT'YE AMERICAN MEN ARE DUMB AS POSTS.

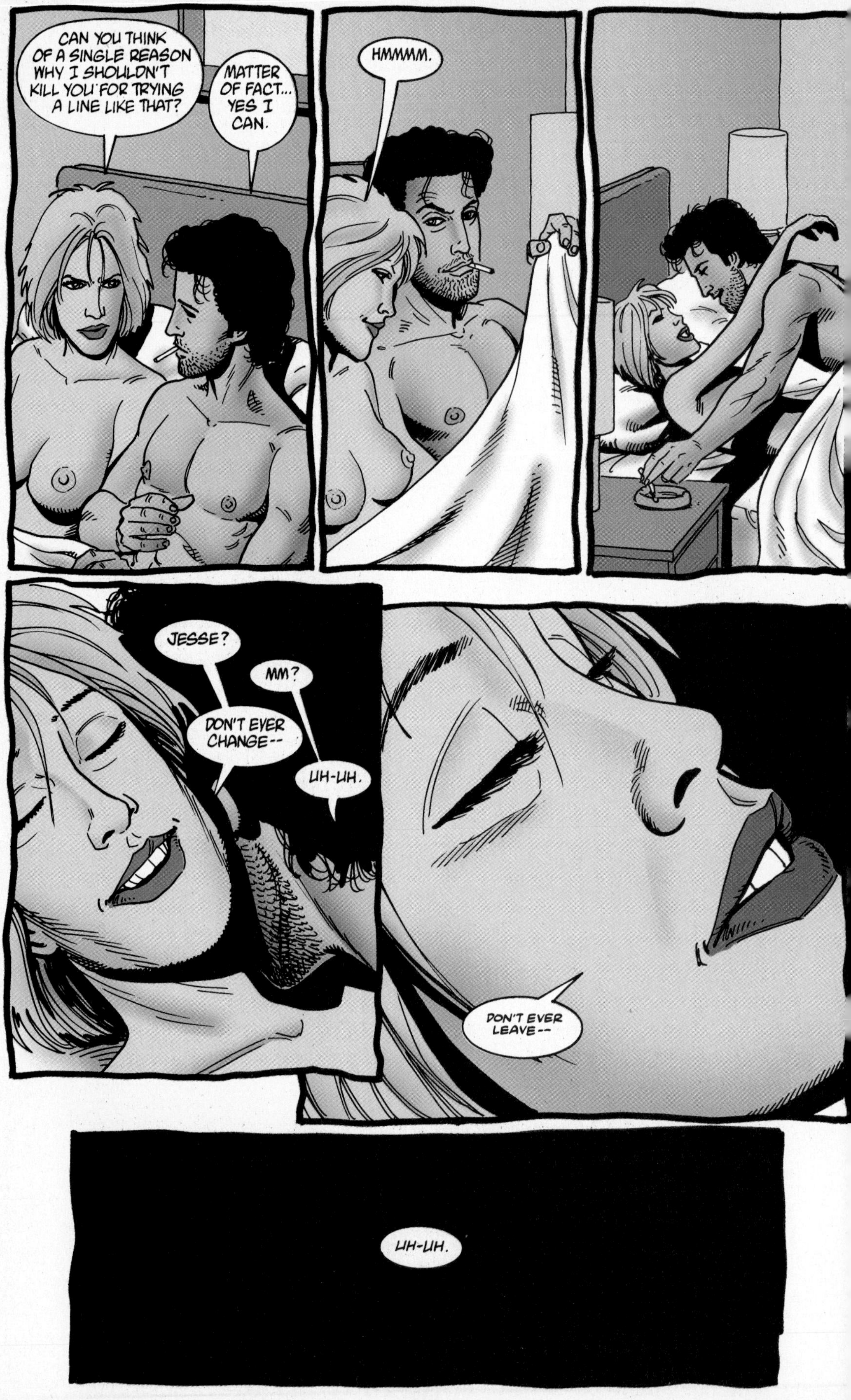
CAN YOU THINK OF A SINGLE REASON WHY I SHOULDN'T KILL YOU FOR TRYING A LINE LIKE THAT?
MATTER OF FACT... YES I CAN.
HMMMM.
JESSE?
MM?
DON'T EVER CHANGE--
UH-UH.
DON'T EVER LEAVE--
UH-UH.

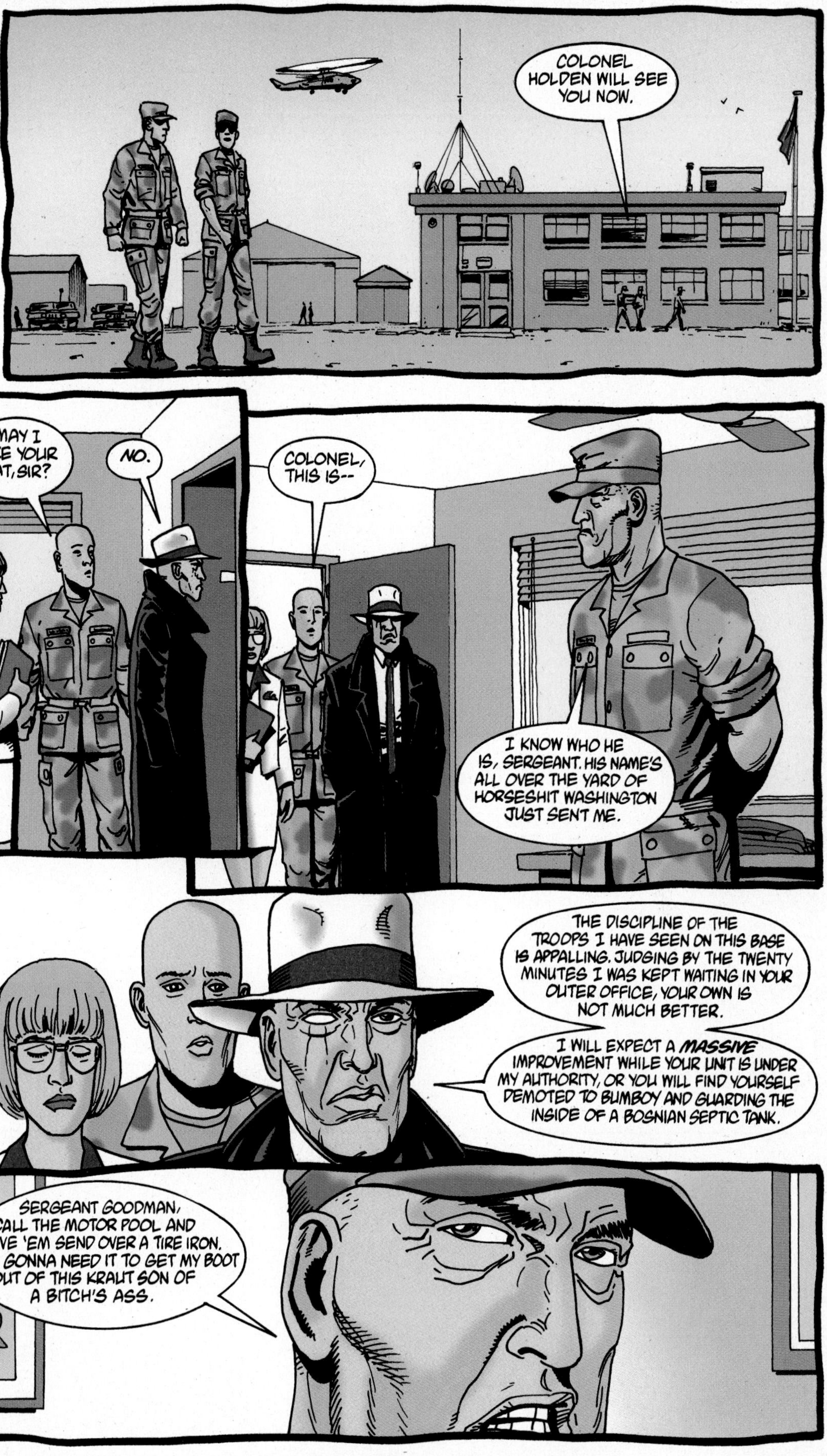
COLONEL HOLDEN WILL SEE YOU NOW.
MAY I TAKE YOUR HAT, SIR?
NO.
COLONEL, THIS IS--
I KNOW WHO HE IS, SERGEANT. HIS NAME'S ALL OVER THE YARD OF HORSESHIT WASHINGTON JUST SENT ME.
THE DISCIPLINE OF THE TROOPS I HAVE SEEN ON THIS BASE IS APPALLING. JUDGING BY THE TWENTY MINUTES I WAS KEPT WAITING IN YOUR OUTER OFFICE, YOUR OWN IS NOT MUCH BETTER.
I WILL EXPECT A *MASSIVE* IMPROVEMENT WHILE YOUR UNIT IS UNDER MY AUTHORITY, OR YOU WILL FIND YOURSELF DEMOTED TO BUMBOY AND GUARDING THE INSIDE OF A BOSNIAN SEPTIC TANK.
SERGEANT GOODMAN, CALL THE MOTOR POOL AND HAVE 'EM SEND OVER A TIRE IRON. I'M GONNA NEED IT TO GET MY BOOT OUT OF THIS KRAUT SON OF A BITCH'S ASS.

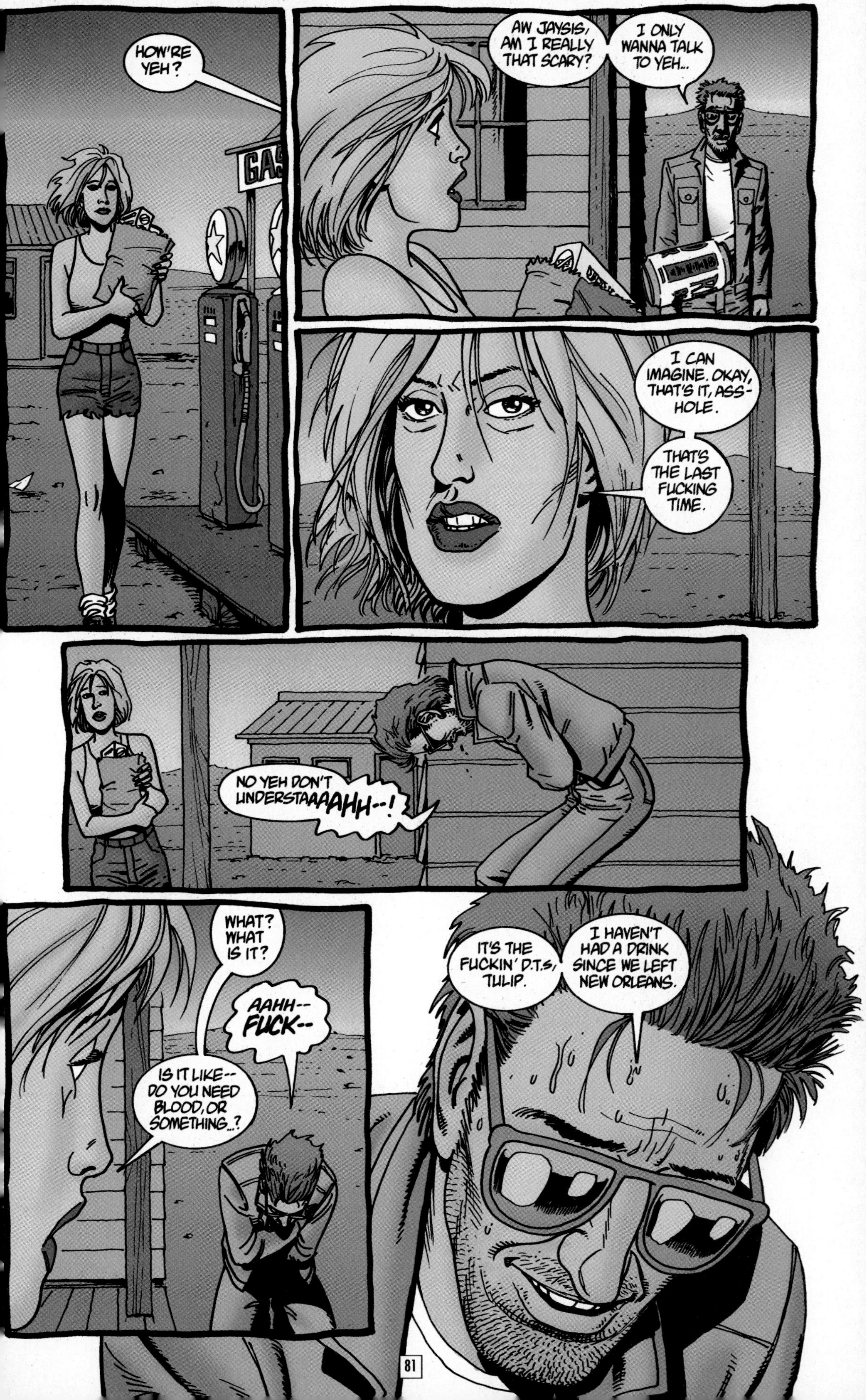

HOW'RE YEH?
AW JAYSIS, AM I REALLY THAT SCARY?
I ONLY WANNA TALK TO YEH...
I CAN IMAGINE. OKAY, THAT'S IT, ASS-HOLE.
THAT'S THE LAST FUCKING TIME.
NO YEH DON'T UNDERSTAAAAHH--!
WHAT? WHAT IS IT?
AAHH-- FUCK--
IS IT LIKE-- DO YOU NEED BLOOD, OR SOMETHING..?
IT'S THE FUCKIN' D.T.s, TULIP.
I HAVEN'T HAD A DRINK SINCE WE LEFT NEW ORLEANS.

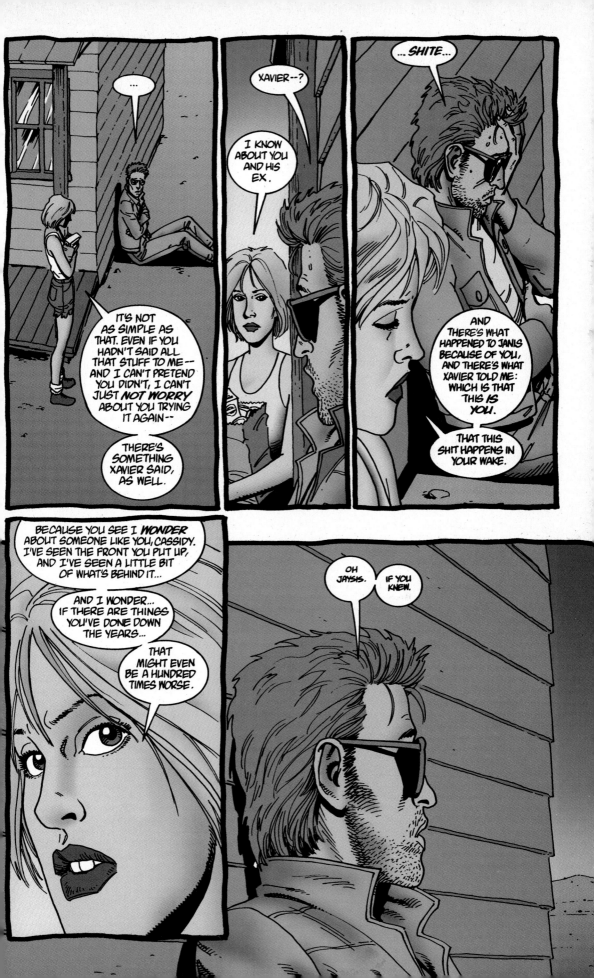

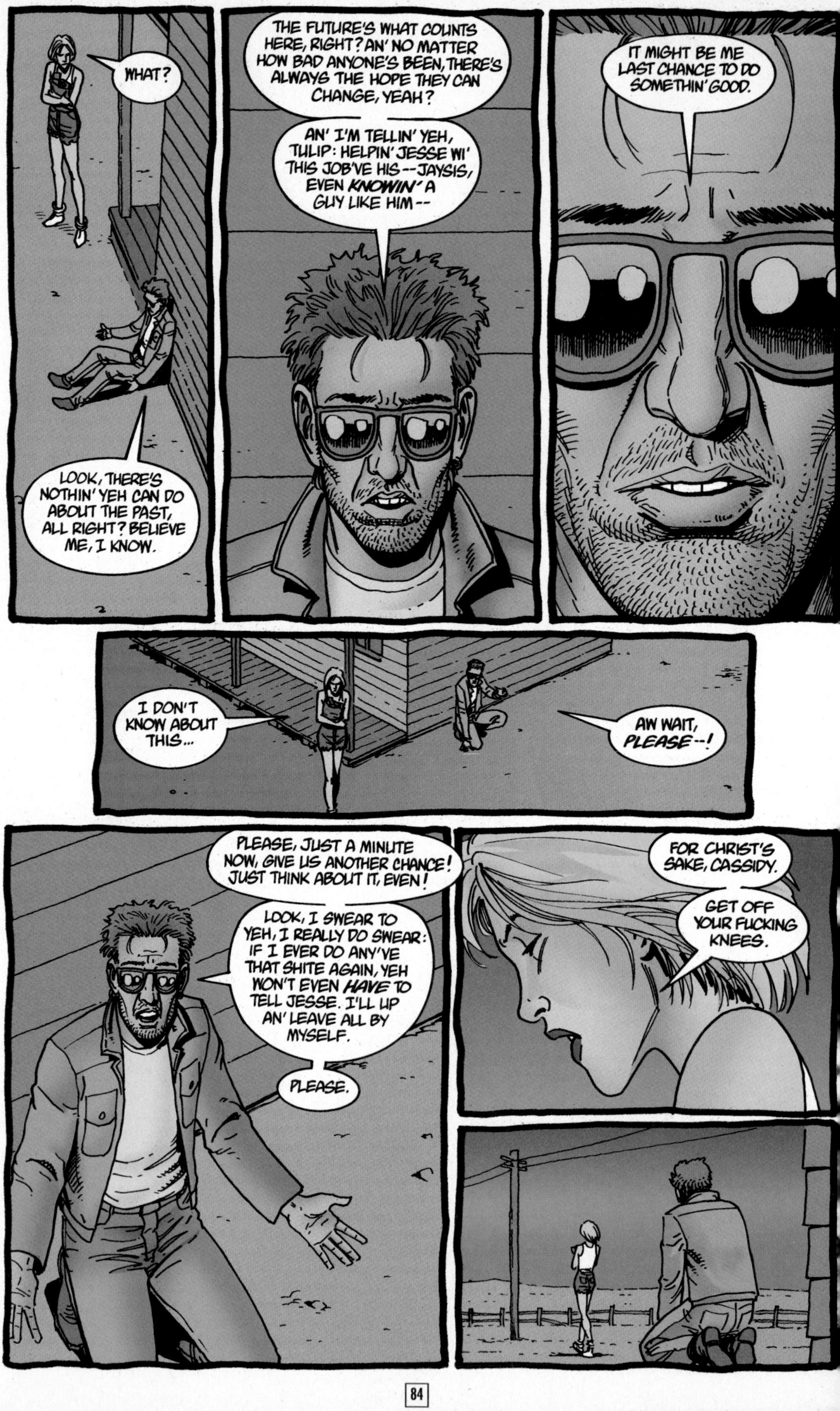
WHAT?
LOOK, THERE'S NOTHIN' YEH CAN DO ABOUT THE PAST, ALL RIGHT? BELIEVE ME, I KNOW.
THE FUTURE'S WHAT COUNTS HERE, RIGHT? AN' NO MATTER HOW BAD ANYONE'S BEEN, THERE'S ALWAYS THE HOPE THEY CAN CHANGE, YEAH?
AN' I'M TELLIN' YEH, TULIP: HELPIN' JESSE WI' THIS JOB'VE HIS--JAYSIS, EVEN *KNOWIN'* A GUY LIKE HIM--
IT MIGHT BE ME LAST CHANCE TO DO SOMETHIN' GOOD.
I DON'T KNOW ABOUT THIS...
AW WAIT, *PLEASE*--!
PLEASE, JUST A MINUTE NOW, GIVE US ANOTHER CHANCE! JUST THINK ABOUT IT, EVEN!
LOOK, I SWEAR TO YEH, I REALLY DO SWEAR: IF I EVER DO ANY'VE THAT SHITE AGAIN, YEH WON'T EVEN *HAVE* TO TELL JESSE. I'LL UP AN' LEAVE ALL BY MYSELF.
PLEASE.
FOR CHRIST'S SAKE, CASSIDY.
GET OFF YOUR FUCKING KNEES.

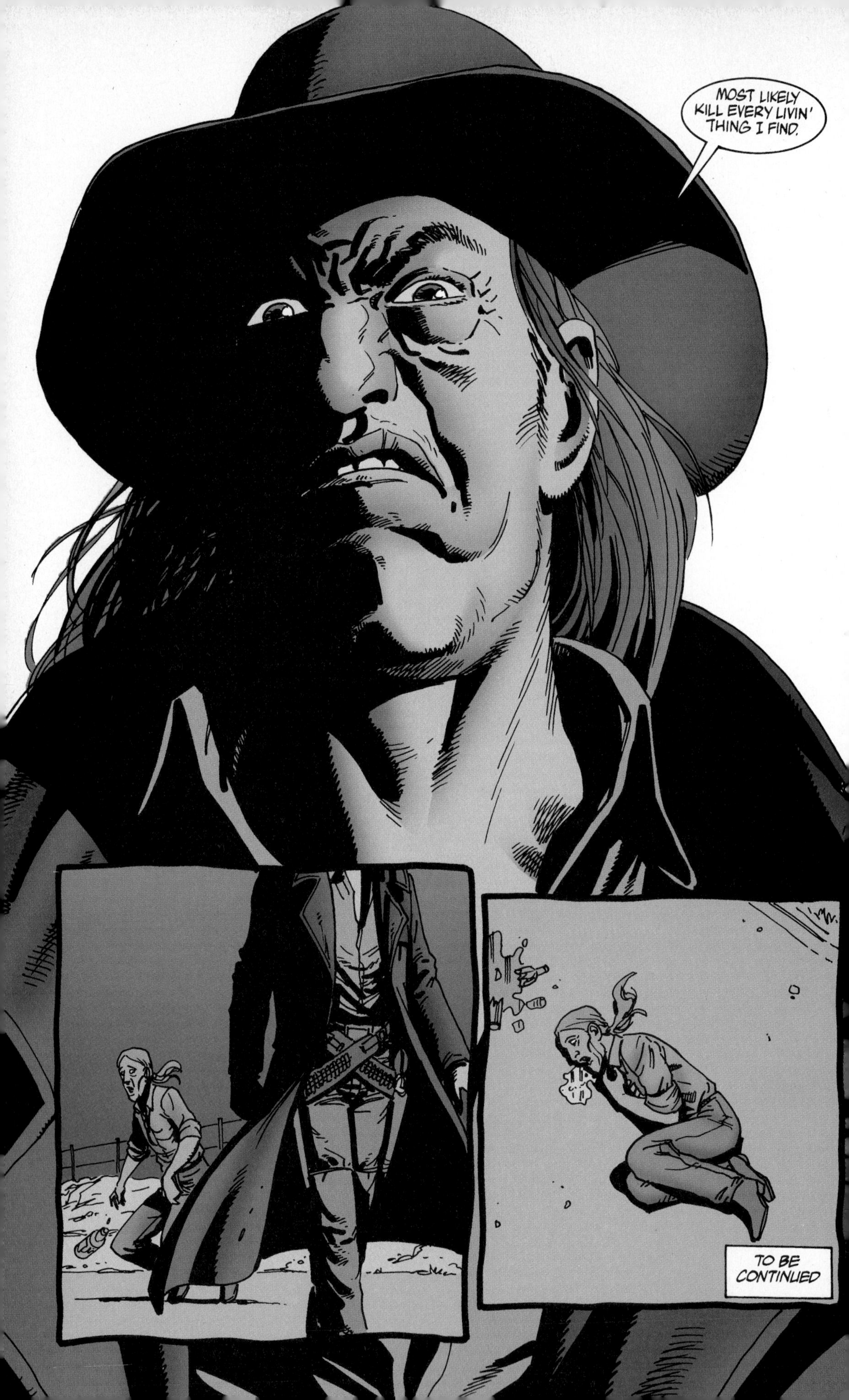
MOST LIKELY KILL EVERY LIVIN' THING I FIND.
TO BE CONTINUED

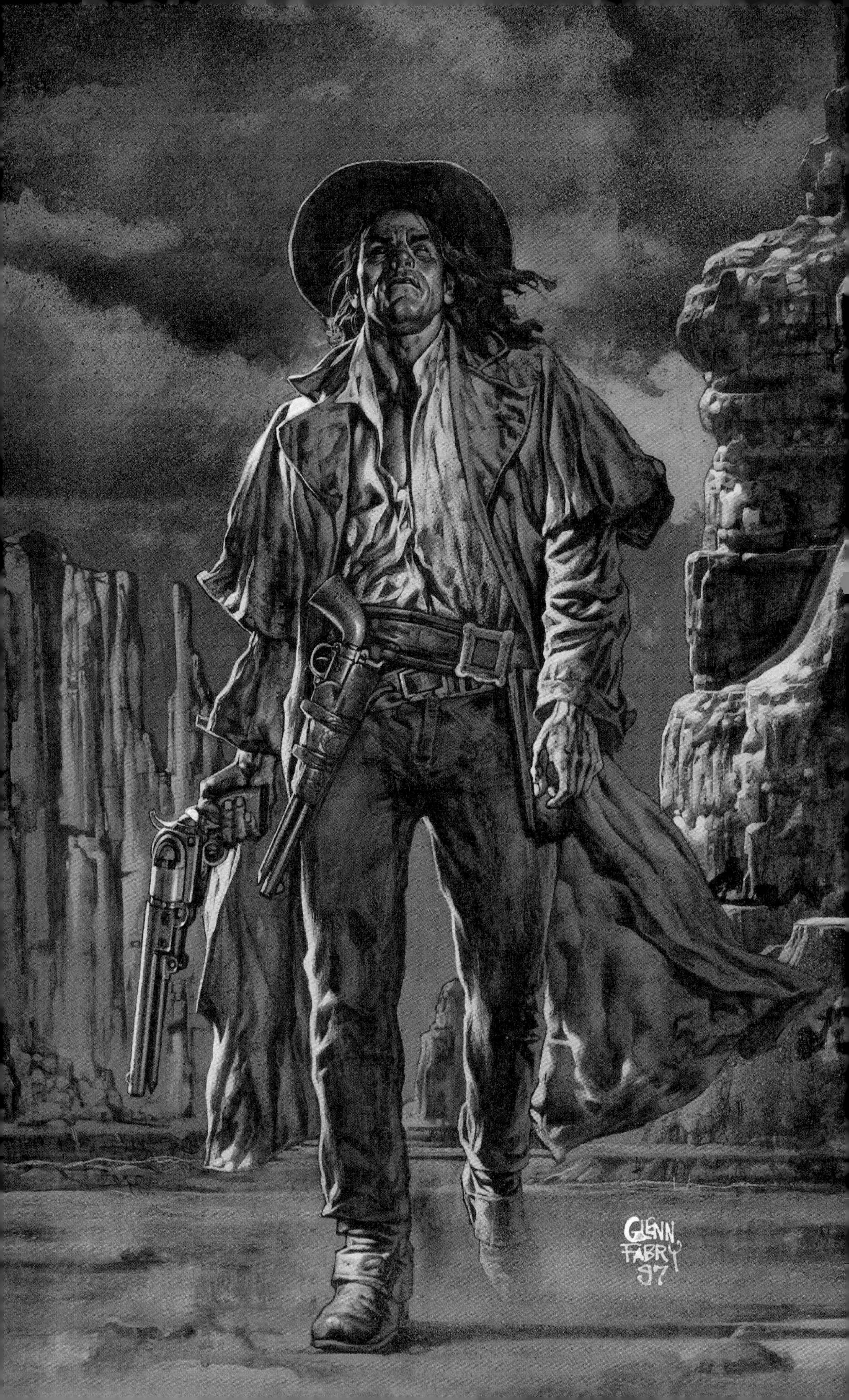
GLENN
FABRY
97

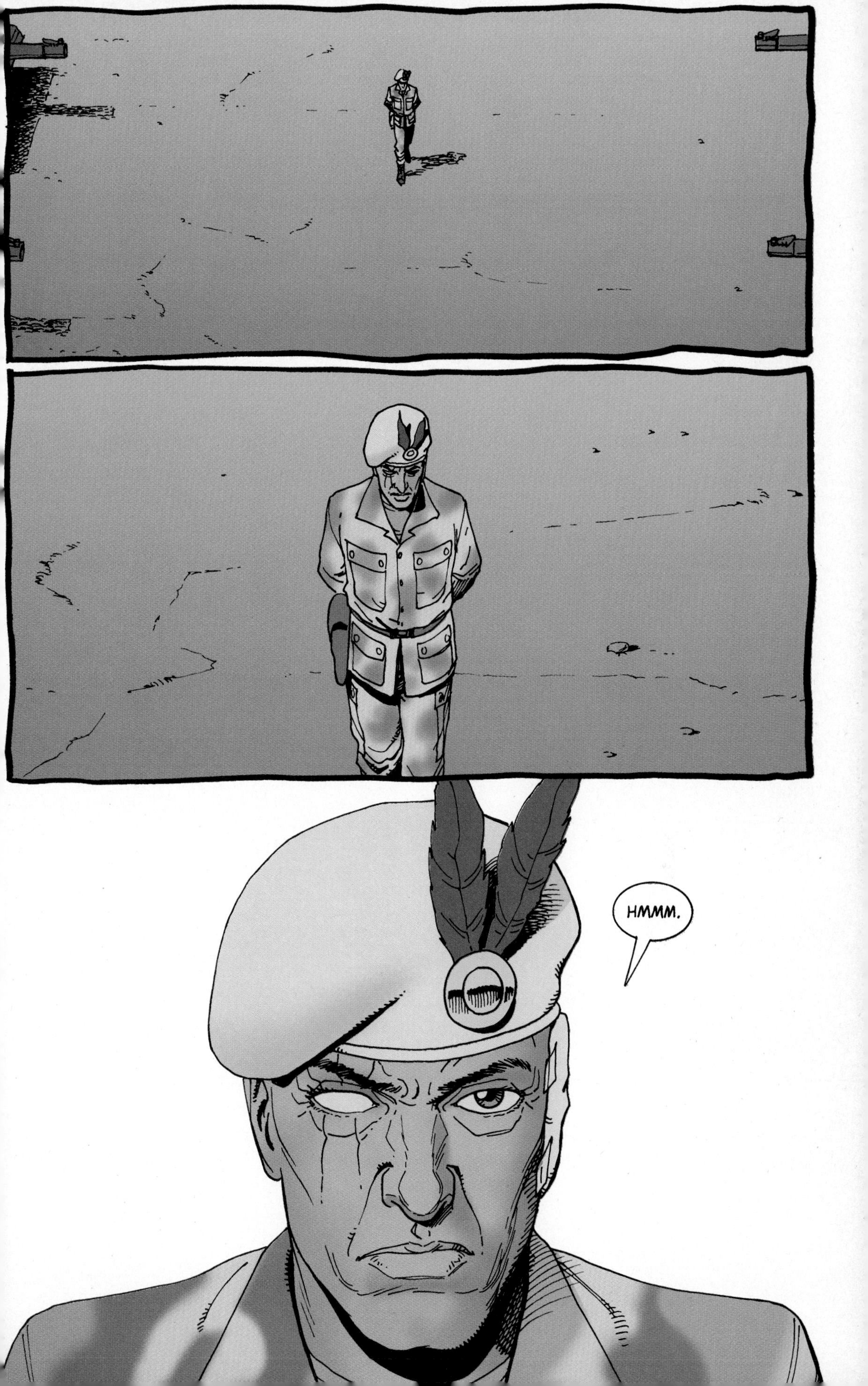
HMMM.

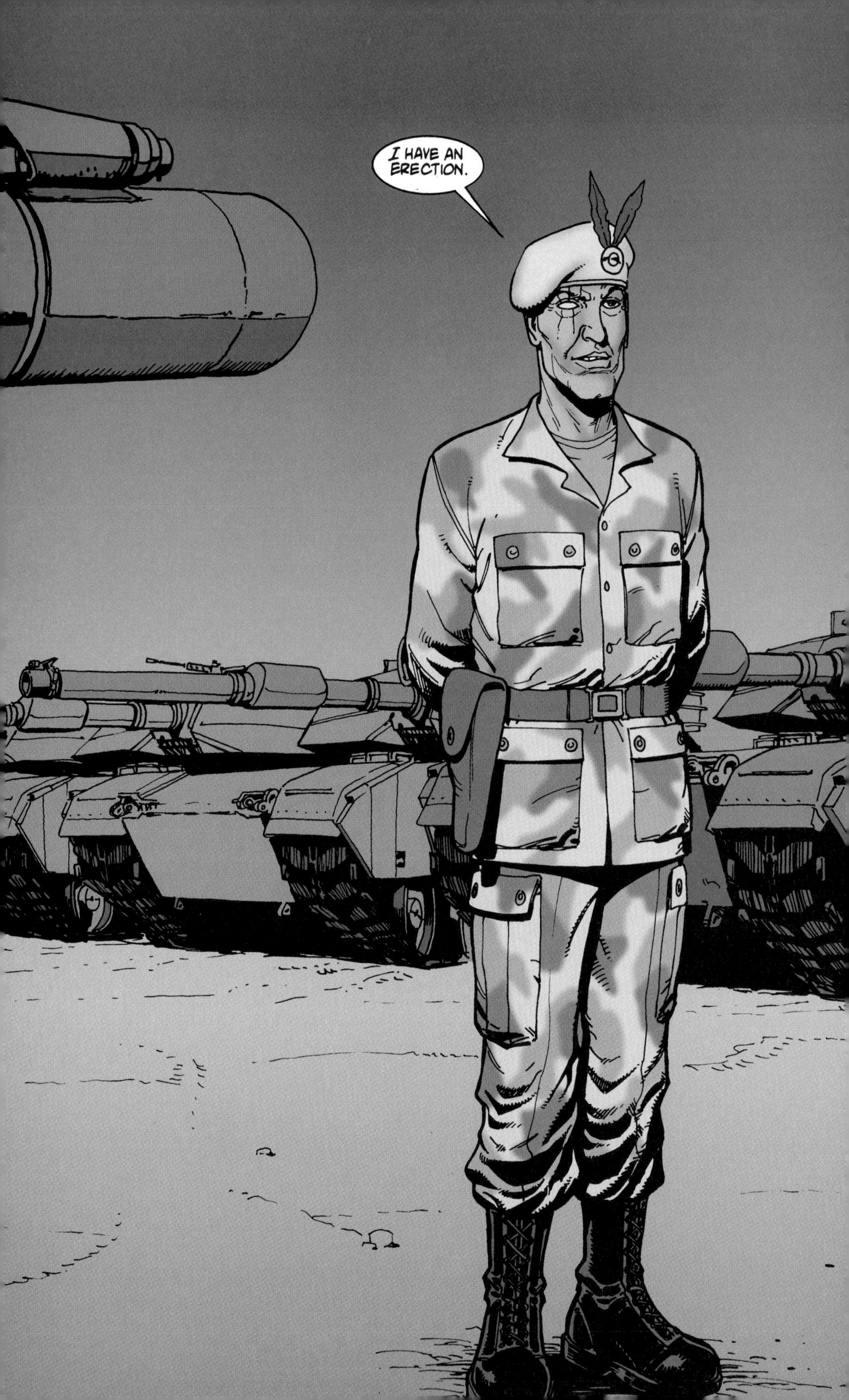
I HAVE AN ERECTION.

You & Me against the WORLD

GARTH ENNIS-Writer
STEVE DILLON-Artist

Pamela Rambo-Colorist, Clem Robins-Letterer,
Axel Alonso-Editor

PREACHER created by Garth Ennis and Steve Dillon

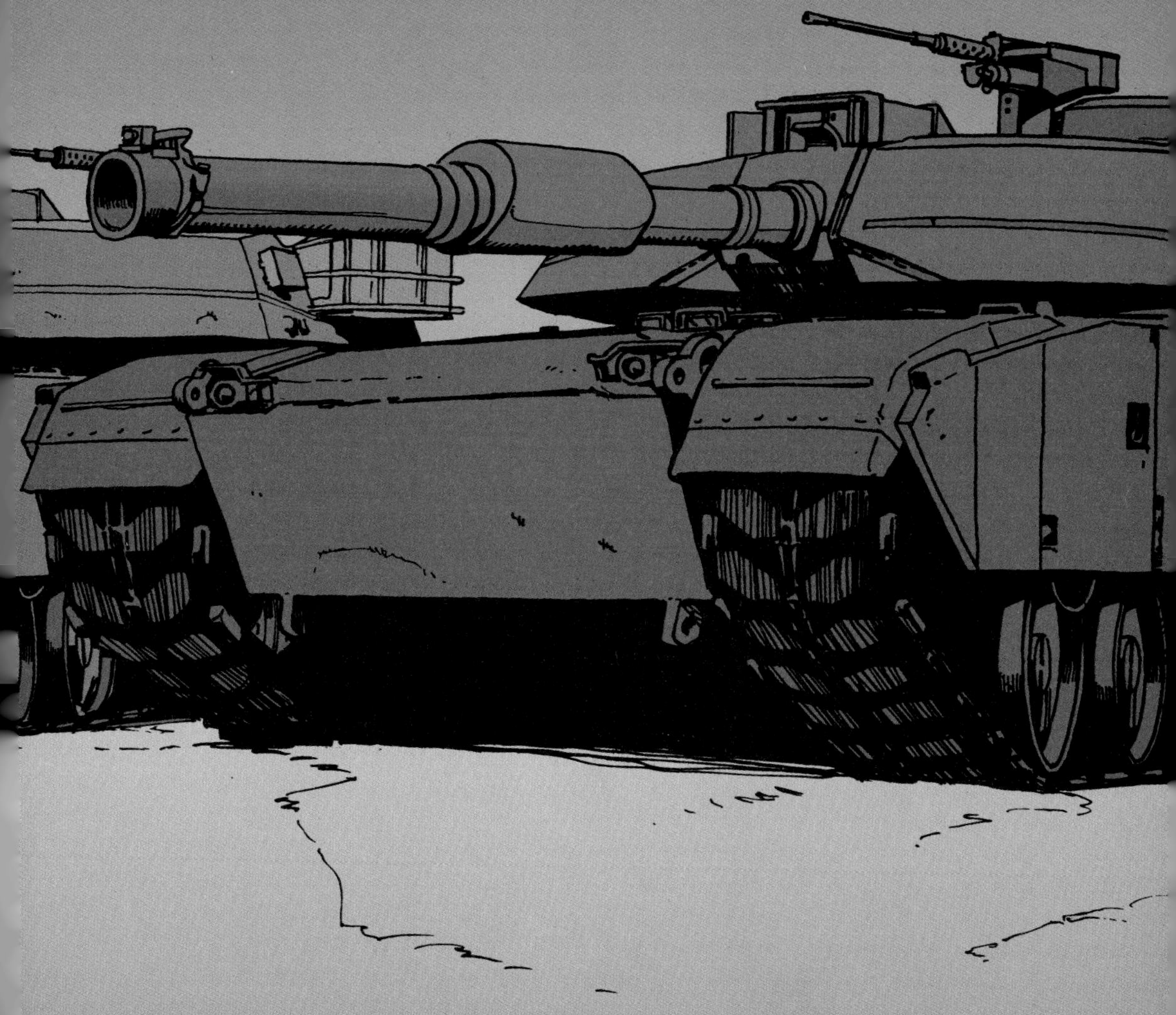

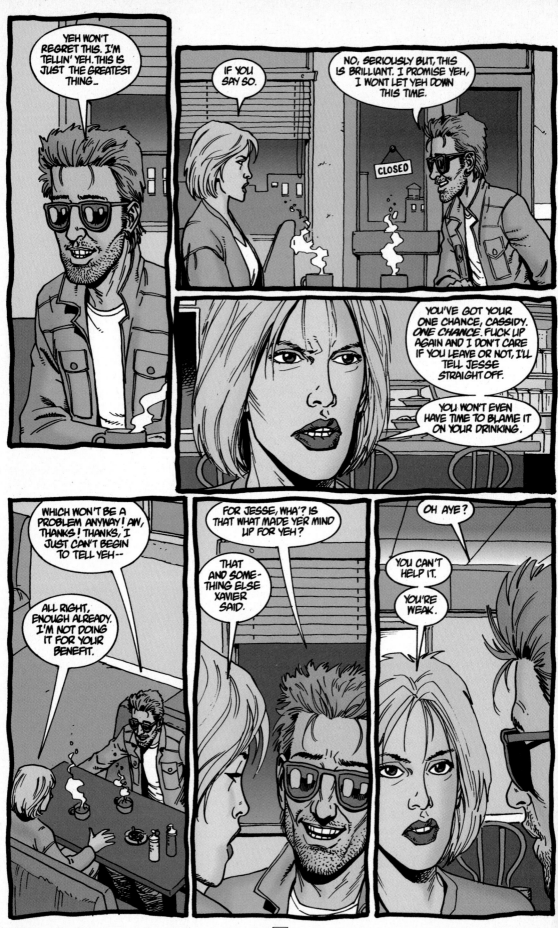

YEH WON'T REGRET THIS. I'M TELLIN' YEH. THIS IS JUST THE GREATEST THING...

IF YOU SAY SO.

NO, SERIOUSLY BUT, THIS IS BRILLIANT. I PROMISE YEH, I WONT LET YEH DOWN THIS TIME.

CLOSED

YOU'VE GOT YOUR ONE CHANCE, CASSIDY. ONE CHANCE. FUCK UP AGAIN AND I DON'T CARE IF YOU LEAVE OR NOT, I'LL TELL JESSE STRAIGHT OFF.

YOU WON'T EVEN HAVE TIME TO BLAME IT ON YOUR DRINKING.

WHICH WON'T BE A PROBLEM ANYWAY! AW, THANKS! THANKS, I JUST CAN'T BEGIN TO TELL YEH--

ALL RIGHT, ENOUGH ALREADY. I'M NOT DOING IT FOR YOUR BENEFIT.

FOR JESSE, WHA'? IS THAT WHAT MADE YER MIND UP FOR YEH?

THAT AND SOMETHING ELSE XAVIER SAID.

OH AYE?

YOU CAN'T HELP IT.

YOU'RE WEAK.

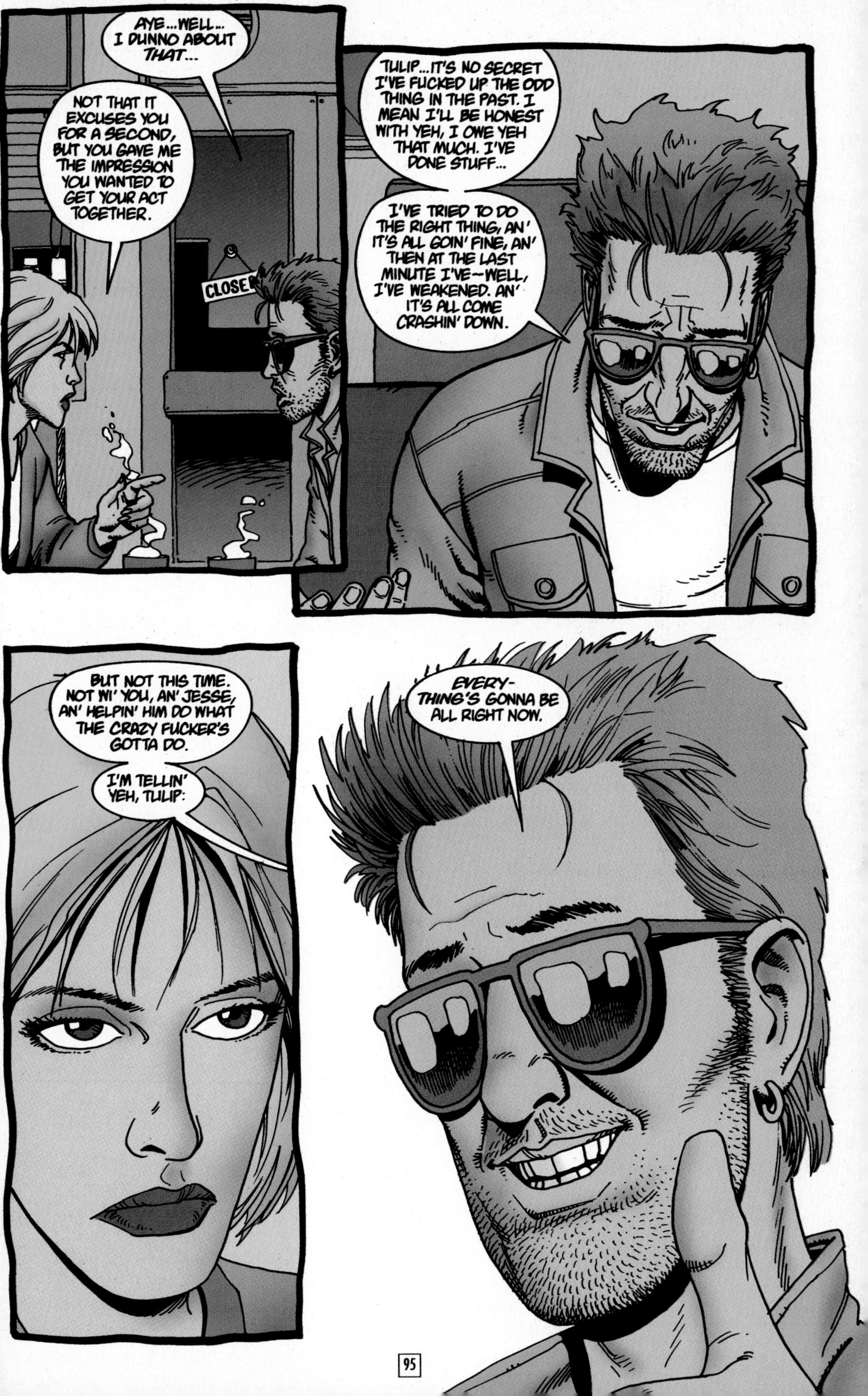
NOT THAT IT EXCUSES YOU FOR A SECOND, BUT YOU GAVE ME THE IMPRESSION YOU WANTED TO GET YOUR ACT TOGETHER.
AYE...WELL... I DUNNO ABOUT THAT...
CLOSE
TULIP...IT'S NO SECRET I'VE FUCKED UP THE ODD THING IN THE PAST. I MEAN I'LL BE HONEST WITH YEH, I OWE YEH THAT MUCH. I'VE DONE STUFF...
I'VE TRIED TO DO THE RIGHT THING, AN' IT'S ALL GOIN' FINE, AN' THEN AT THE LAST MINUTE I'VE--WELL, I'VE WEAKENED. AN' IT'S ALL COME CRASHIN' DOWN.
BUT NOT THIS TIME. NOT WI' YOU, AN' JESSE, AN' HELPIN' HIM DO WHAT THE CRAZY FUCKER'S GOTTA DO.
I'M TELLIN' YEH, TULIP:
EVERY-THING'S GONNA BE ALL RIGHT NOW.

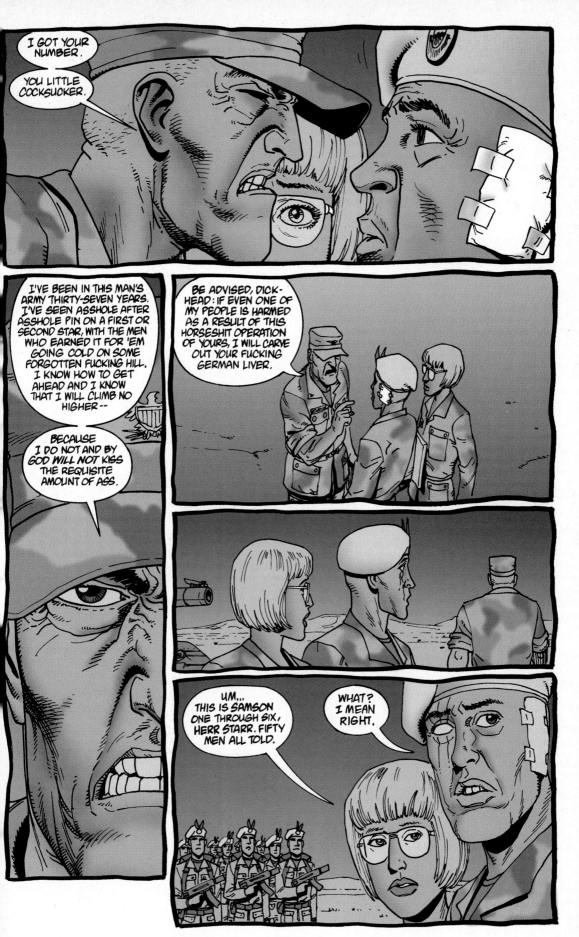

I GOT YOUR NUMBER.

YOU LITTLE COCKSUCKER.

I'VE BEEN IN THIS MAN'S ARMY THIRTY-SEVEN YEARS. I'VE SEEN ASSHOLE AFTER ASSHOLE PIN ON A FIRST OR SECOND STAR, WITH THE MEN WHO EARNED IT FOR 'EM GOING COLD ON SOME FORGOTTEN FUCKING HILL. I KNOW HOW TO GET AHEAD AND I KNOW THAT I WILL CLIMB NO HIGHER--

BECAUSE I DO NOT AND BY GOD WILL NOT KISS THE REQUISITE AMOUNT OF ASS.

BE ADVISED, DICK-HEAD: IF EVEN ONE OF MY PEOPLE IS HARMED AS A RESULT OF THIS HORSESHIT OPERATION OF YOURS, I WILL CARVE OUT YOUR FUCKING GERMAN LIVER.

UM... THIS IS SAMSON ONE THROUGH SIX, HERR STARR. FIFTY MEN ALL TOLD.

WHAT? I MEAN RIGHT.

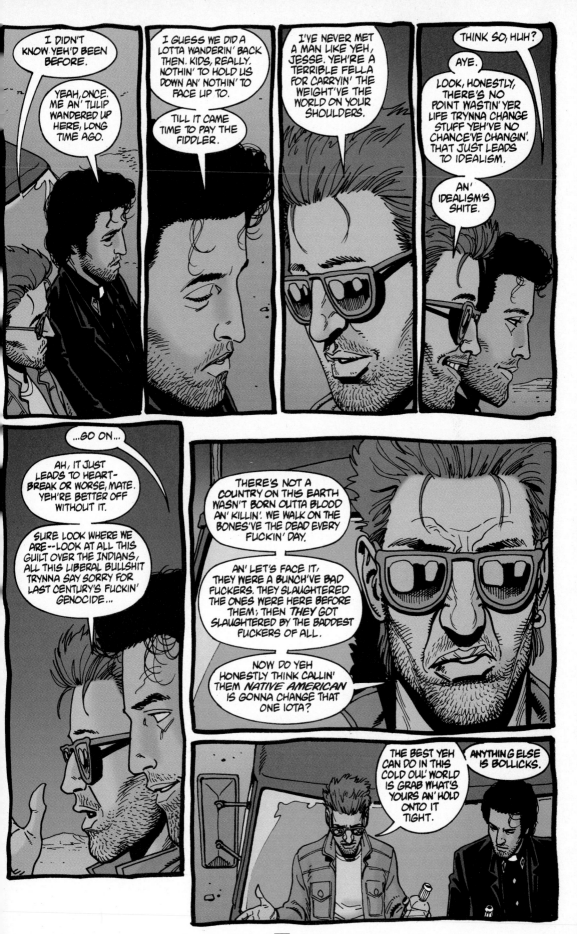

I DIDN'T KNOW YEH'D BEEN BEFORE.

YEAH, ONCE. ME AN' TULIP WANDERED UP HERE, LONG TIME AGO.

I GUESS WE DID A LOTTA WANDERIN' BACK THEN. KIDS, REALLY. NOTHIN' TO HOLD US DOWN AN' NOTHIN' TO FACE UP TO.

TILL IT CAME TIME TO PAY THE FIDDLER.

I'VE NEVER MET A MAN LIKE YEH, JESSE. YEH'RE A TERRIBLE FELLA FOR CARRYIN' THE WEIGHT'VE THE WORLD ON YOUR SHOULDERS.

THINK SO, HUH?

AYE.

LOOK, HONESTLY, THERE'S NO POINT WASTIN' YER LIFE TRYNNA CHANGE STUFF YEH'VE NO CHANCE'VE CHANGIN'. THAT JUST LEADS TO IDEALISM.

AN' IDEALISM'S SHITE.

...GO ON...

AH, IT JUST LEADS TO HEART-BREAK OR WORSE, MATE. YEH'RE BETTER OFF WITHOUT IT.

SURE LOOK WHERE WE ARE -- LOOK AT ALL THIS GUILT OVER THE INDIANS, ALL THIS LIBERAL BULLSHIT TRYNNA SAY SORRY FOR LAST CENTURY'S FUCKIN' GENOCIDE...

THERE'S NOT A COUNTRY ON THIS EARTH WASN'T BORN OUTTA BLOOD AN' KILLIN'. WE WALK ON THE BONES'VE THE DEAD EVERY FUCKIN' DAY.

AN' LET'S FACE IT, THEY WERE A BUNCH'VE BAD FUCKERS. THEY SLAUGHTERED THE ONES WERE HERE BEFORE THEM; THEN THEY GOT SLAUGHTERED BY THE BADDEST FUCKERS OF ALL.

NOW DO YEH HONESTLY THINK CALLIN' THEM NATIVE AMERICAN IS GONNA CHANGE THAT ONE IOTA?

THE BEST YEH CAN DO IN THIS COLD OUL' WORLD IS GRAB WHAT'S YOURS AN' HOLD ONTO IT TIGHT.

ANYTHING ELSE IS BOLLICKS.

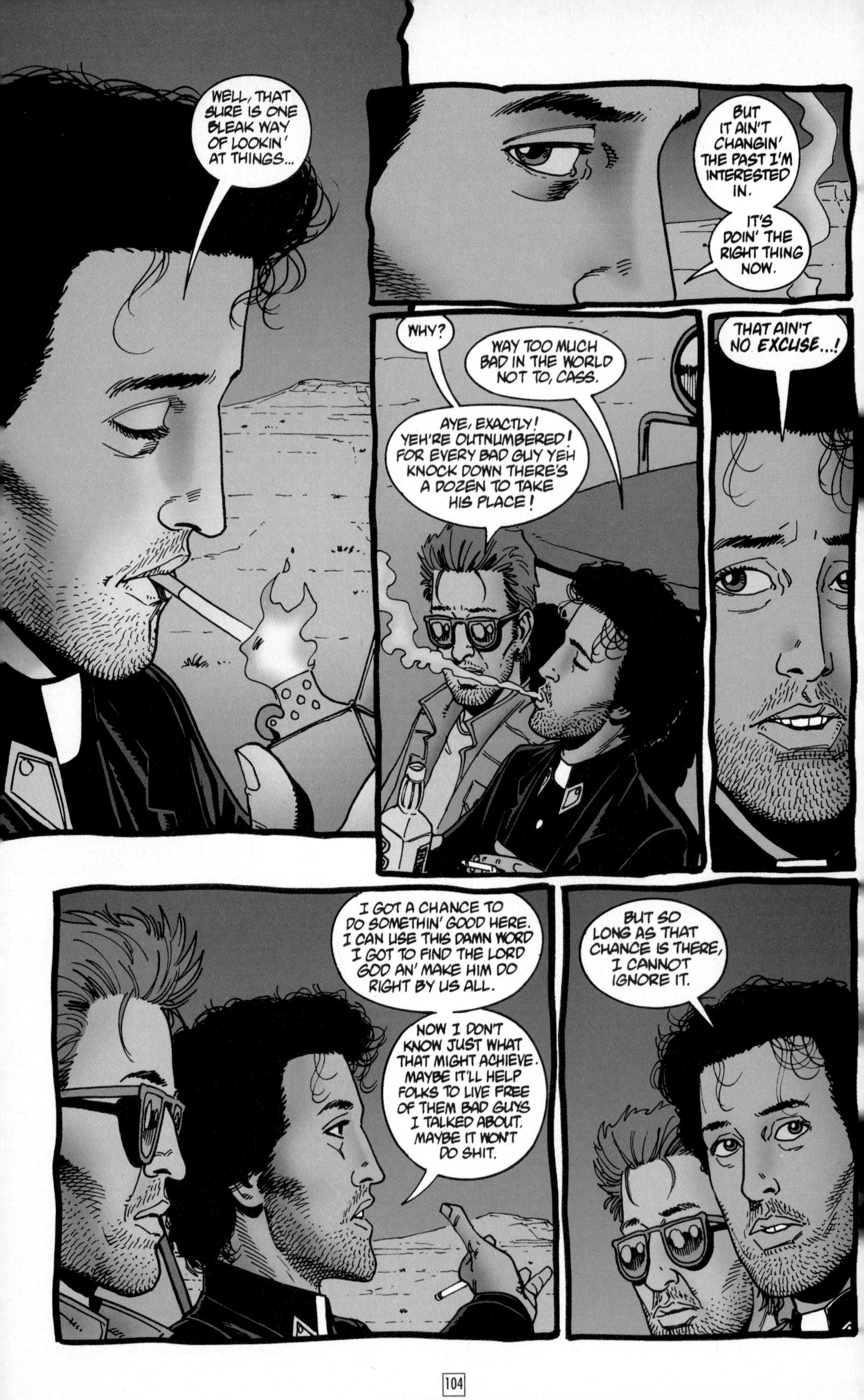
WELL, THAT SURE IS ONE BLEAK WAY OF LOOKIN' AT THINGS...
BUT IT AIN'T CHANGIN' THE PAST I'M INTERESTED IN.
IT'S DOIN' THE RIGHT THING NOW.
WHY?
WAY TOO MUCH BAD IN THE WORLD NOT TO, CASS.
AYE, EXACTLY! YEH'RE OUTNUMBERED! FOR EVERY BAD GUY YEH KNOCK DOWN THERE'S A DOZEN TO TAKE HIS PLACE!
THAT AIN'T NO *EXCUSE*...!
I GOT A CHANCE TO DO SOMETHIN' GOOD HERE. I CAN USE THIS DAMN WORD I GOT TO FIND THE LORD GOD AN' MAKE HIM DO RIGHT BY US ALL.
NOW I DON'T KNOW JUST WHAT THAT MIGHT ACHIEVE. MAYBE IT'LL HELP FOLKS TO LIVE FREE OF THEM BAD GUYS I TALKED ABOUT. MAYBE IT WON'T DO SHIT.
BUT SO LONG AS THAT CHANCE IS THERE, I CANNOT IGNORE IT.

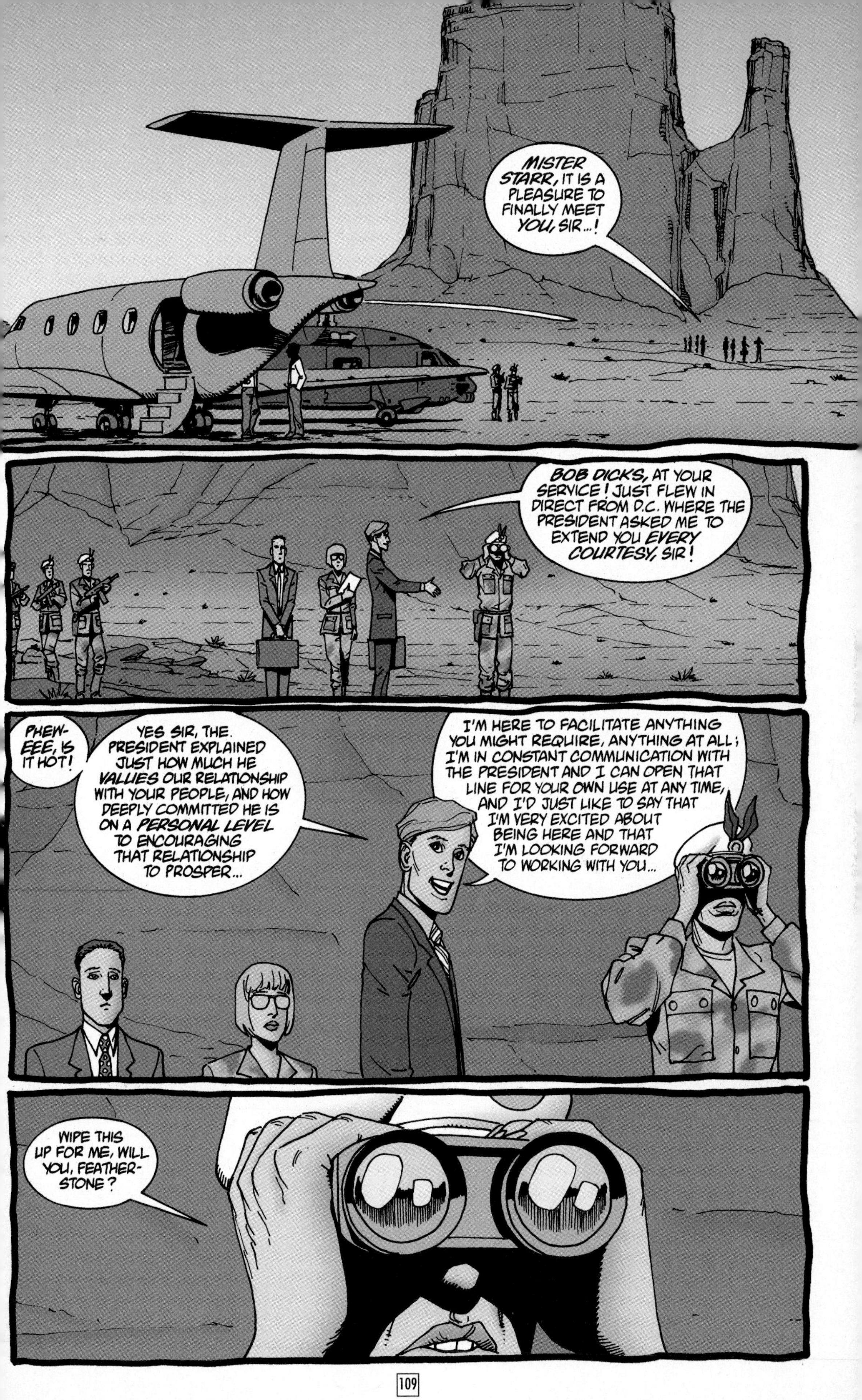
MISTER STARR, IT IS A PLEASURE TO FINALLY MEET YOU, SIR...!
BOB DICKS, AT YOUR SERVICE! JUST FLEW IN DIRECT FROM D.C. WHERE THE PRESIDENT ASKED ME TO EXTEND YOU EVERY COURTESY, SIR!
PHEW-EEE, IS IT HOT!
YES SIR, THE. PRESIDENT EXPLAINED JUST HOW MUCH HE VALUES OUR RELATIONSHIP WITH YOUR PEOPLE, AND HOW DEEPLY COMMITTED HE IS ON A PERSONAL LEVEL TO ENCOURAGING THAT RELATIONSHIP TO PROSPER...
I'M HERE TO FACILITATE ANYTHING YOU MIGHT REQUIRE, ANYTHING AT ALL; I'M IN CONSTANT COMMUNICATION WITH THE PRESIDENT AND I CAN OPEN THAT LINE FOR YOUR OWN USE AT ANY TIME, AND I'D JUST LIKE TO SAY THAT I'M VERY EXCITED ABOUT BEING HERE AND THAT I'M LOOKING FORWARD TO WORKING WITH YOU...
WIPE THIS UP FOR ME, WILL YOU, FEATHER-STONE?

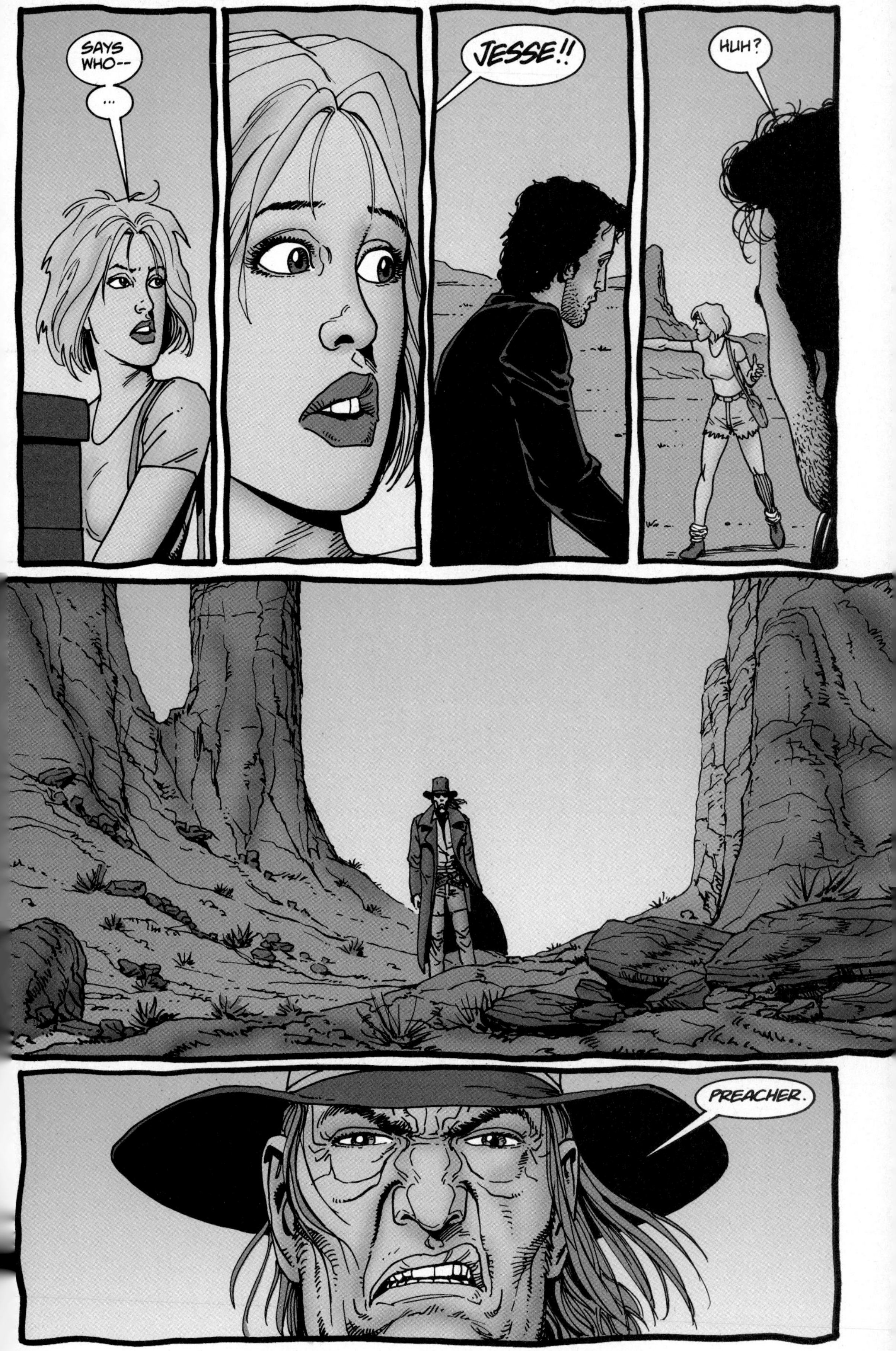
SAYS WHO--
...
JESSE!!
HUH?
PREACHER.

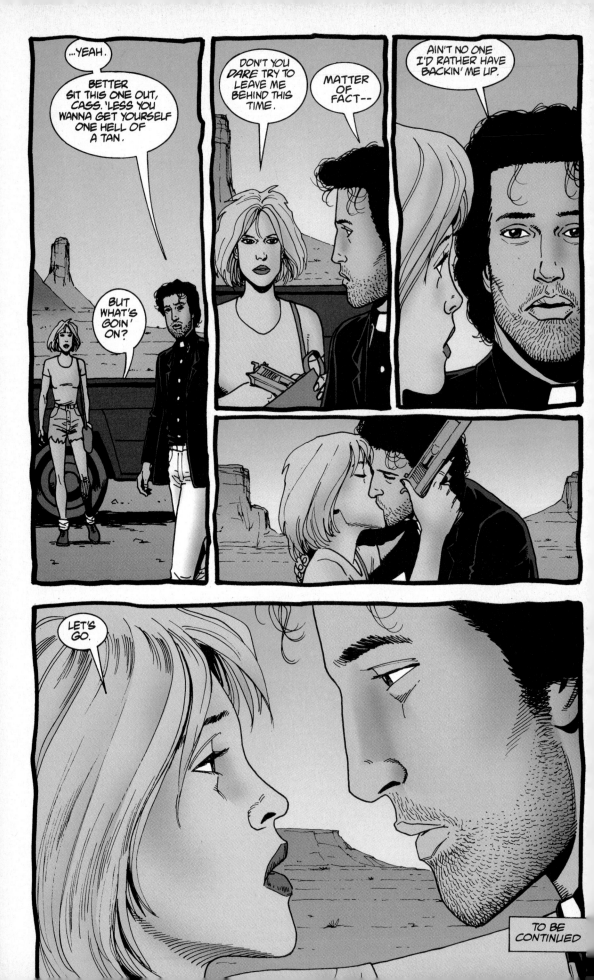

TO BE
CONTINUED

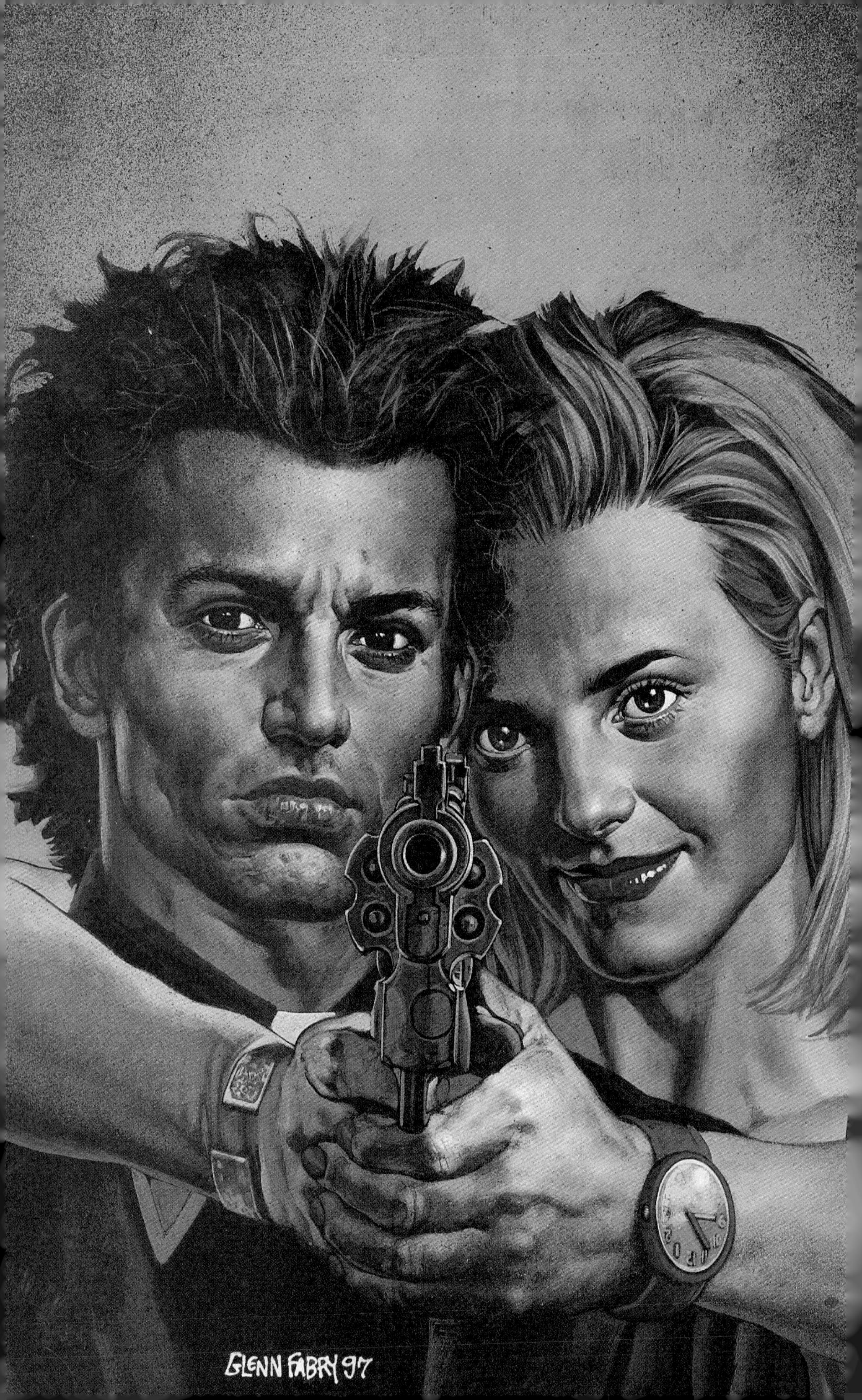
GLENN FABRY 97

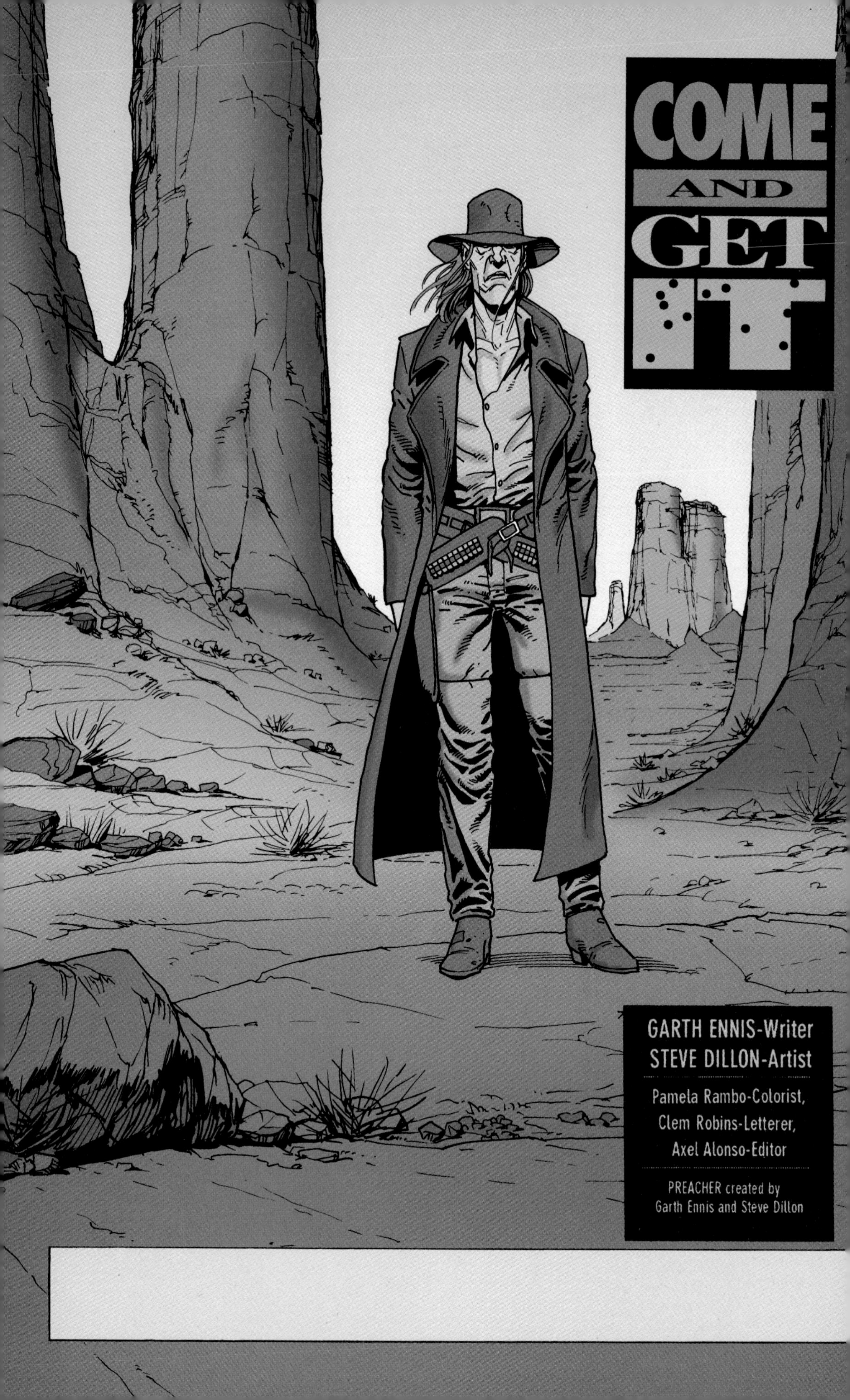
COME AND GET IT
GARTH ENNIS-Writer
STEVE DILLON-Artist
Pamela Rambo-Colorist,
Clem Robins-Letterer,
Axel Alonso-Editor
PREACHER created by
Garth Ennis and Steve Dillon

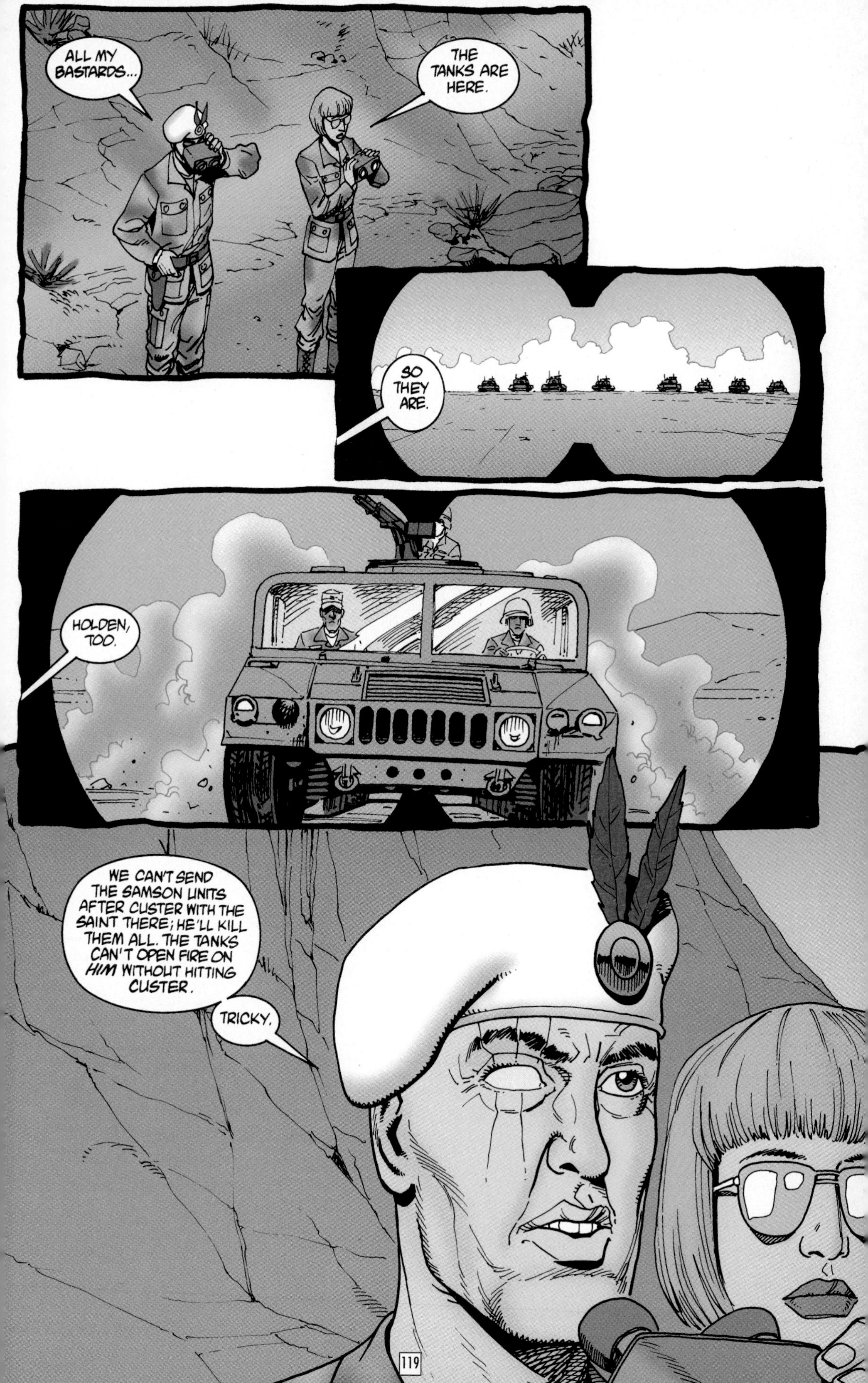
ALL MY BASTARDS...
THE TANKS ARE HERE.
SO THEY ARE.
HOLDEN, TOO.
WE CAN'T SEND THE SAMSON UNITS AFTER CUSTER WITH THE SAINT THERE; HE'LL KILL THEM ALL. THE TANKS CAN'T OPEN FIRE ON *HIM* WITHOUT HITTING CUSTER.
TRICKY.

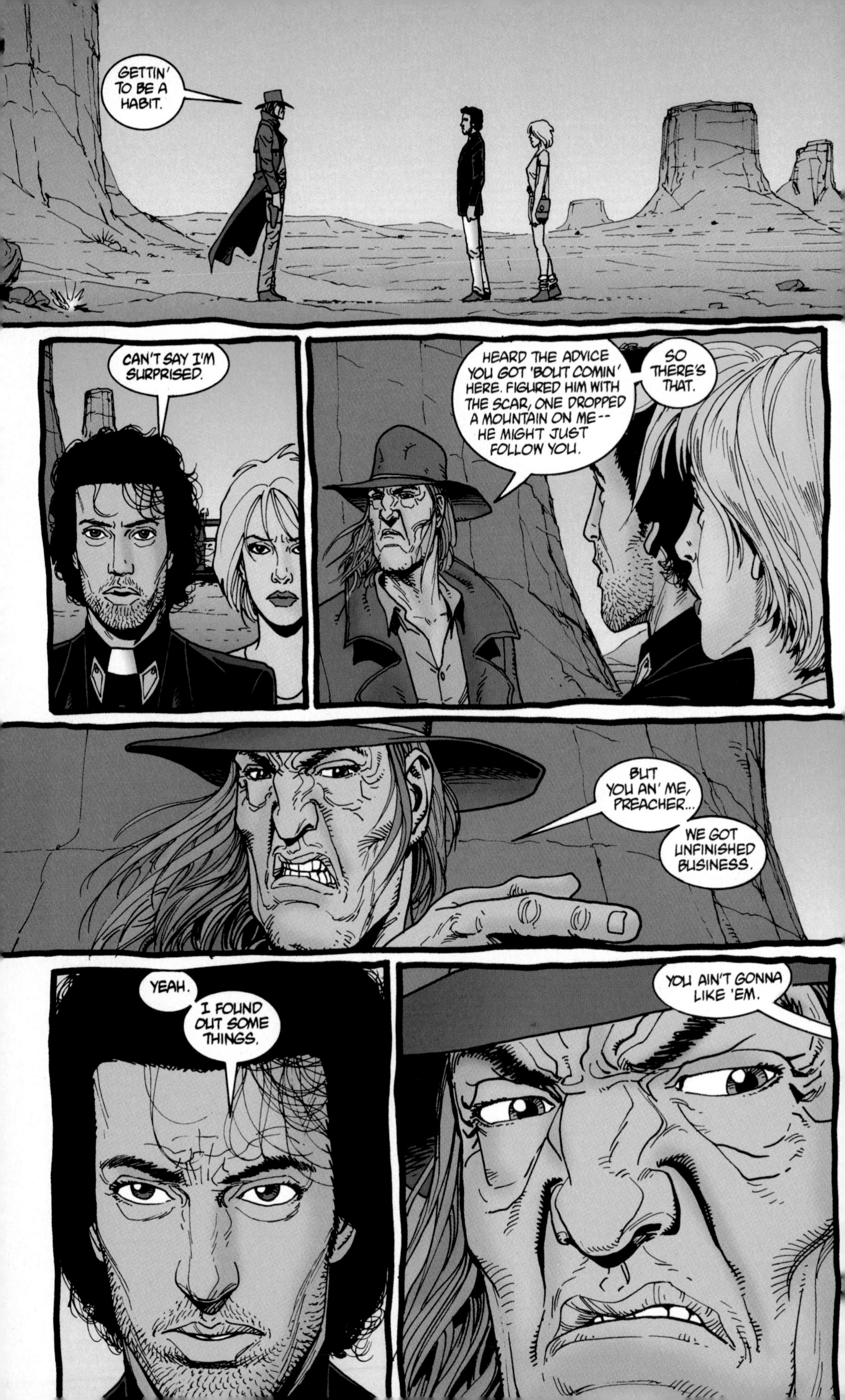
GETTIN' TO BE A HABIT.
CAN'T SAY I'M SURPRISED.
HEARD THE ADVICE YOU GOT 'BOUT COMIN' HERE. FIGURED HIM WITH THE SCAR, ONE DROPPED A MOUNTAIN ON ME-- HE MIGHT JUST FOLLOW YOU.
SO THERE'S THAT.
BUT YOU AN' ME, PREACHER...
WE GOT UNFINISHED BUSINESS.
YEAH.
I FOUND OUT SOME THINGS.
YOU AIN'T GONNA LIKE 'EM.

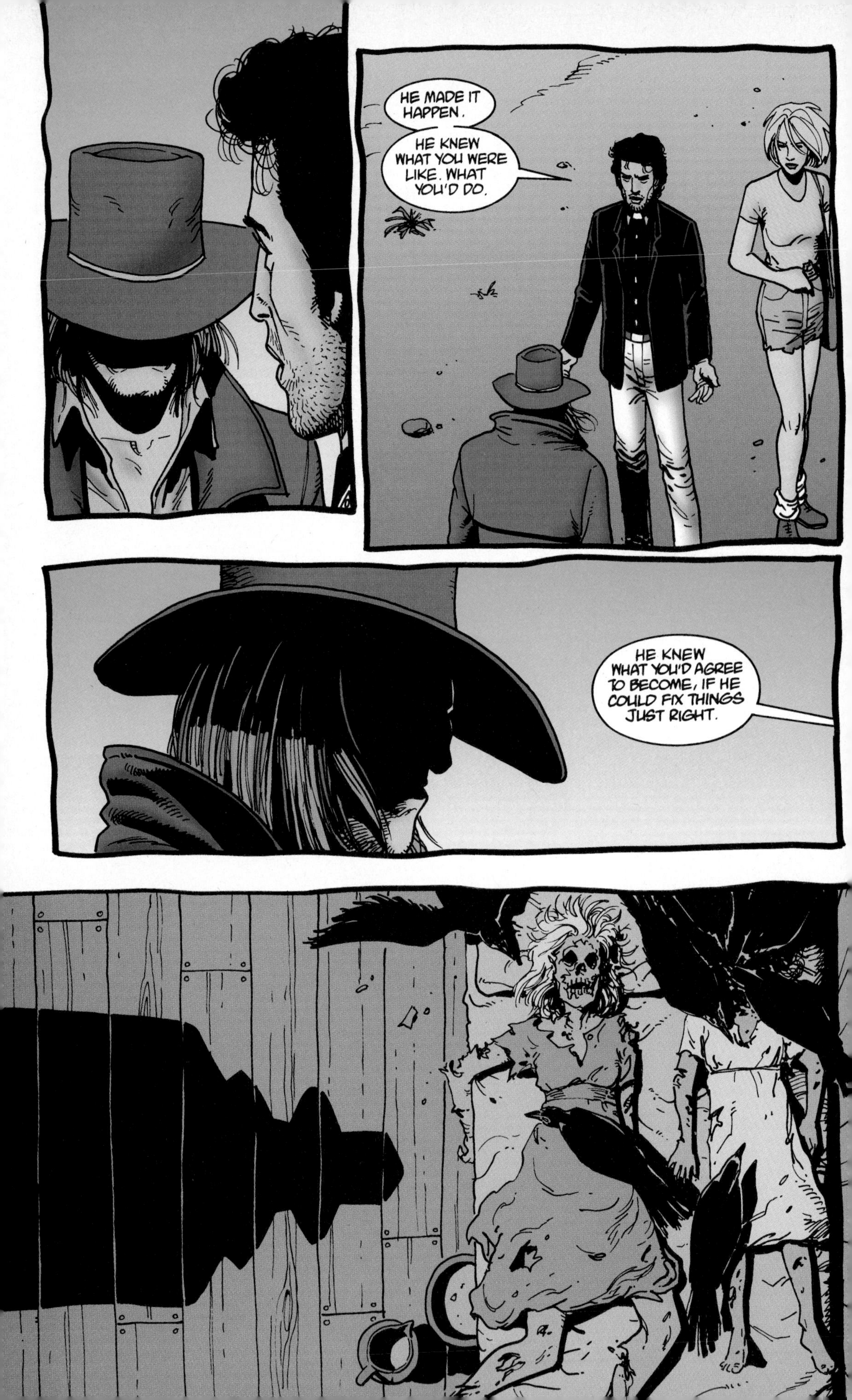
HE MADE IT HAPPEN.
HE KNEW WHAT YOU WERE LIKE. WHAT YOU'D DO.
HE KNEW WHAT YOU'D AGREE TO BECOME, IF HE COULD FIX THINGS JUST RIGHT.

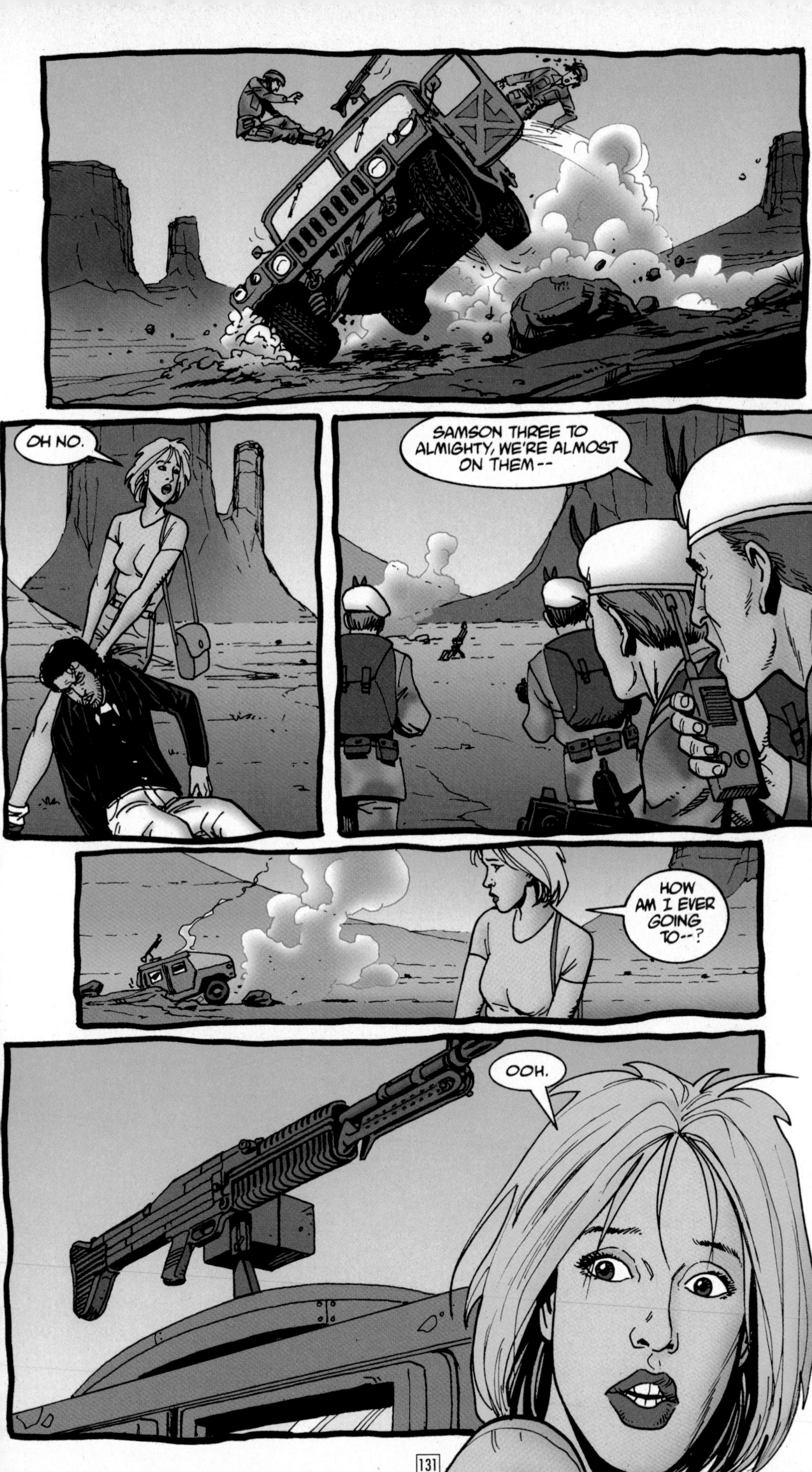
OH NO.
SAMSON THREE TO ALMIGHTY, WE'RE ALMOST ON THEM --
HOW AM I EVER GOING TO--?
OOH.

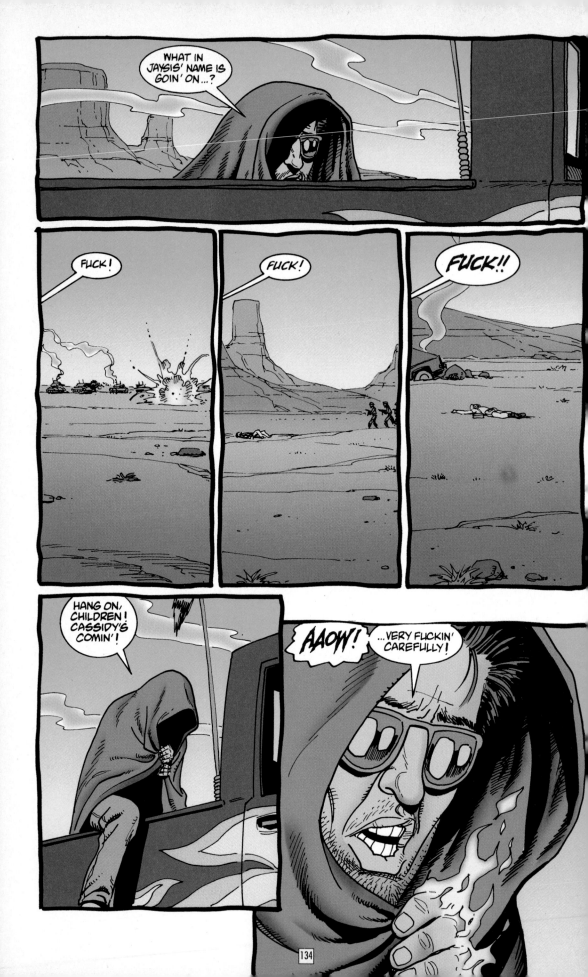

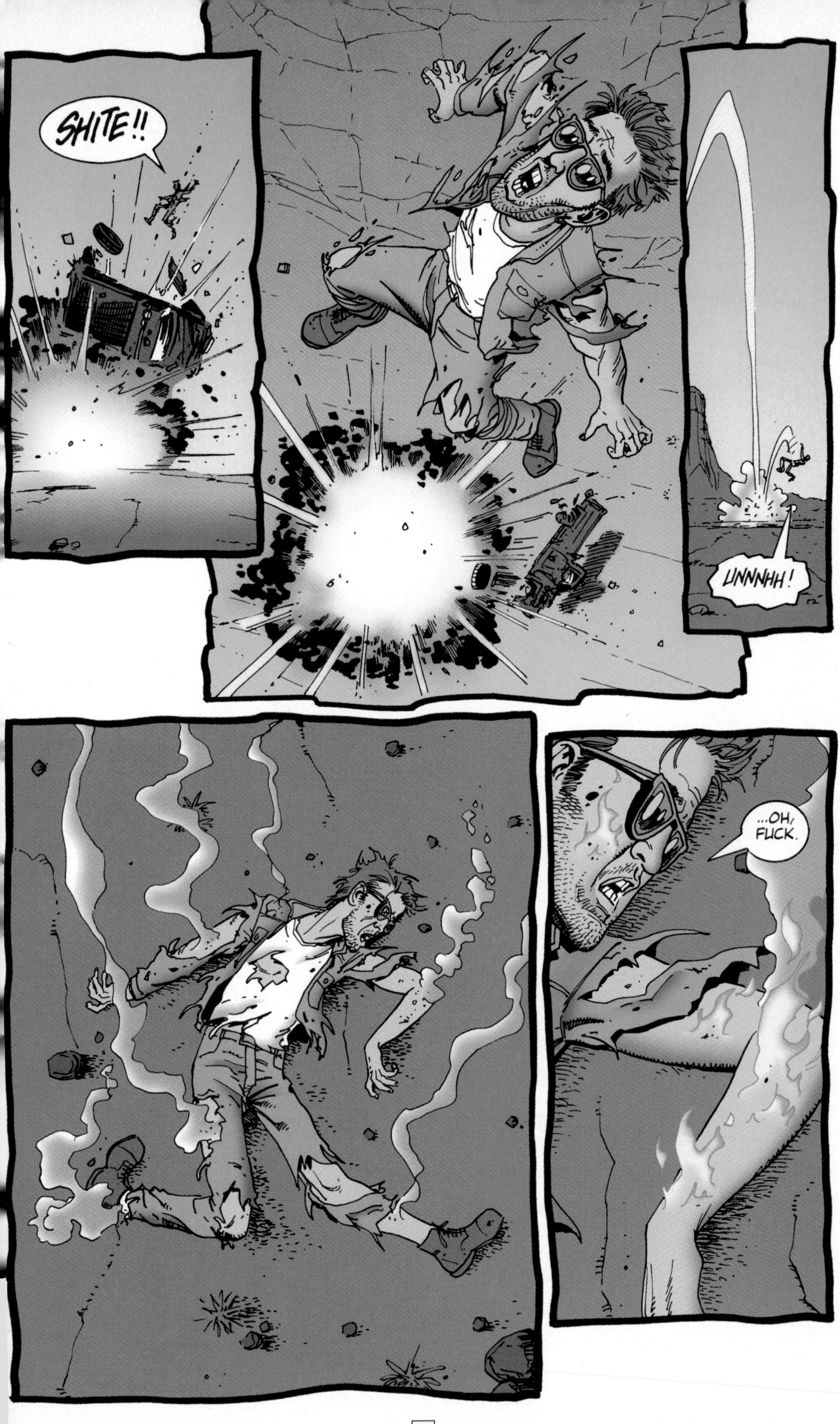
SHITE!!
UNNNHH!
...OH, FUCK.

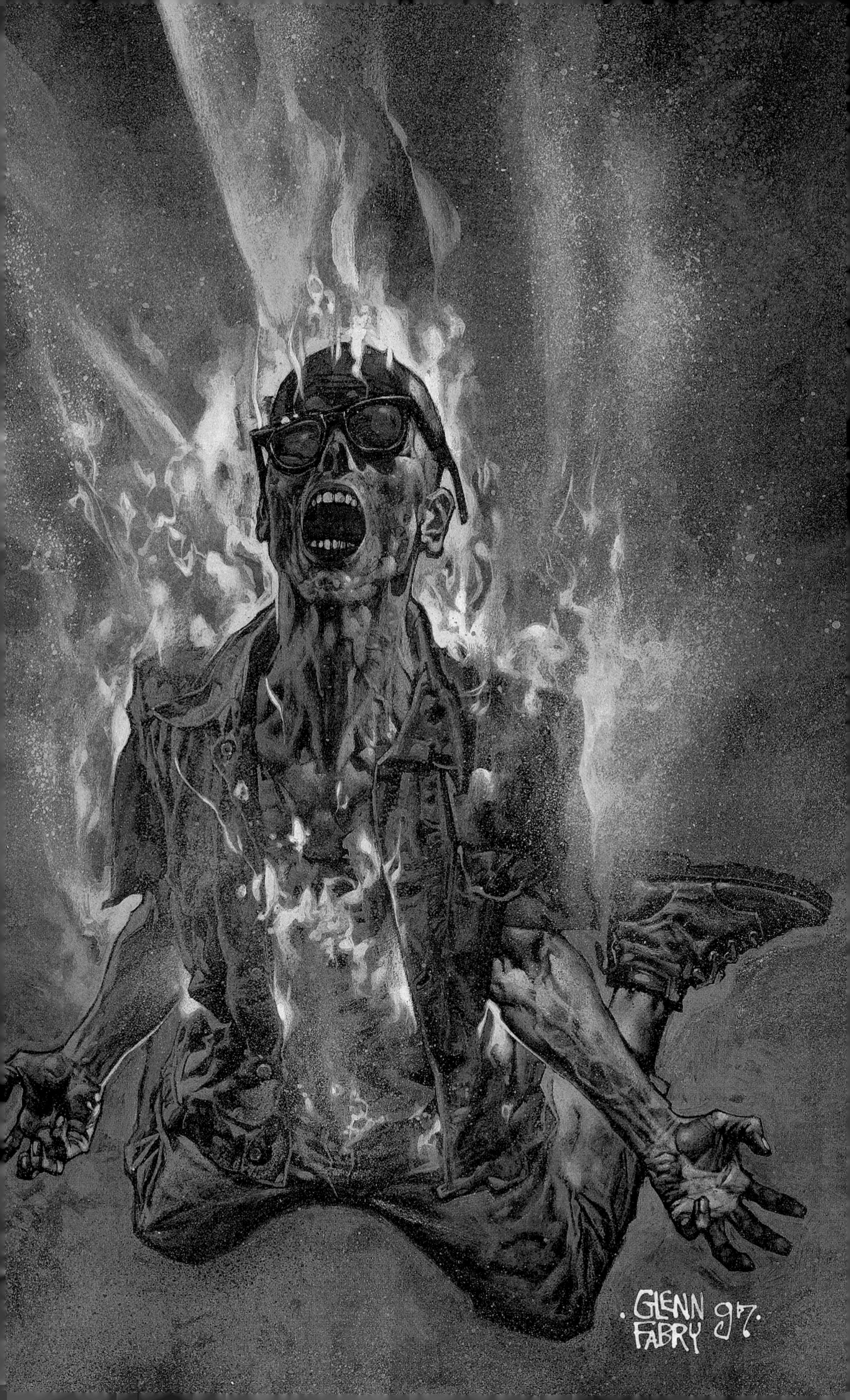
GLENN FABRY 97.

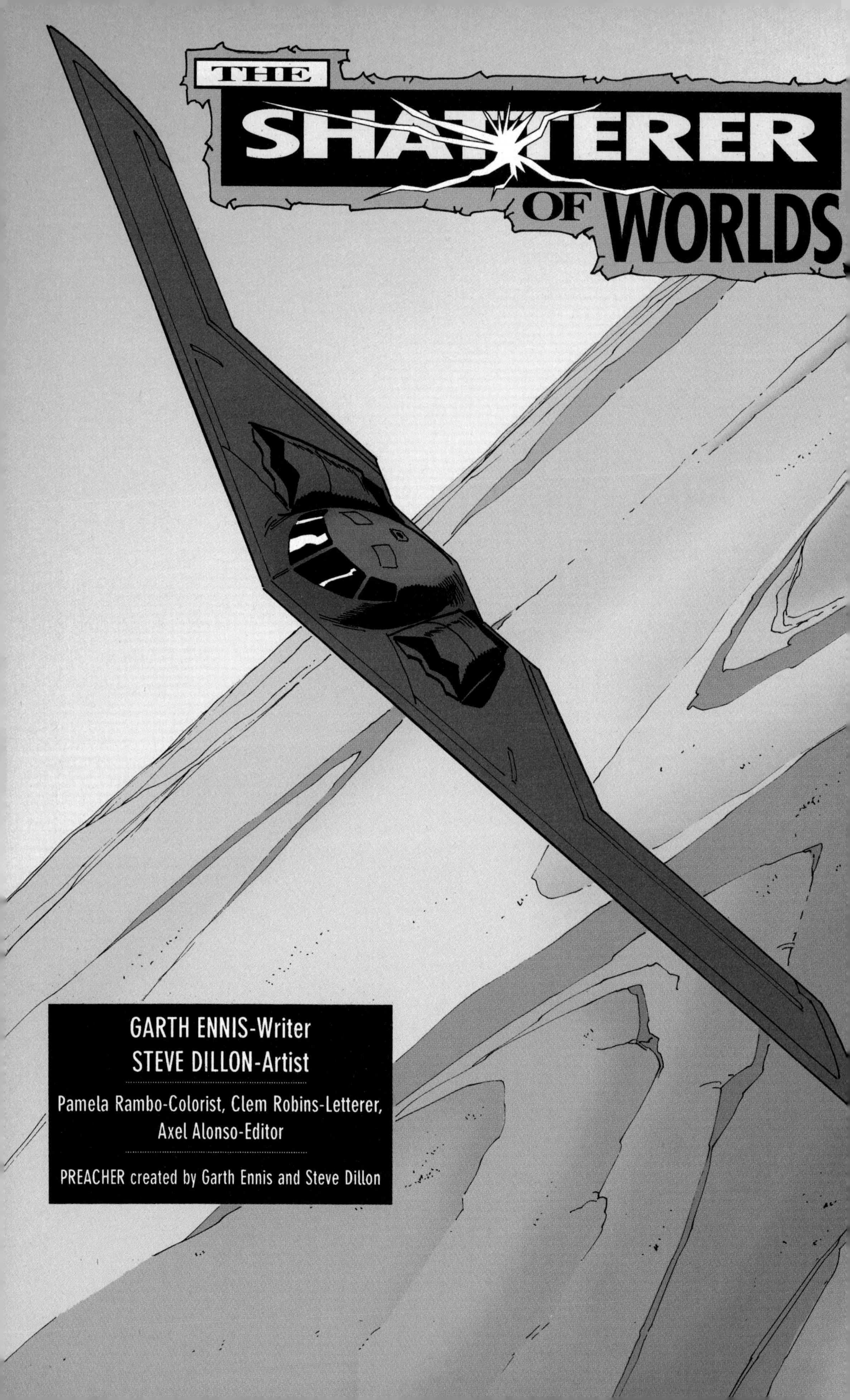
THE SHATTERER OF WORLDS
GARTH ENNIS-Writer
STEVE DILLON-Artist
Pamela Rambo-Colorist, Clem Robins-Letterer,
Axel Alonso-Editor
PREACHER created by Garth Ennis and Steve Dillon

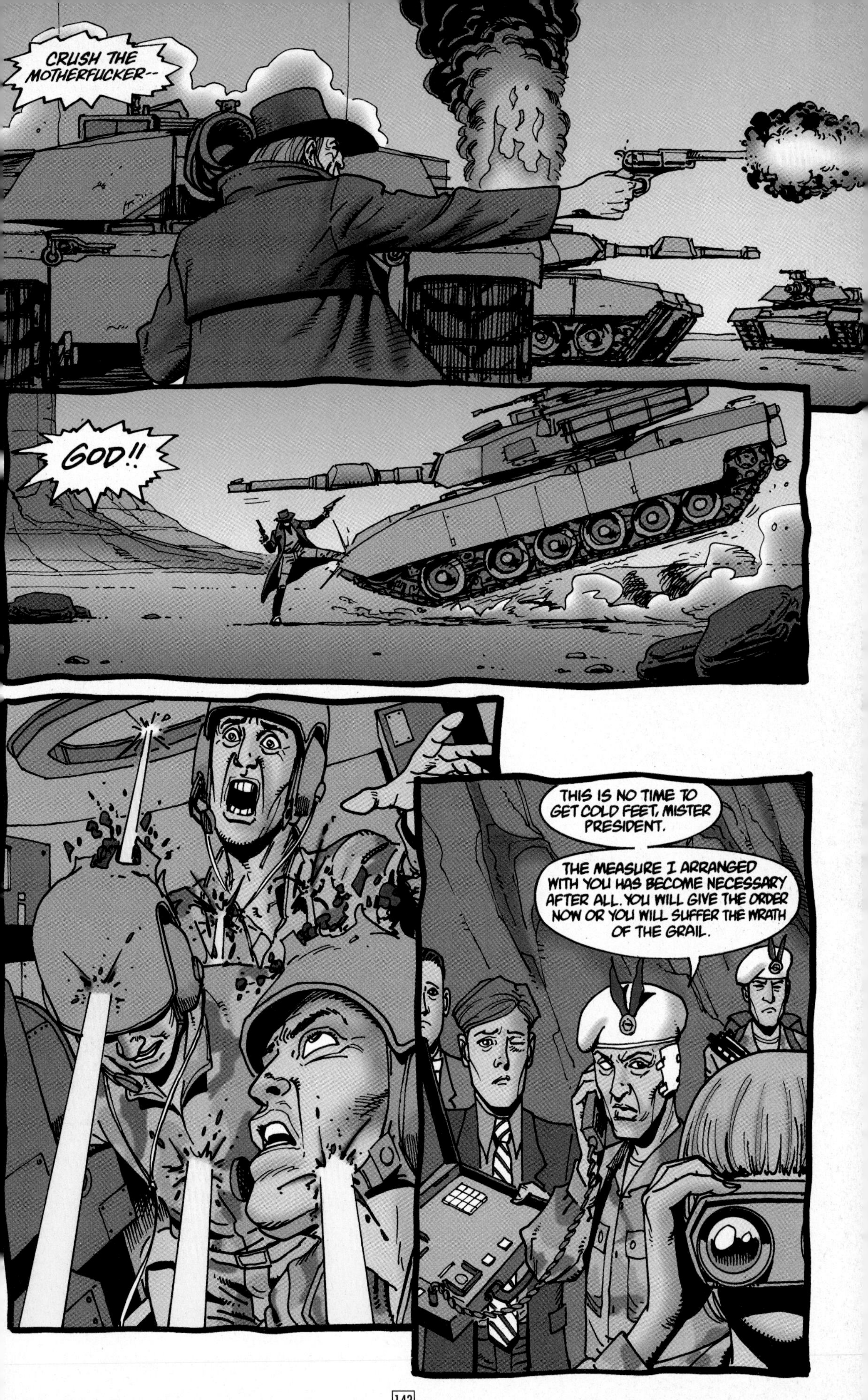

CRUSH THE MOTHERFUCKER--
GOD!!
THIS IS NO TIME TO GET COLD FEET, MISTER PRESIDENT.
THE MEASURE I ARRANGED WITH YOU HAS BECOME NECESSARY AFTER ALL. YOU WILL GIVE THE ORDER NOW OR YOU WILL SUFFER THE WRATH OF THE GRAIL.

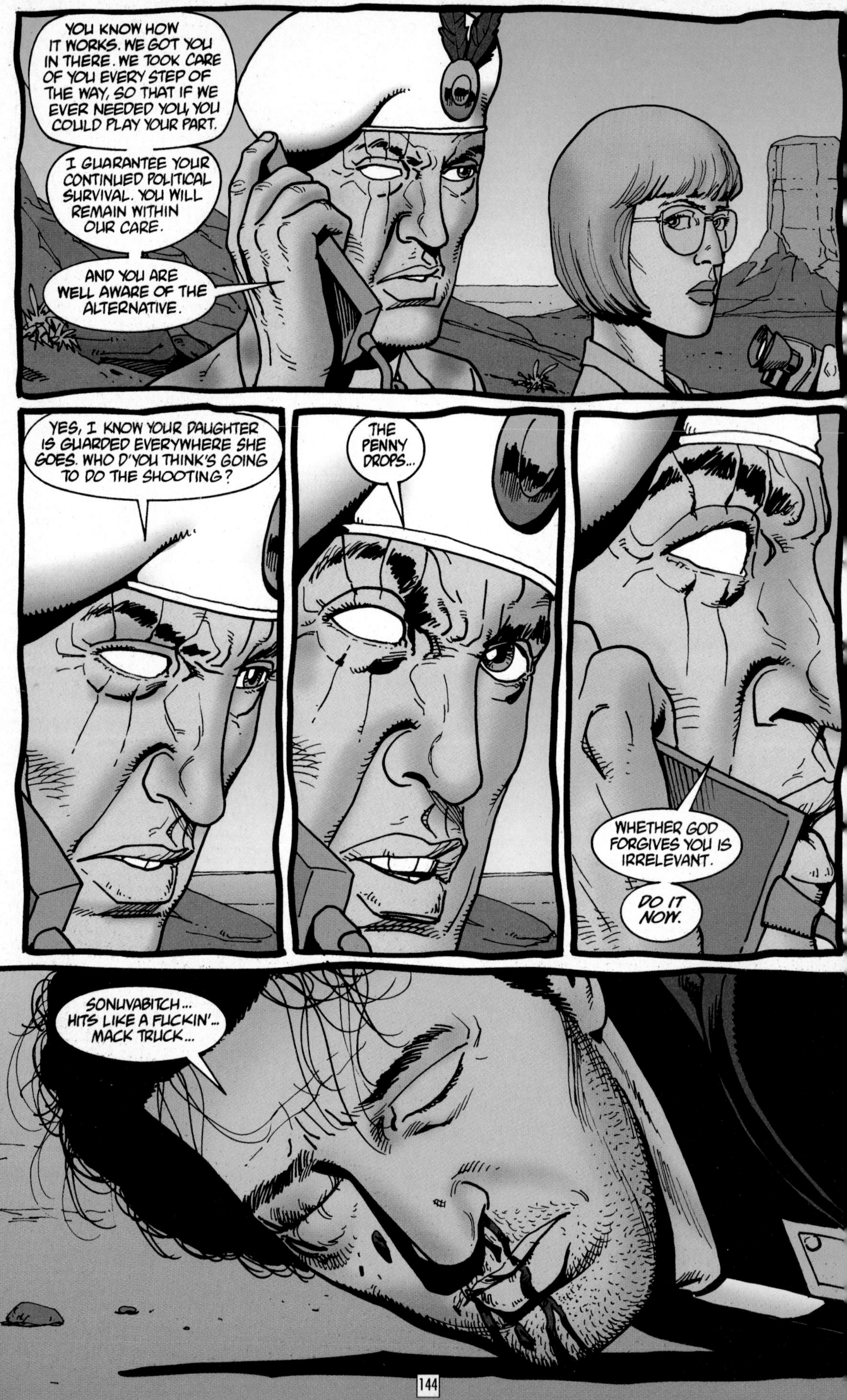
YOU KNOW HOW IT WORKS. WE GOT YOU IN THERE. WE TOOK CARE OF YOU EVERY STEP OF THE WAY, SO THAT IF WE EVER NEEDED YOU, YOU COULD PLAY YOUR PART.
I GUARANTEE YOUR CONTINUED POLITICAL SURVIVAL. YOU WILL REMAIN WITHIN OUR CARE.
AND YOU ARE WELL AWARE OF THE ALTERNATIVE.
YES, I KNOW YOUR DAUGHTER IS GUARDED EVERYWHERE SHE GOES. WHO D'YOU THINK'S GOING TO DO THE SHOOTING?
THE PENNY DROPS...
WHETHER GOD FORGIVES YOU IS IRRELEVANT.
DO IT NOW.
SONUVABITCH... HITS LIKE A FUCKIN'... MACK TRUCK...

149

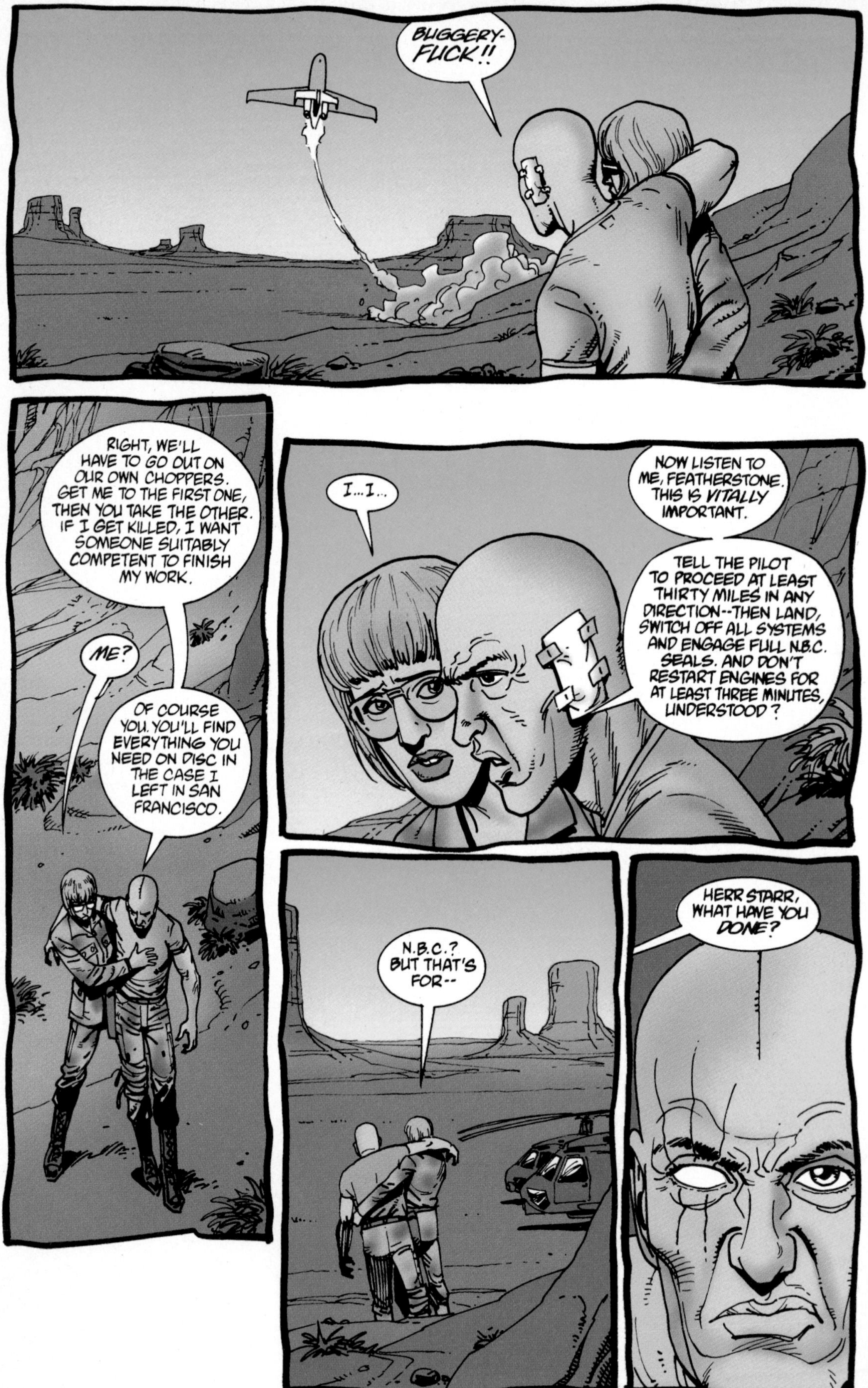
BUGGERY-FUCK!!
RIGHT, WE'LL HAVE TO GO OUT ON OUR OWN CHOPPERS. GET ME TO THE FIRST ONE, THEN YOU TAKE THE OTHER. IF I GET KILLED, I WANT SOMEONE SUITABLY COMPETENT TO FINISH MY WORK.
ME?
OF COURSE YOU. YOU'LL FIND EVERYTHING YOU NEED ON DISC IN THE CASE I LEFT IN SAN FRANCISCO.
I... I...
NOW LISTEN TO ME, FEATHERSTONE. THIS IS VITALLY IMPORTANT.
TELL THE PILOT TO PROCEED AT LEAST THIRTY MILES IN ANY DIRECTION--THEN LAND, SWITCH OFF ALL SYSTEMS AND ENGAGE FULL N.B.C. SEALS. AND DON'T RESTART ENGINES FOR AT LEAST THREE MINUTES, UNDERSTOOD?
N.B.C.? BUT THAT'S FOR--
HERR STARR, WHAT HAVE YOU DONE?

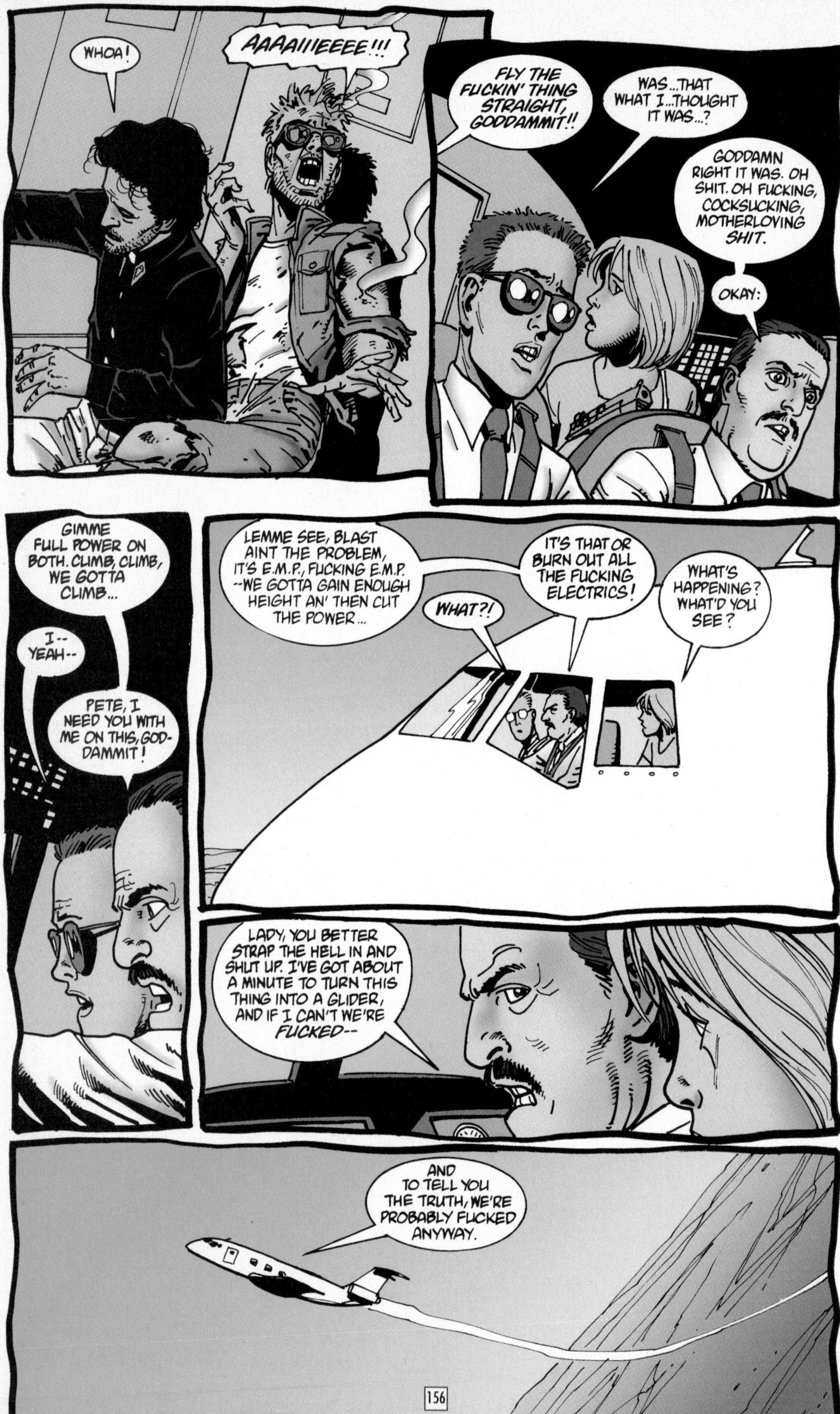

WHOA!
AAAAIIIEEEE!!!
FLY THE FUCKIN' THING STRAIGHT, GODDAMMIT!!
WAS...THAT WHAT I...THOUGHT IT WAS...?
GODDAMN RIGHT IT WAS. OH SHIT. OH FUCKING, COCKSUCKING, MOTHERLOVING SHIT.
OKAY:
GIMME FULL POWER ON BOTH. CLIMB, CLIMB, WE GOTTA CLIMB...
I-- YEAH--
PETE, I NEED YOU WITH ME ON THIS, GOD-DAMMIT!
LEMME SEE, BLAST AINT THE PROBLEM, IT'S E.M.P., FUCKING E.M.P. --WE GOTTA GAIN ENOUGH HEIGHT AN' THEN CUT THE POWER...
WHAT?!
IT'S THAT OR BURN OUT ALL THE FUCKING ELECTRICS!
WHAT'S HAPPENING? WHAT'D YOU SEE?
LADY, YOU BETTER STRAP THE HELL IN AND SHUT UP. I'VE GOT ABOUT A MINUTE TO TURN THIS THING INTO A GLIDER, AND IF I CAN'T WE'RE FUCKED--
AND TO TELL YOU THE TRUTH, WE'RE PROBABLY FUCKED ANYWAY.

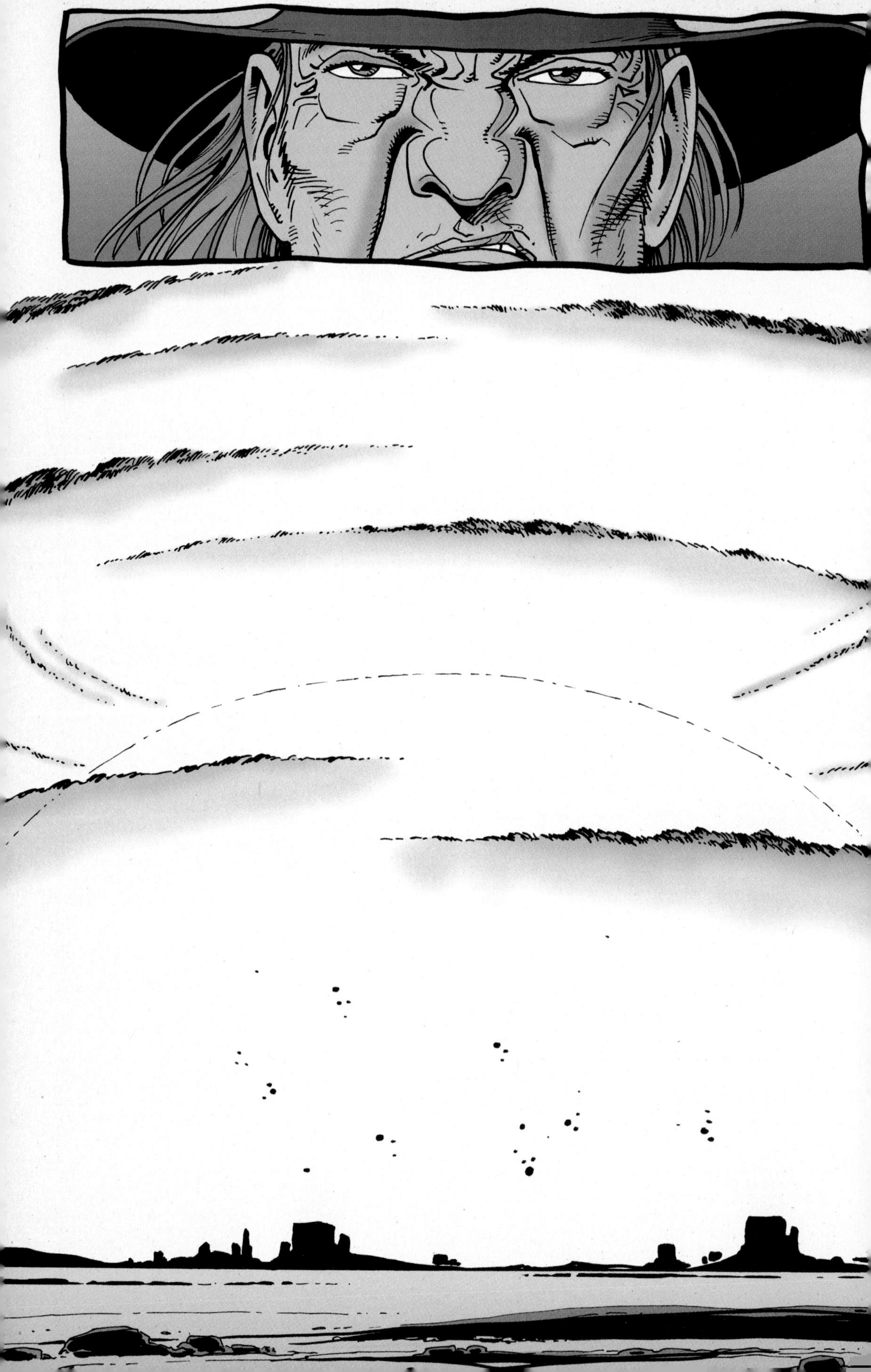

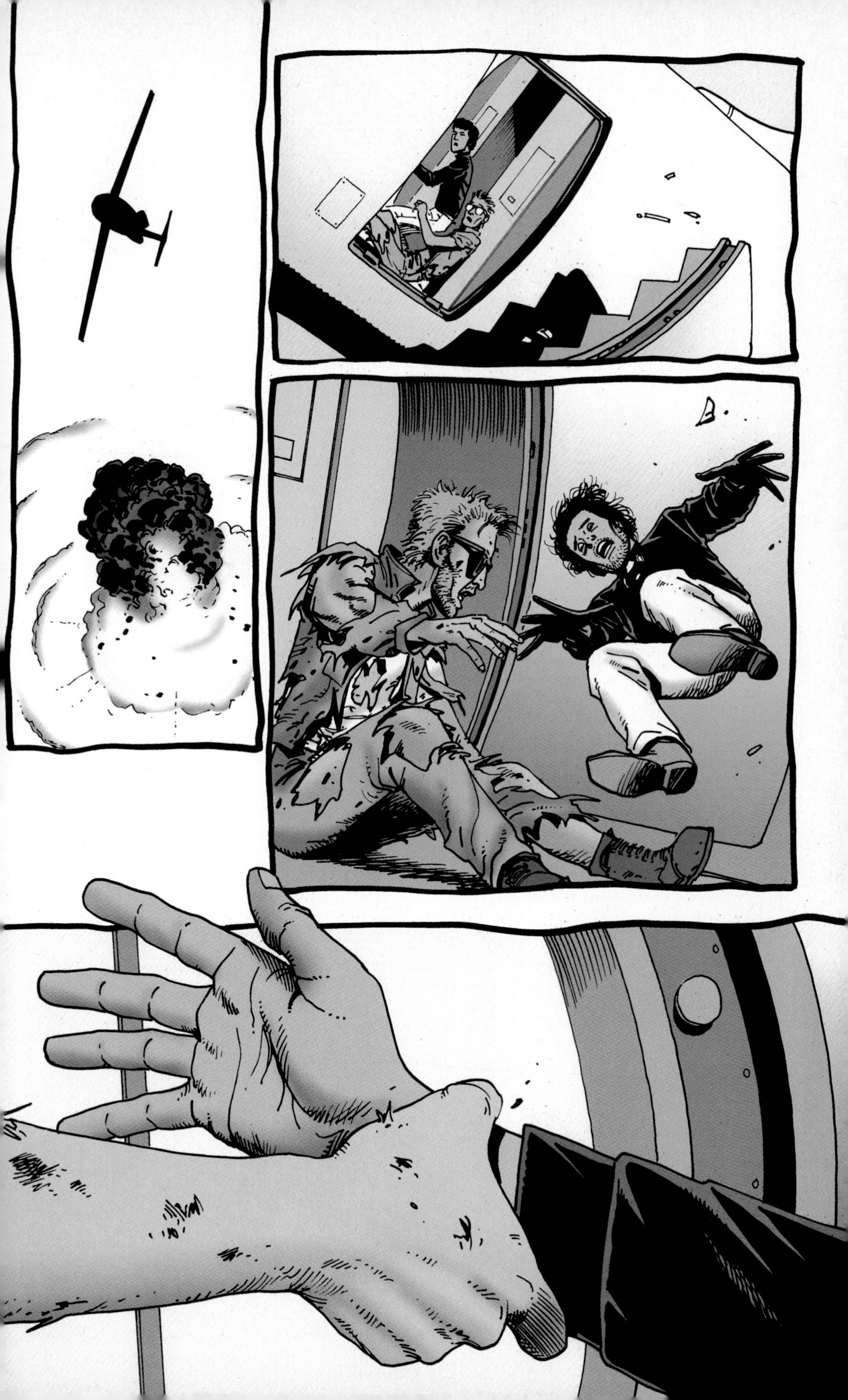

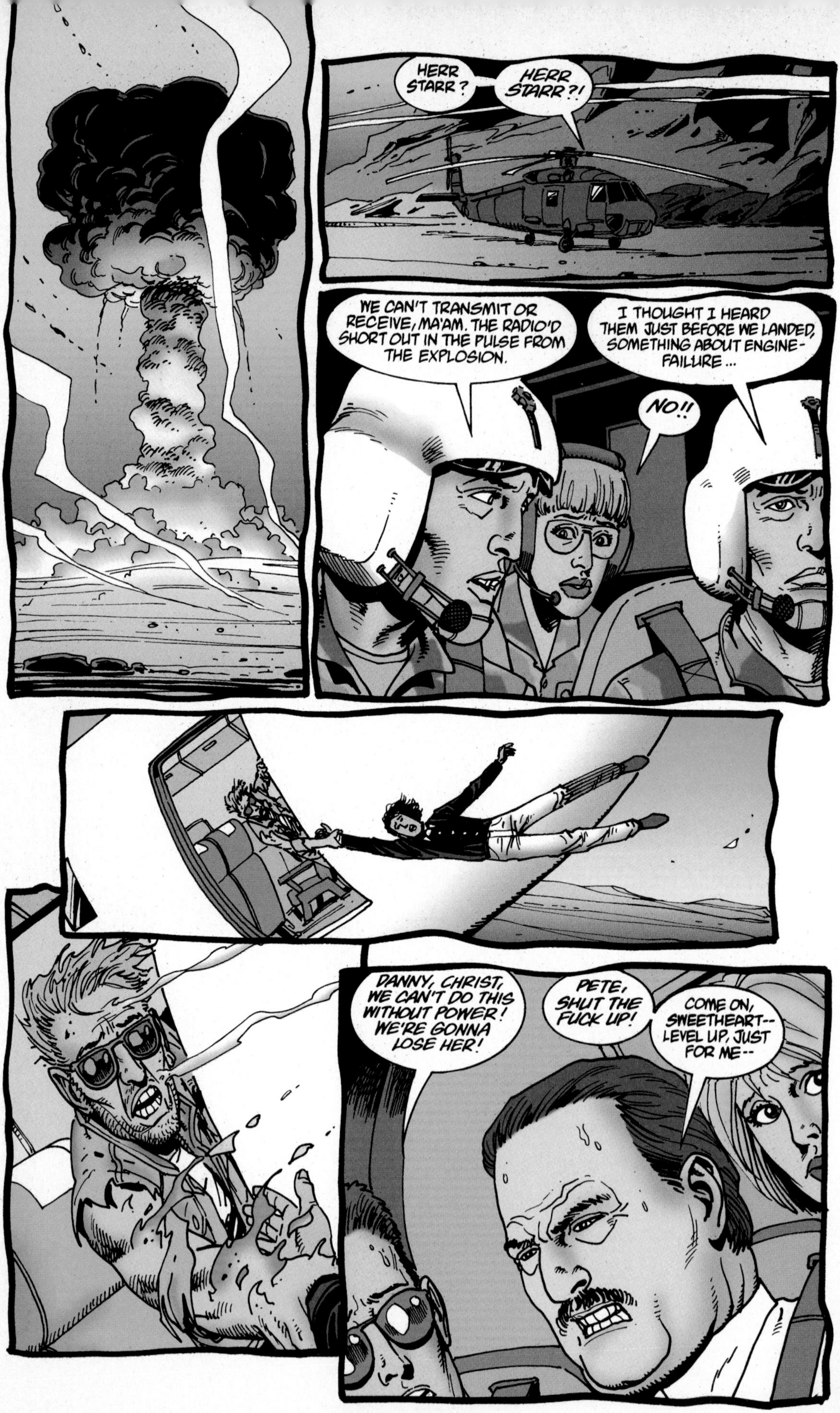
HERR STARR?
HERR STARR?!
WE CAN'T TRANSMIT OR RECEIVE, MA'AM. THE RADIO'D SHORT OUT IN THE PULSE FROM THE EXPLOSION.
I THOUGHT I HEARD THEM JUST BEFORE WE LANDED, SOMETHING ABOUT ENGINE-FAILURE...
NO!!
DANNY, CHRIST, WE CAN'T DO THIS WITHOUT POWER! WE'RE GONNA LOSE HER!
PETE, SHUT THE FUCK UP!
COME ON, SWEETHEART-- LEVEL UP, JUST FOR ME--

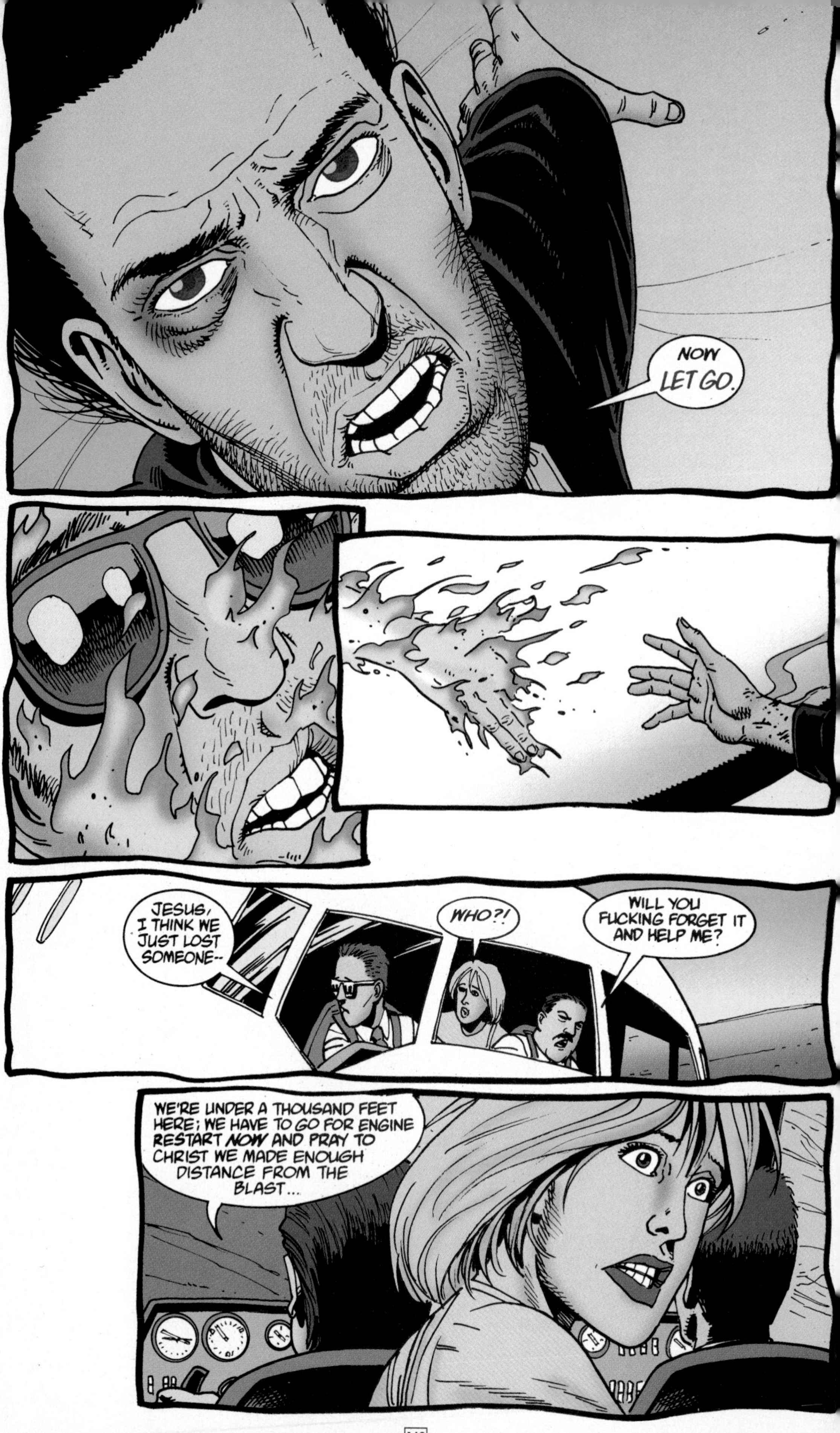
NOW LET GO.
JESUS, I THINK WE JUST LOST SOMEONE--
WHO?!
WILL YOU FUCKING FORGET IT AND HELP ME?
WE'RE UNDER A THOUSAND FEET HERE; WE HAVE TO GO FOR ENGINE RESTART NOW AND PRAY TO CHRIST WE MADE ENOUGH DISTANCE FROM THE BLAST...

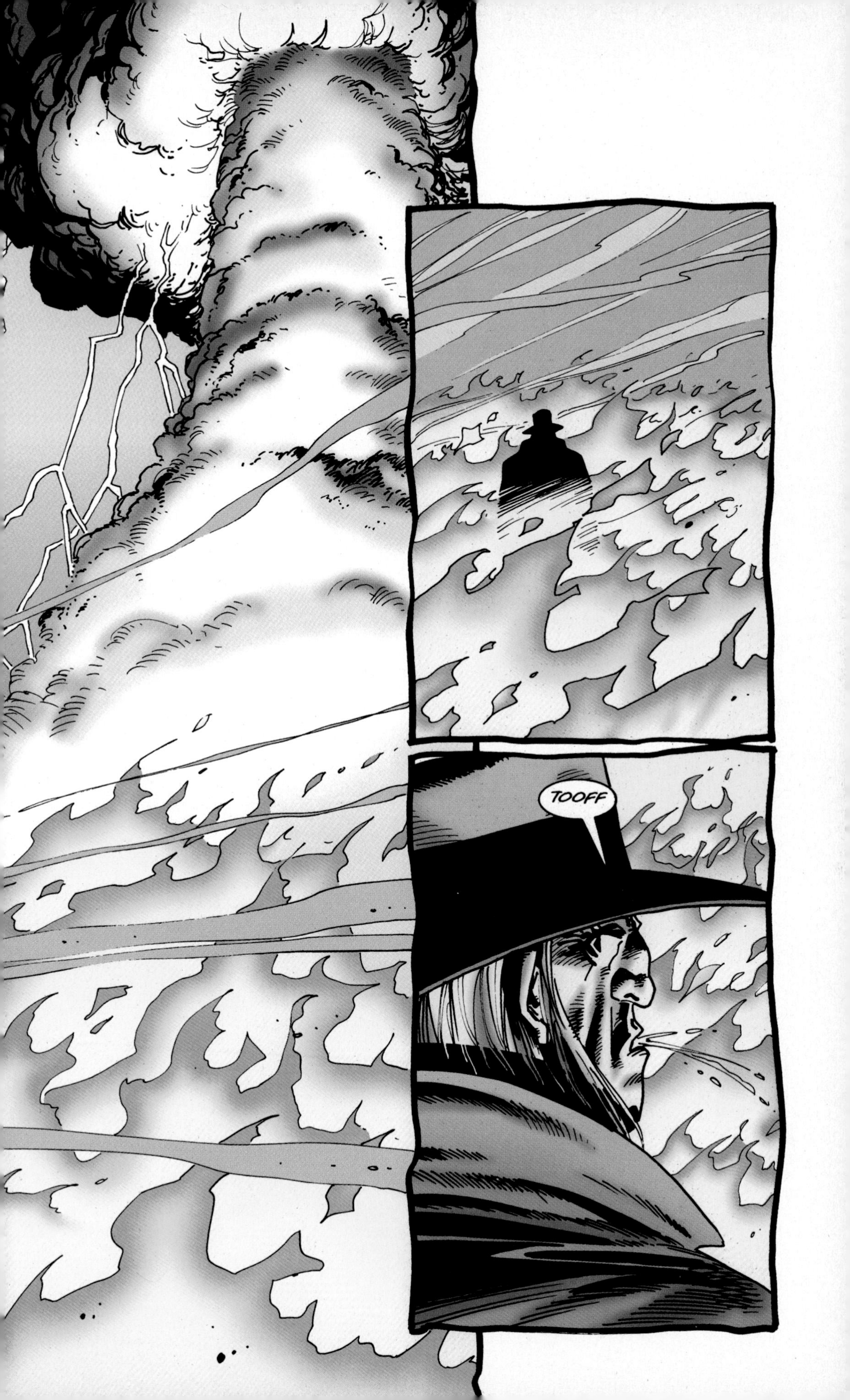
TOOFF

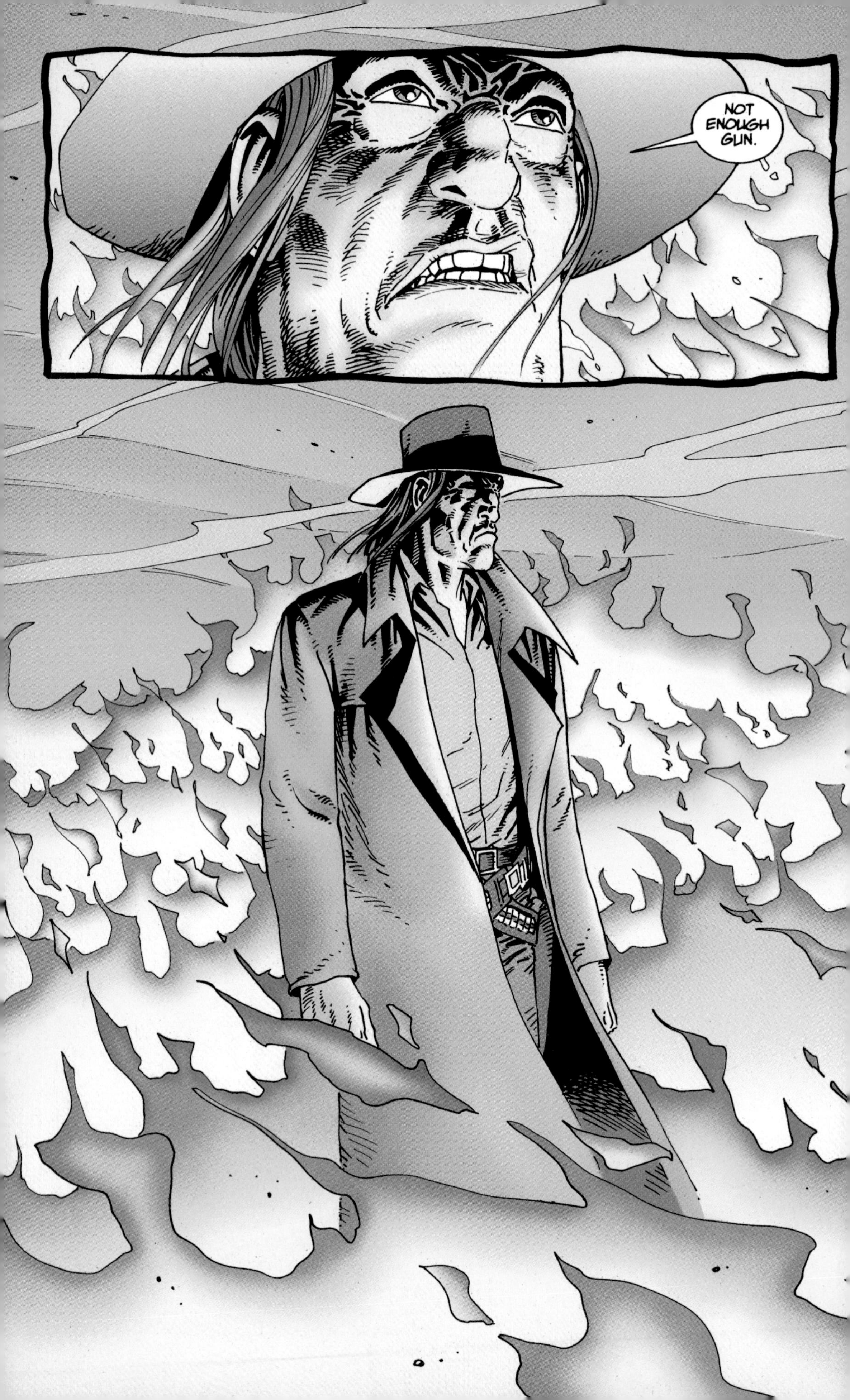
NOT ENOUGH GUN.

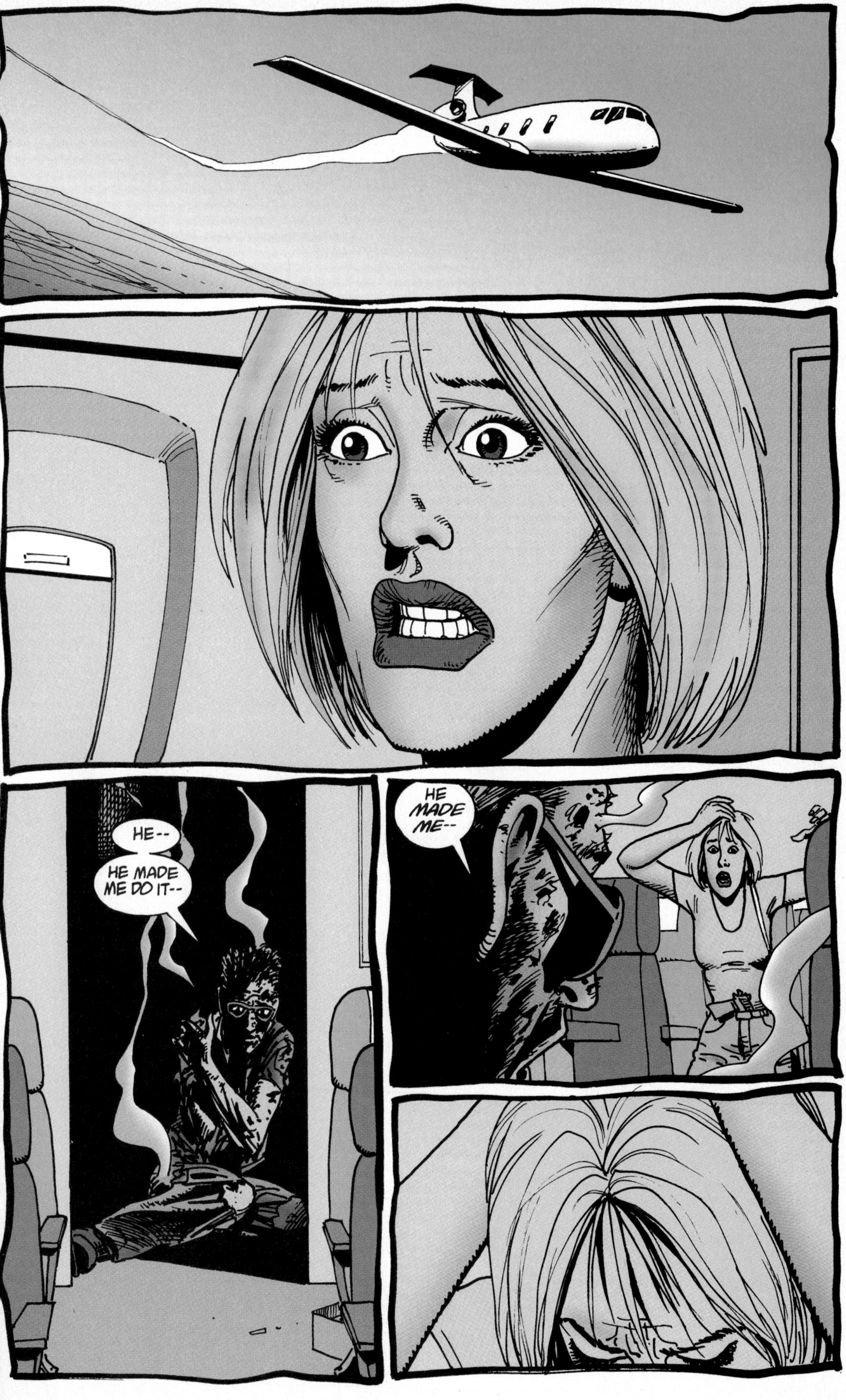
HE--
HE MADE ME DO IT--
HE MADE ME--

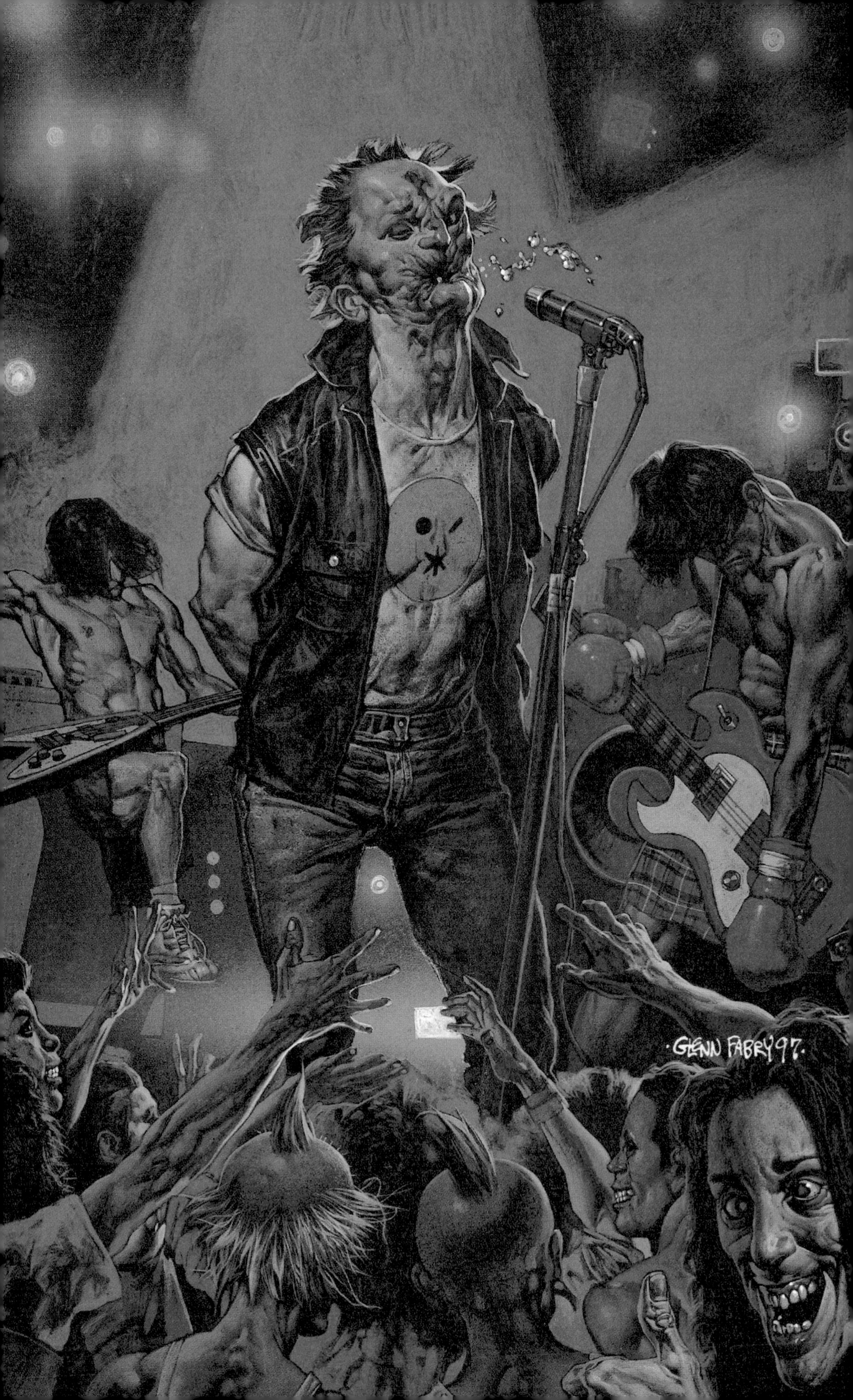
·GLENN FABRY 97.

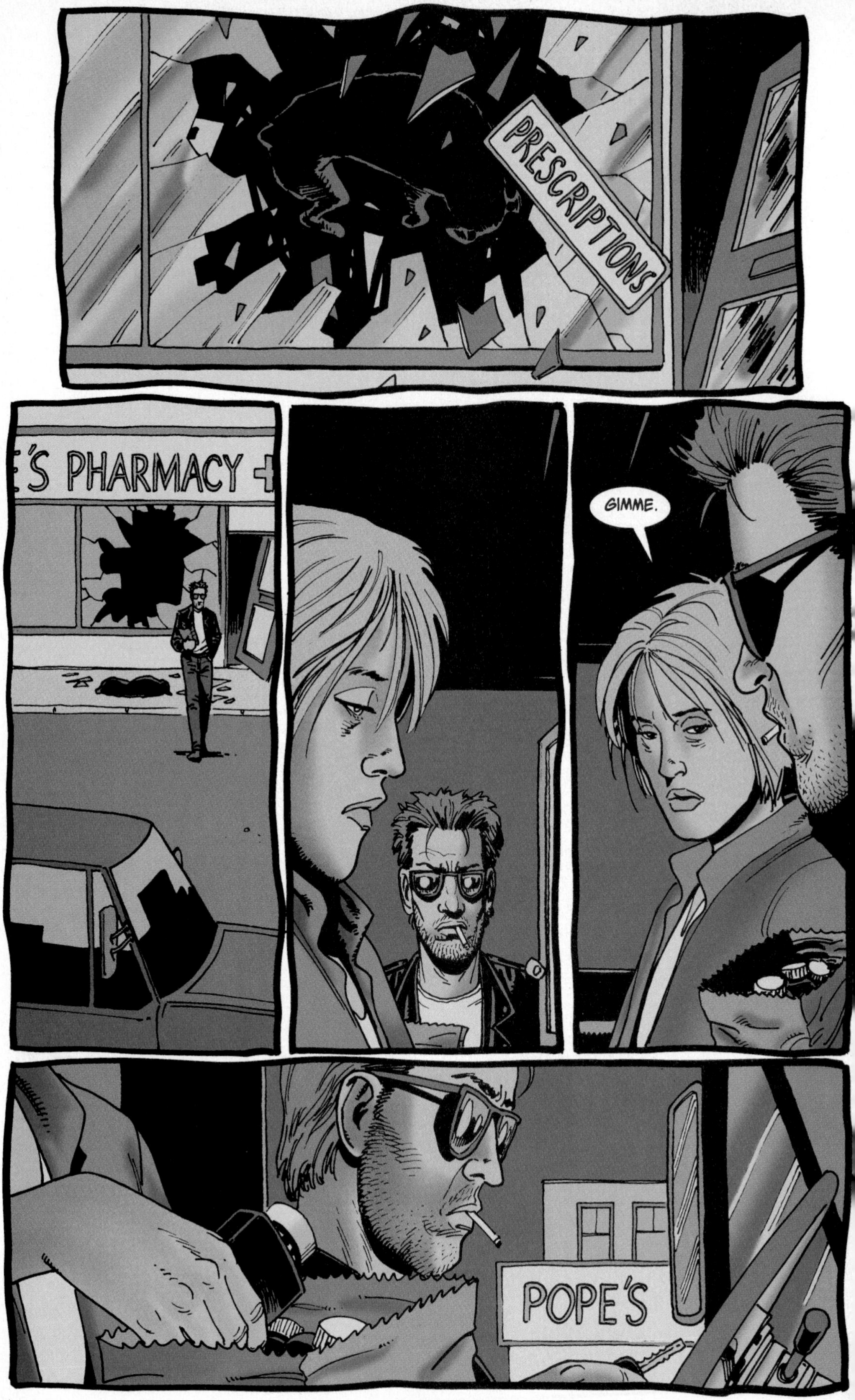
PRESCRIPTIONS
E'S PHARMACY
GIMME.
POPE'S

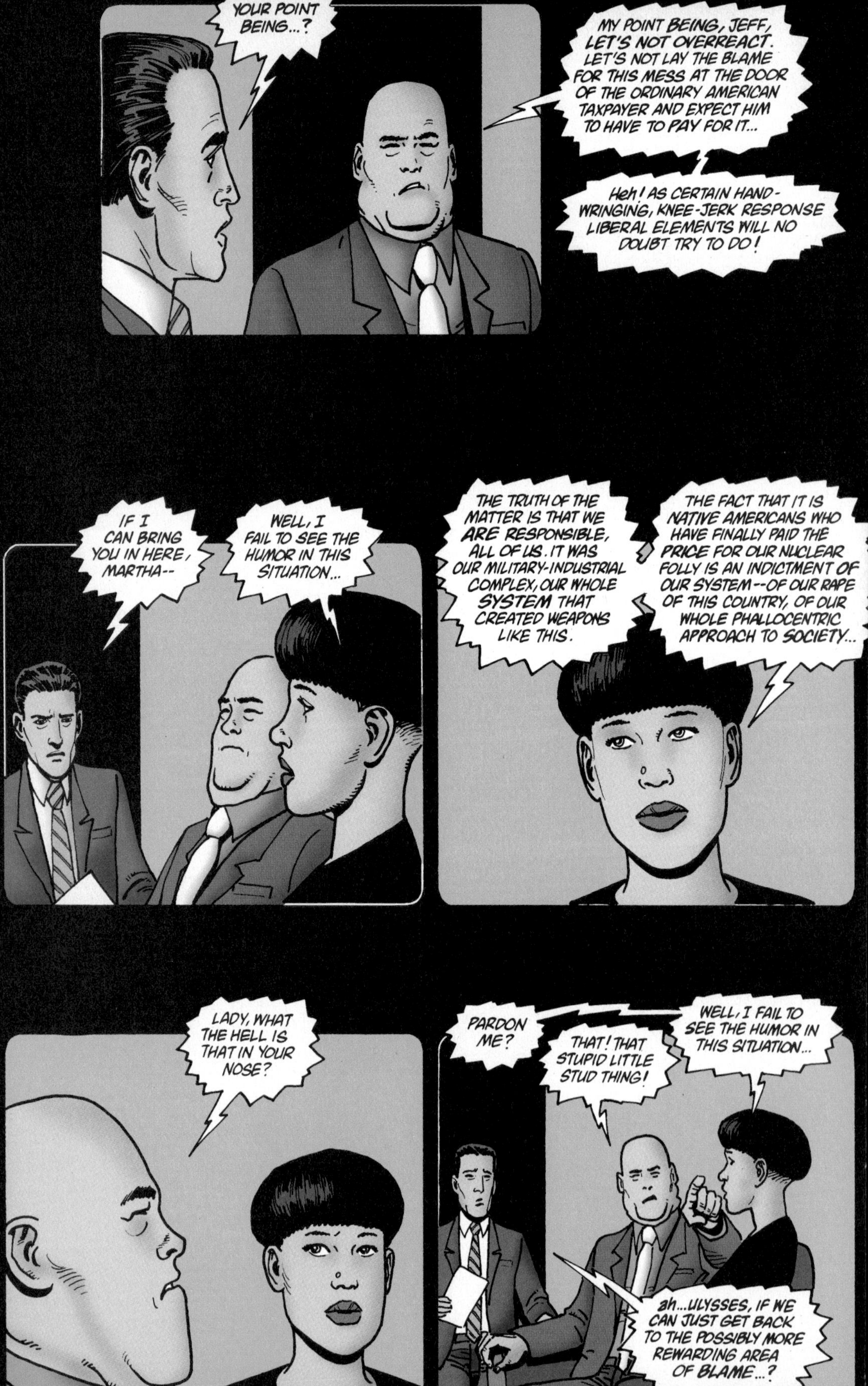

YOUR POINT BEING...?
MY POINT BEING, JEFF, LET'S NOT OVERREACT. LET'S NOT LAY THE BLAME FOR THIS MESS AT THE DOOR OF THE ORDINARY AMERICAN TAXPAYER AND EXPECT HIM TO HAVE TO PAY FOR IT...
Heh! AS CERTAIN HAND-WRINGING, KNEE-JERK RESPONSE LIBERAL ELEMENTS WILL NO DOUBT TRY TO DO!
IF I CAN BRING YOU IN HERE, MARTHA--
WELL, I FAIL TO SEE THE HUMOR IN THIS SITUATION...
THE TRUTH OF THE MATTER IS THAT WE ARE RESPONSIBLE, ALL OF US. IT WAS OUR MILITARY-INDUSTRIAL COMPLEX, OUR WHOLE SYSTEM THAT CREATED WEAPONS LIKE THIS.
THE FACT THAT IT IS NATIVE AMERICANS WHO HAVE FINALLY PAID THE PRICE FOR OUR NUCLEAR FOLLY IS AN INDICTMENT OF OUR SYSTEM--OF OUR RAPE OF THIS COUNTRY, OF OUR WHOLE PHALLOCENTRIC APPROACH TO SOCIETY...
LADY, WHAT THE HELL IS THAT IN YOUR NOSE?
PARDON ME?
THAT! THAT STUPID LITTLE STUD THING!
WELL, I FAIL TO SEE THE HUMOR IN THIS SITUATION...
ah...ULYSSES, IF WE CAN JUST GET BACK TO THE POSSIBLY MORE REWARDING AREA OF BLAME...?

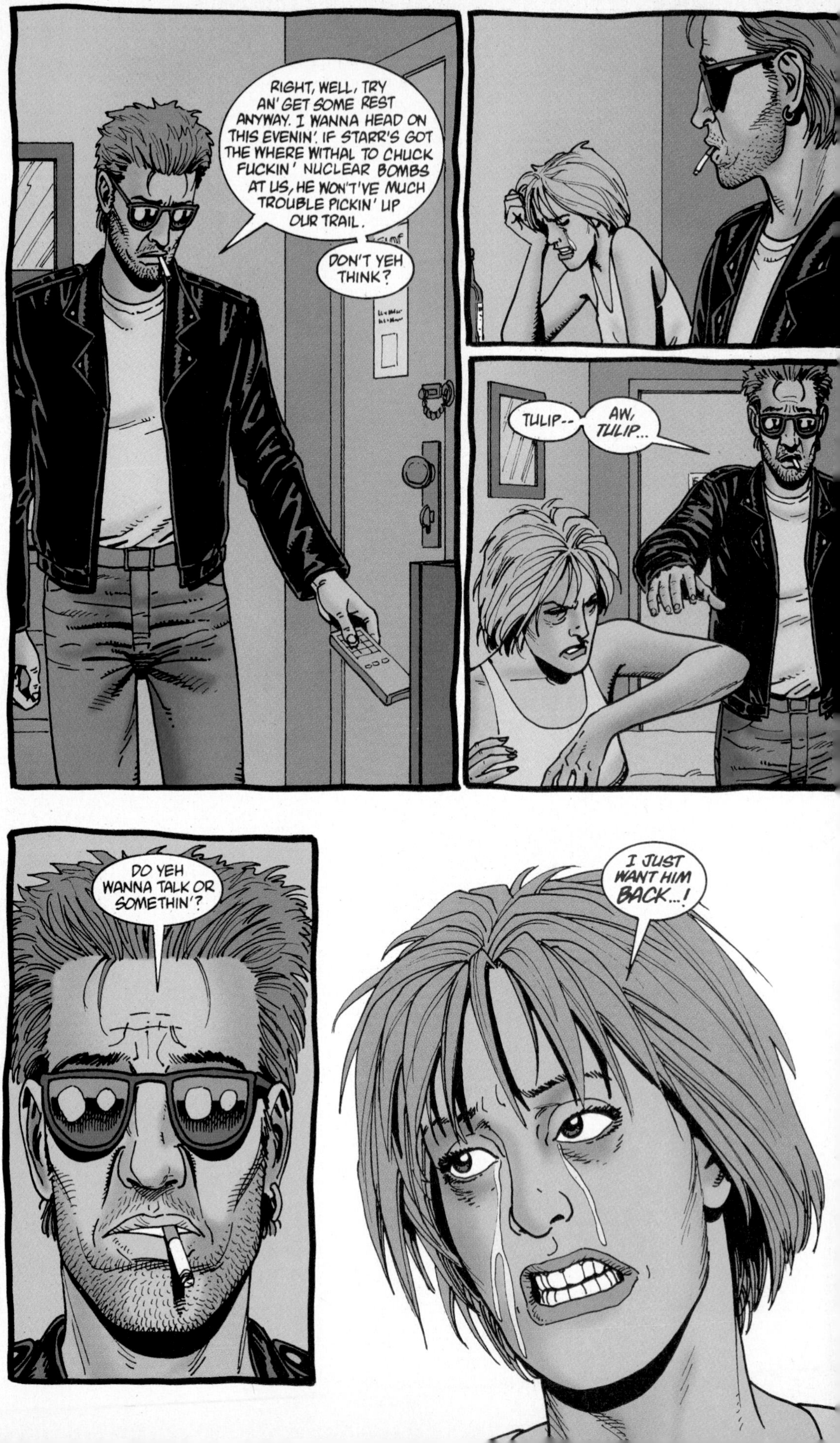
RIGHT, WELL, TRY AN' GET SOME REST ANYWAY. I WANNA HEAD ON THIS EVENIN'. IF STARR'S GOT THE WHERE WITHAL TO CHUCK FUCKIN' NUCLEAR BOMBS AT US, HE WON'T'VE MUCH TROUBLE PICKIN' UP OUR TRAIL.
DON'T YEH THINK?
TULIP--
AW, TULIP...
DO YEH WANNA TALK OR SOMETHIN'?
I JUST WANT HIM BACK...!

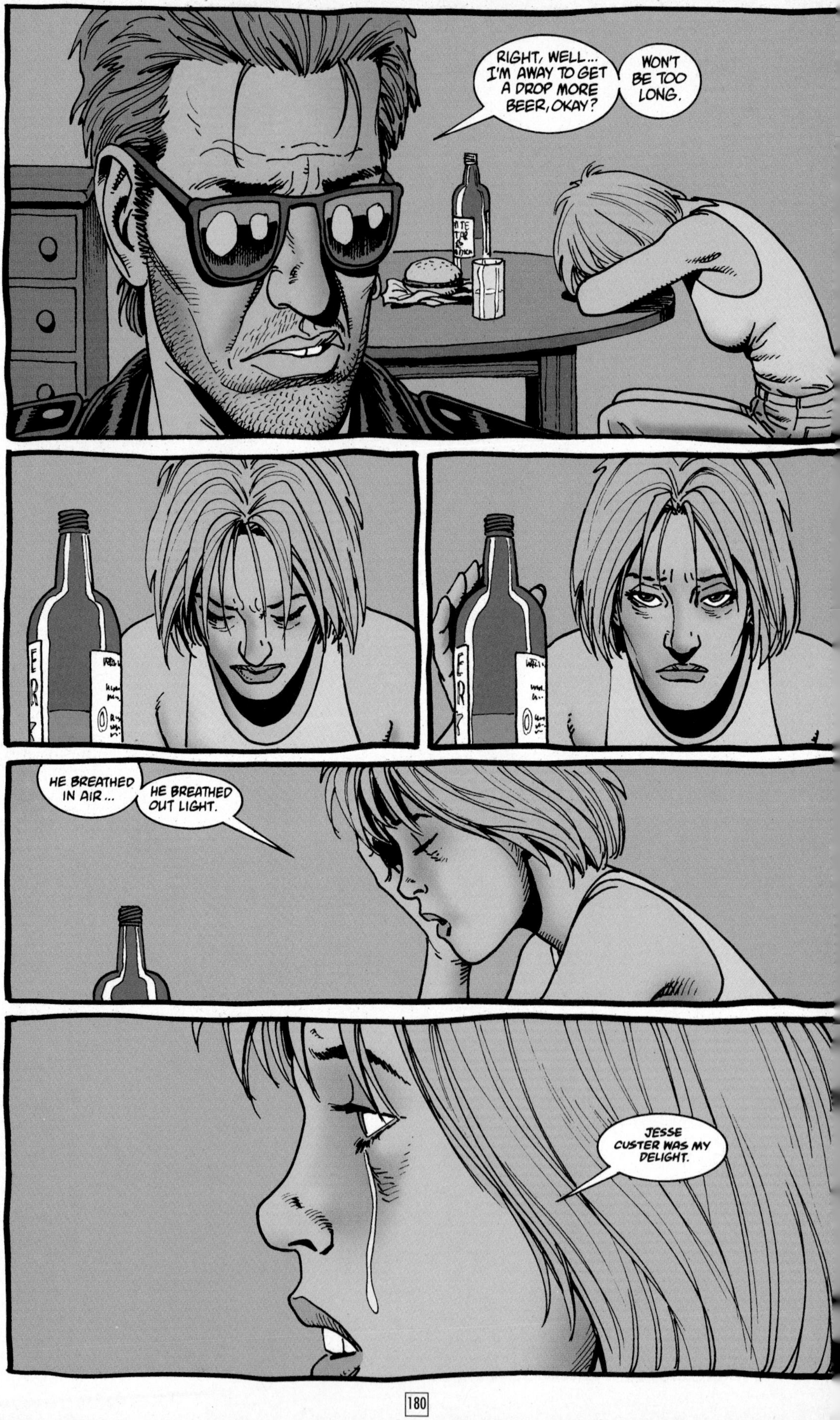
RIGHT, WELL... I'M AWAY TO GET A DROP MORE BEER, OKAY?
WON'T BE TOO LONG.
HE BREATHED IN AIR...
HE BREATHED OUT LIGHT.
JESSE CUSTER WAS MY DELIGHT.

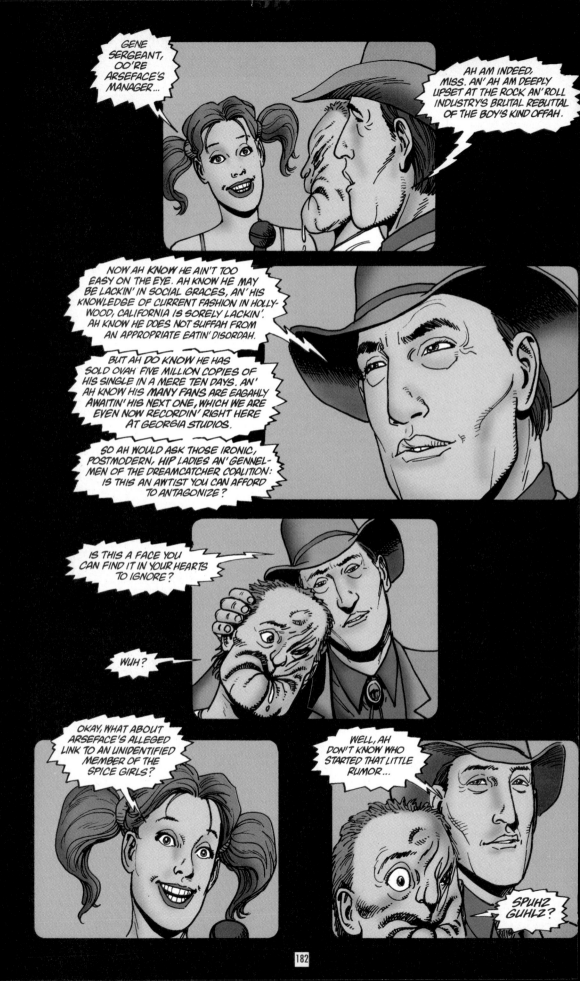

GENE SERGEANT, OO'RE ARSEFACE'S MANAGER...

AH AM INDEED, MISS. AN' AH AM DEEPLY UPSET AT THE ROCK AN' ROLL INDUSTRY'S BRUTAL REBUTTAL OF THE BOY'S KIND OFFAH.

NOW AH KNOW HE AIN'T TOO EASY ON THE EYE. AH KNOW HE MAY BE LACKIN' IN SOCIAL GRACES, AN' HIS KNOWLEDGE OF CURRENT FASHION IN HOLLY-WOOD, CALIFORNIA IS SORELY LACKIN'. AH KNOW HE DOES NOT SUFFAH FROM AN APPROPRIATE EATIN' DISORDAH.

BUT AH DO KNOW HE HAS SOLD OVAH FIVE MILLION COPIES OF HIS SINGLE IN A MERE TEN DAYS. AN' AH KNOW HIS MANY FANS ARE EAGAHLY AWAITIN' HIS NEXT ONE, WHICH WE ARE EVEN NOW RECORDIN' RIGHT HERE AT GEORGIA STUDIOS.

SO AH WOULD ASK THOSE IRONIC, POSTMODERN, HIP LADIES AN' GENNEL-MEN OF THE DREAMCATCHER COALITION: IS THIS AN AWTIST YOU CAN AFFORD TO ANTAGONIZE?

IS THIS A FACE YOU CAN FIND IT IN YOUR HEARTS TO IGNORE?

WUH?

OKAY, WHAT ABOUT ARSEFACE'S ALLEGED LINK TO AN UNIDENTIFIED MEMBER OF THE SPICE GIRLS?

WELL, AH DON'T KNOW WHO STARTED THAT LITTLE RUMOR...

SPUHZ GUHLZ?

182

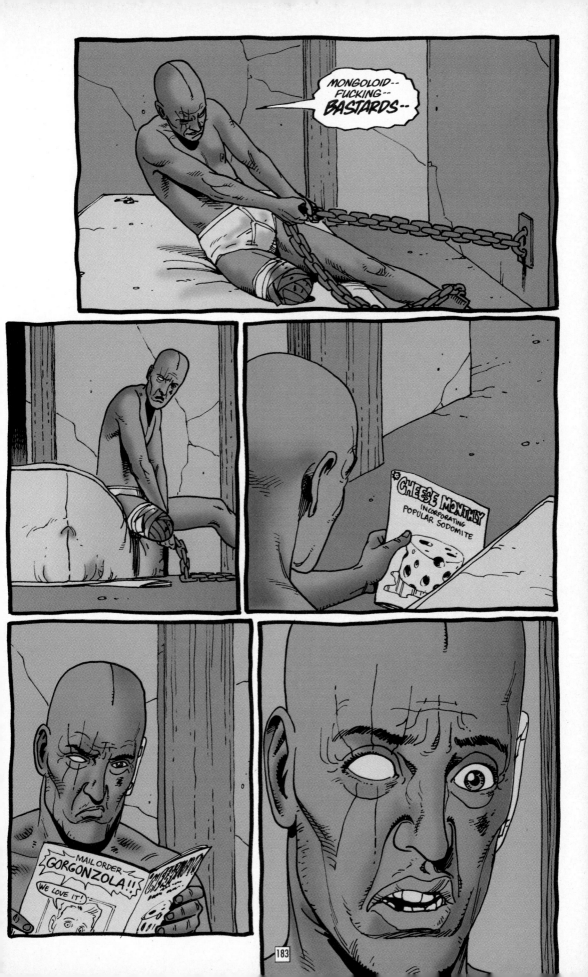

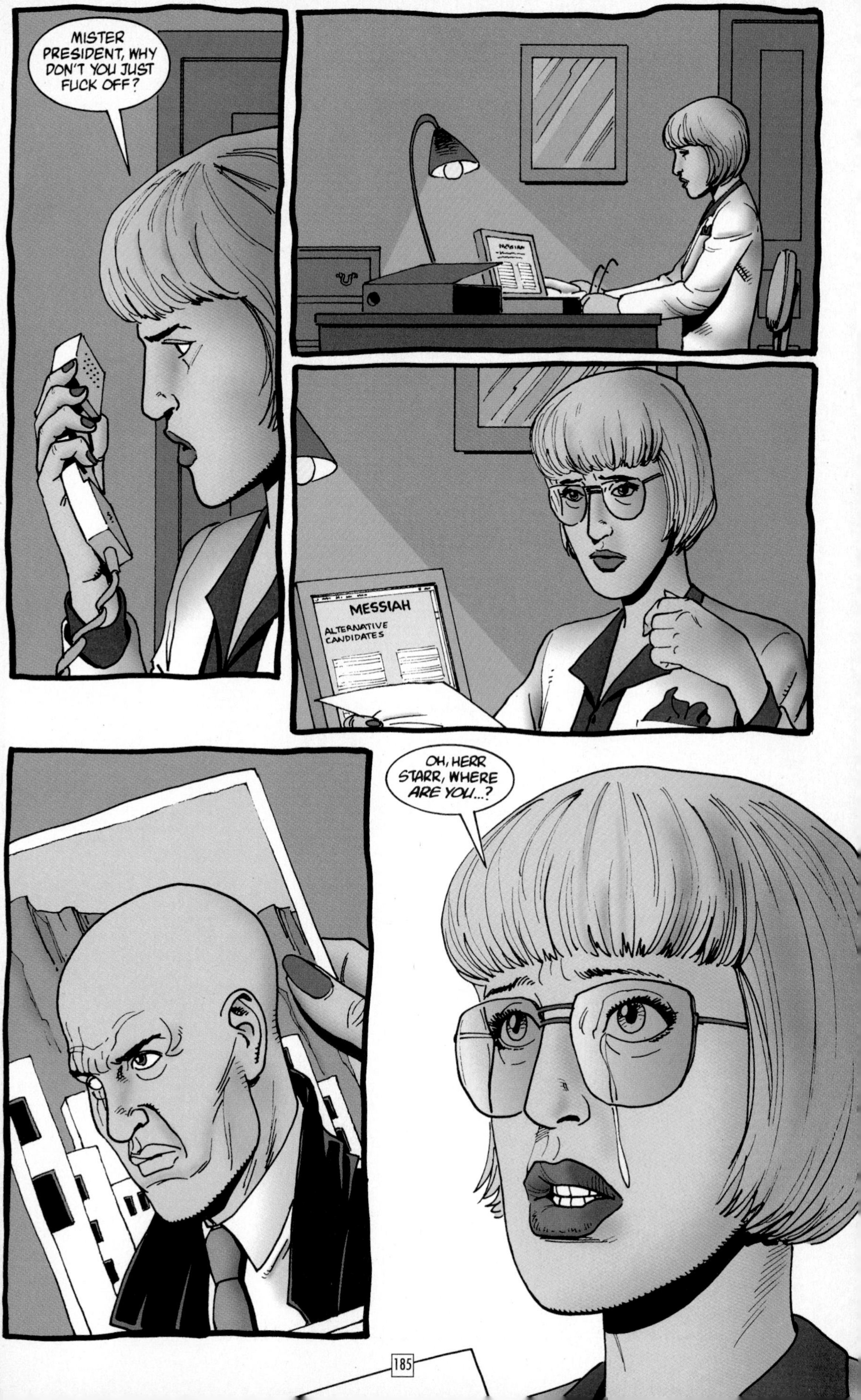
MISTER PRESIDENT, WHY DON'T YOU JUST FUCK OFF?
MESSIAH
ALTERNATIVE CANDIDATES
OH, HERR STARR, WHERE *ARE YOU...?*

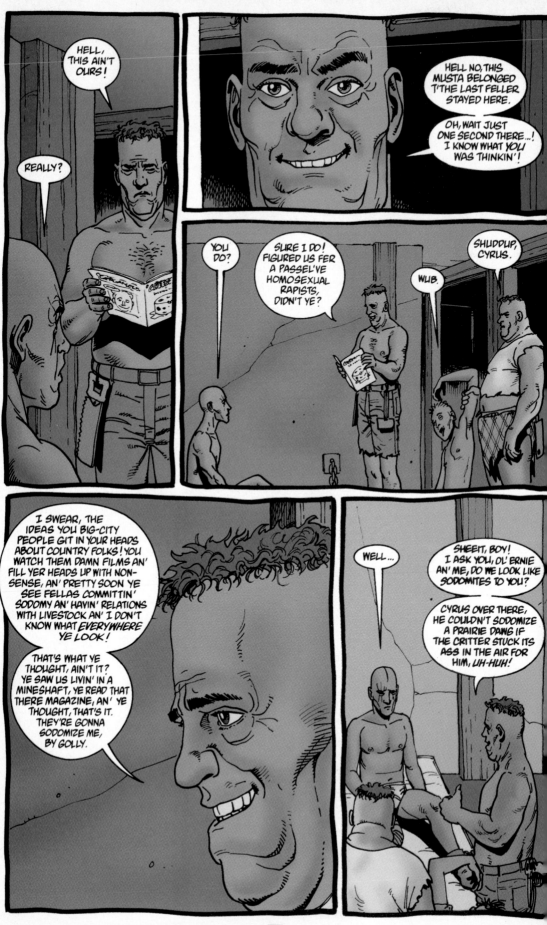

189

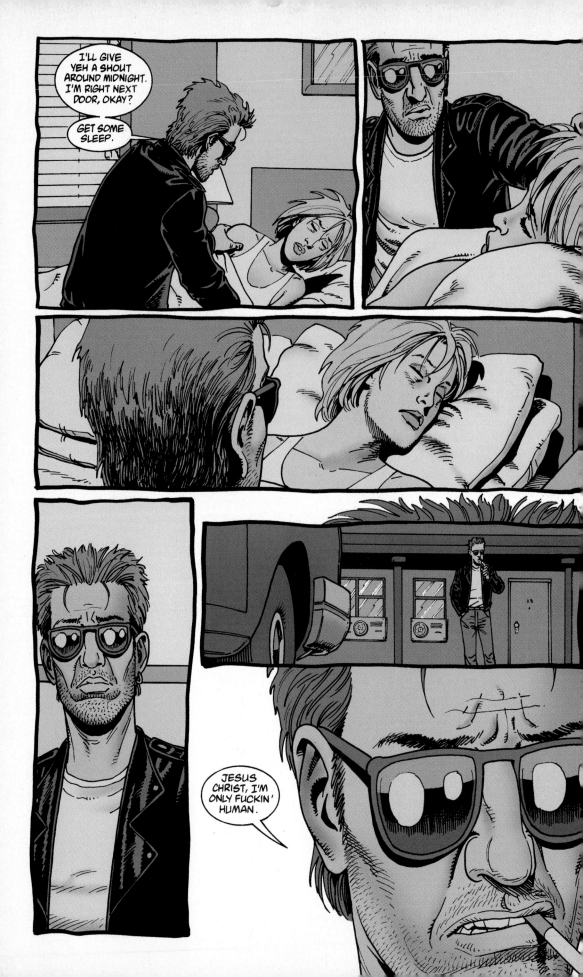

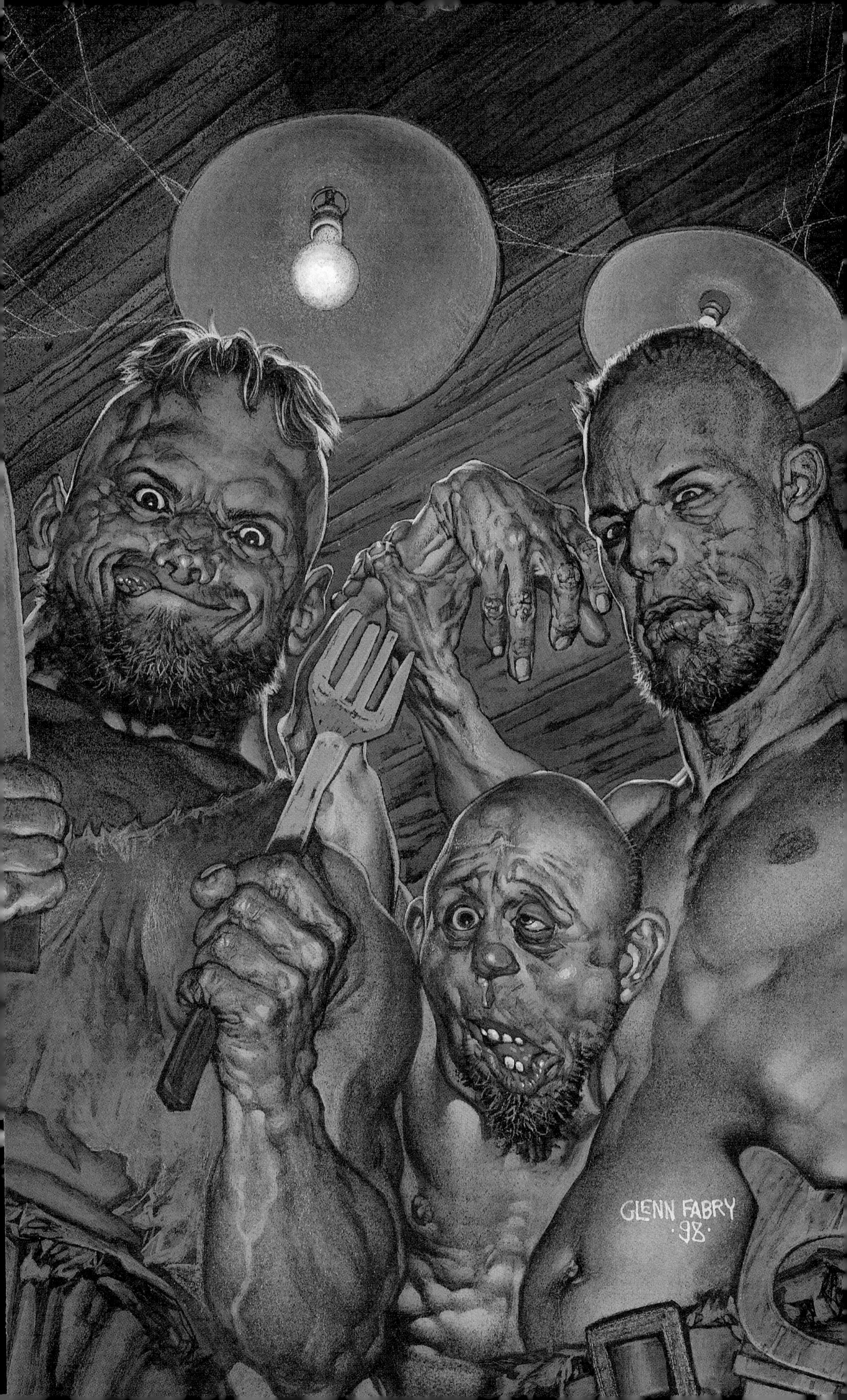
GLENN FABRY
·98·

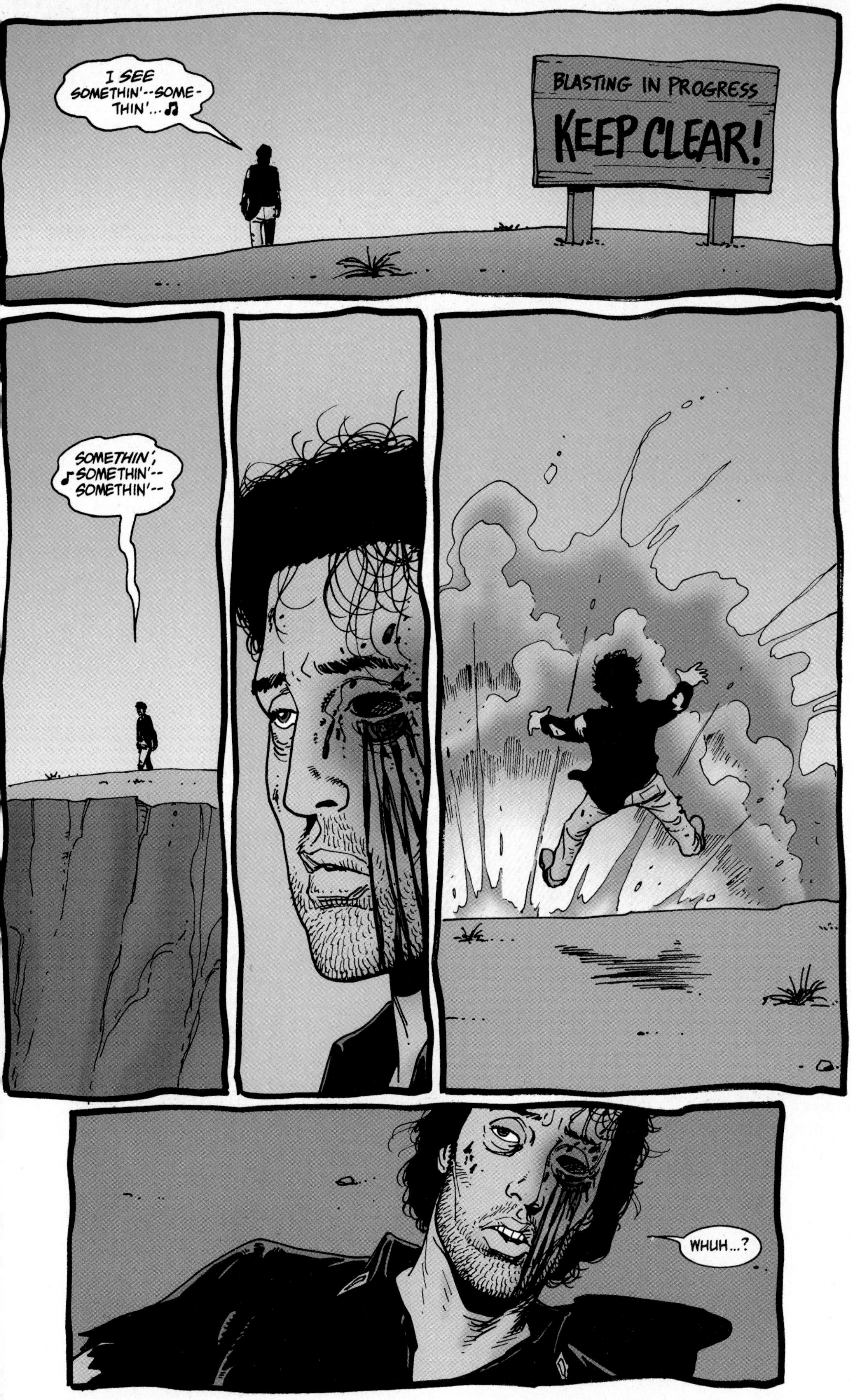
I SEE SOMETHIN'--SOME-THIN'... ♫
BLASTING IN PROGRESS
KEEP CLEAR!
SOMETHIN', ♪SOMETHIN'-- SOMETHIN'--
WHUH...?

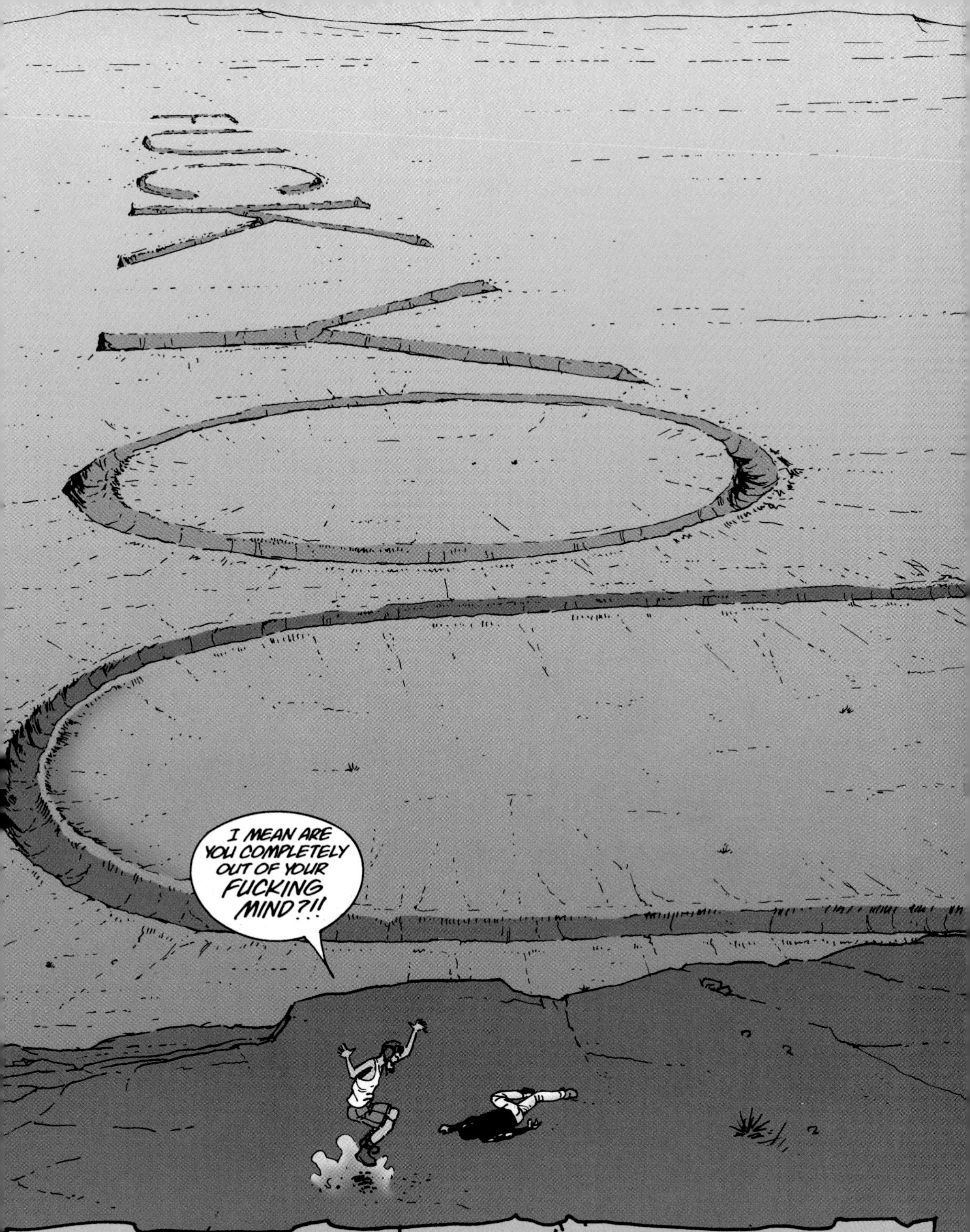
I MEAN ARE YOU COMPLETELY OUT OF YOUR FUCKING MIND?!!

FOR ALL MANKIND

GARTH ENNIS-Writer STEVE DILLON-Artist

Pamela Rambo-Colorist, Clem Robins-Letterer, Axel Alonso-Editor

PREACHER created by Garth Ennis and Steve Dillon

197

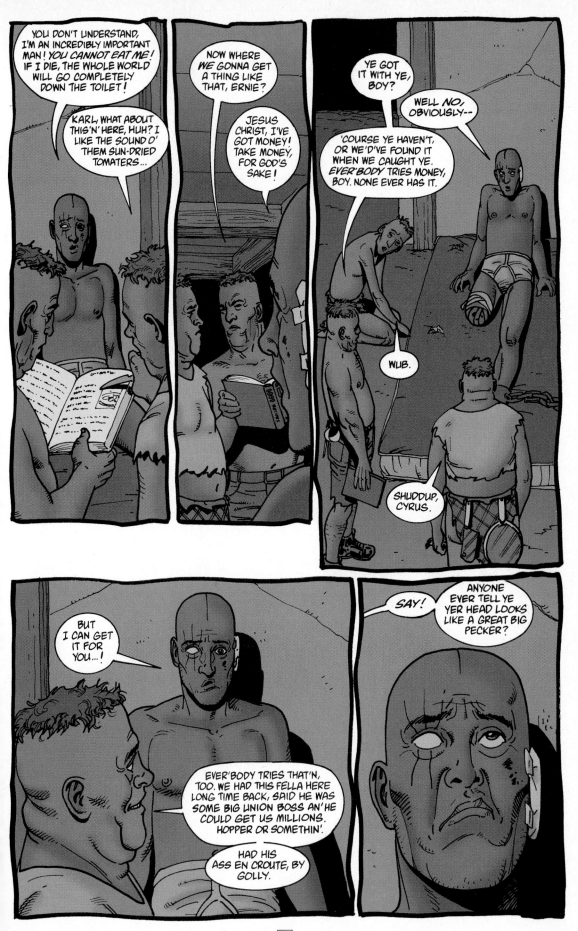

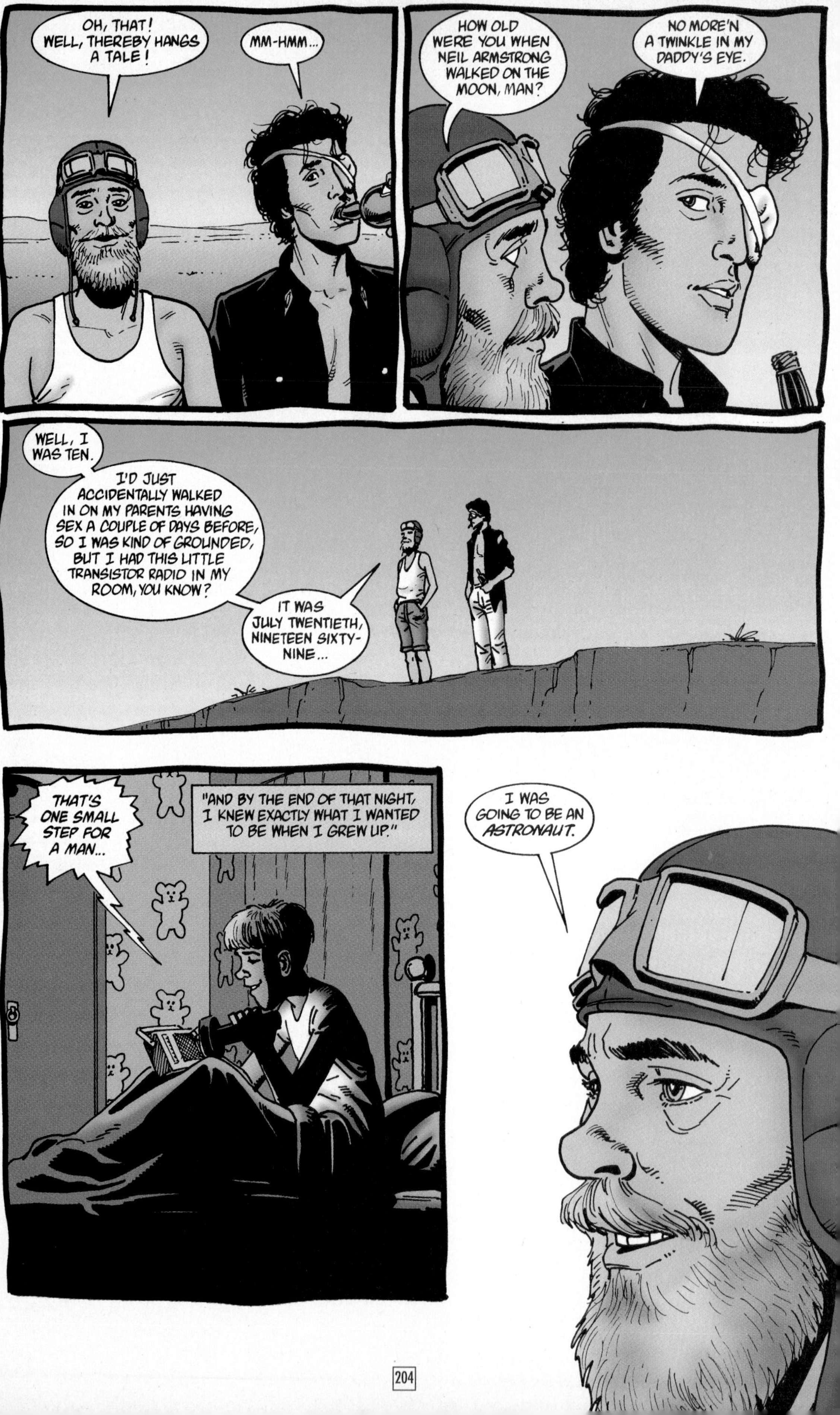
OH, THAT! WELL, THEREBY HANGS A TALE!
MM-HMM...
HOW OLD WERE YOU WHEN NEIL ARMSTRONG WALKED ON THE MOON, MAN?
NO MORE'N A TWINKLE IN MY DADDY'S EYE.
WELL, I WAS TEN.
I'D JUST ACCIDENTALLY WALKED IN ON MY PARENTS HAVING SEX A COUPLE OF DAYS BEFORE, SO I WAS KIND OF GROUNDED, BUT I HAD THIS LITTLE TRANSISTOR RADIO IN MY ROOM, YOU KNOW?
IT WAS JULY TWENTIETH, NINETEEN SIXTY-NINE...
THAT'S ONE SMALL STEP FOR A MAN...
"AND BY THE END OF THAT NIGHT, I KNEW EXACTLY WHAT I WANTED TO BE WHEN I GREW UP."
I WAS GOING TO BE AN *ASTRONAUT*.

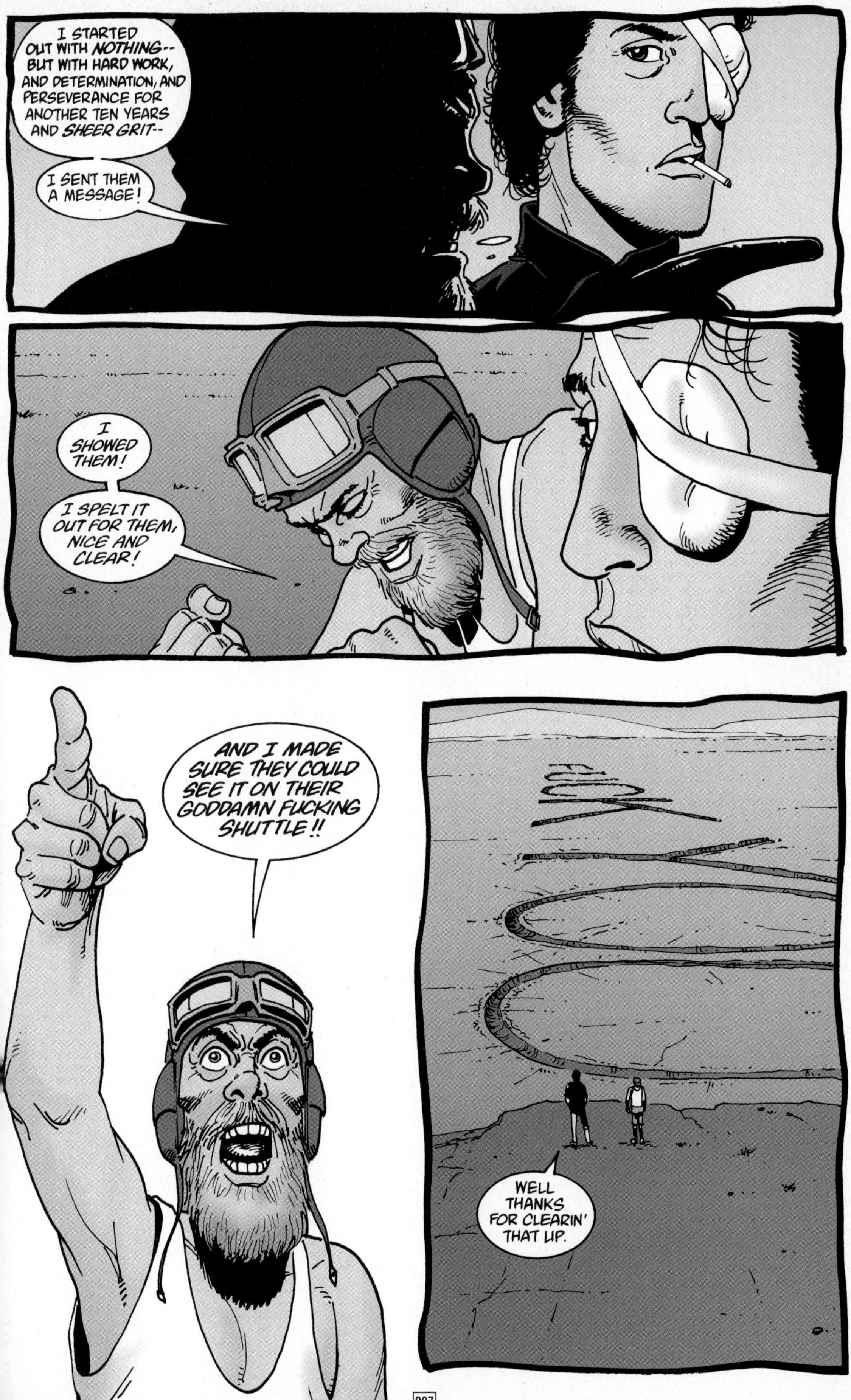
I STARTED OUT WITH NOTHING-- BUT WITH HARD WORK, AND DETERMINATION, AND PERSEVERANCE FOR ANOTHER TEN YEARS AND SHEER GRIT--
I SENT THEM A MESSAGE!
I SHOWED THEM!
I SPELT IT OUT FOR THEM, NICE AND CLEAR!
AND I MADE SURE THEY COULD SEE IT ON THEIR GODDAMN FUCKING SHUTTLE!!
WELL THANKS FOR CLEARIN' THAT UP.

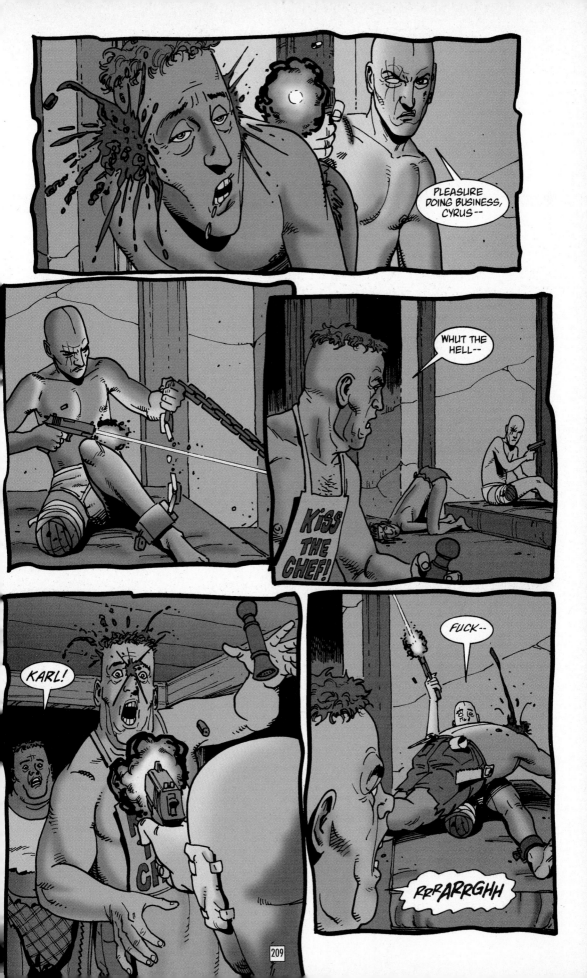

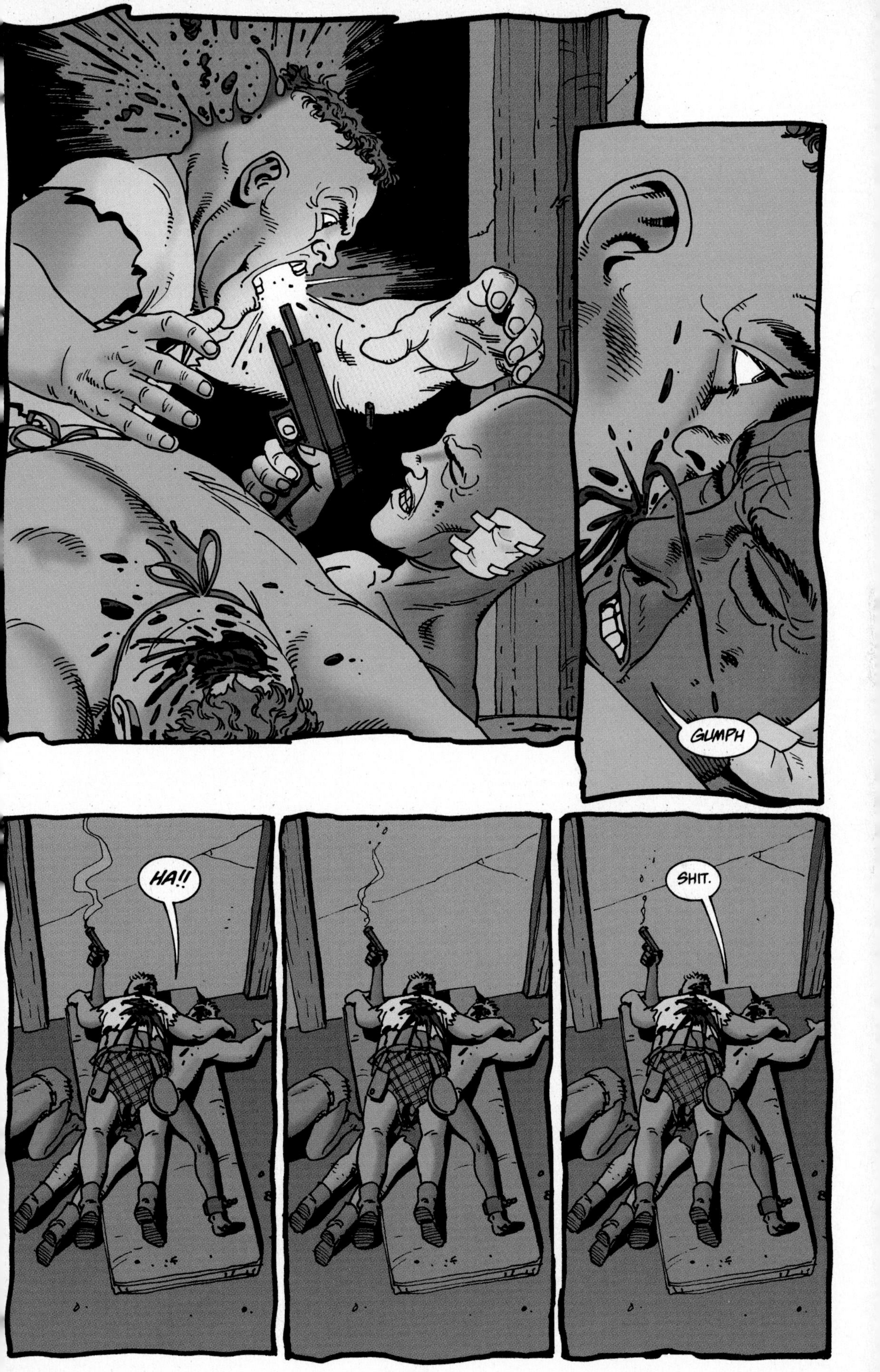
GUMPH
HA!!
SHIT.

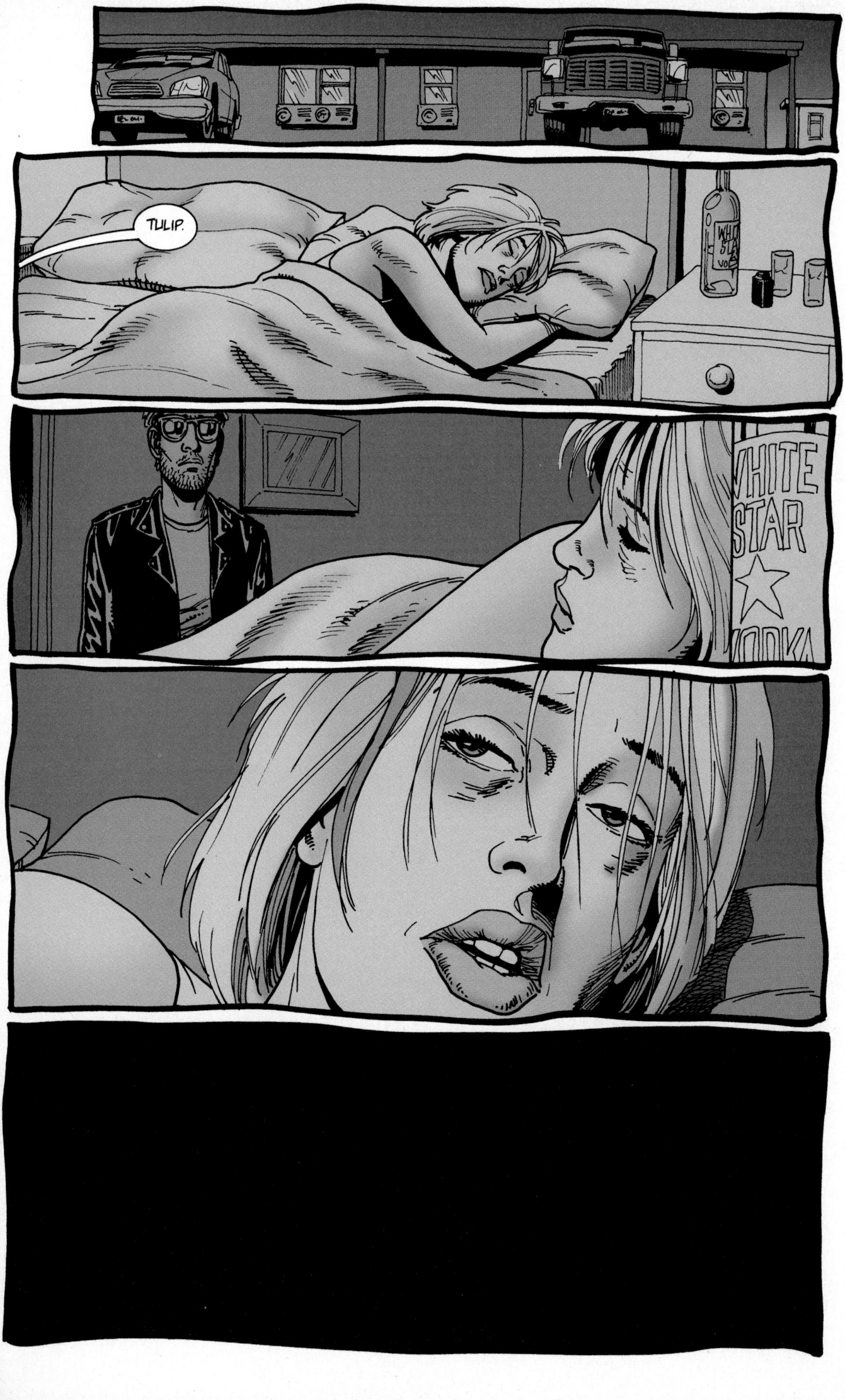
TULIP.
WHITE STAR VODKA

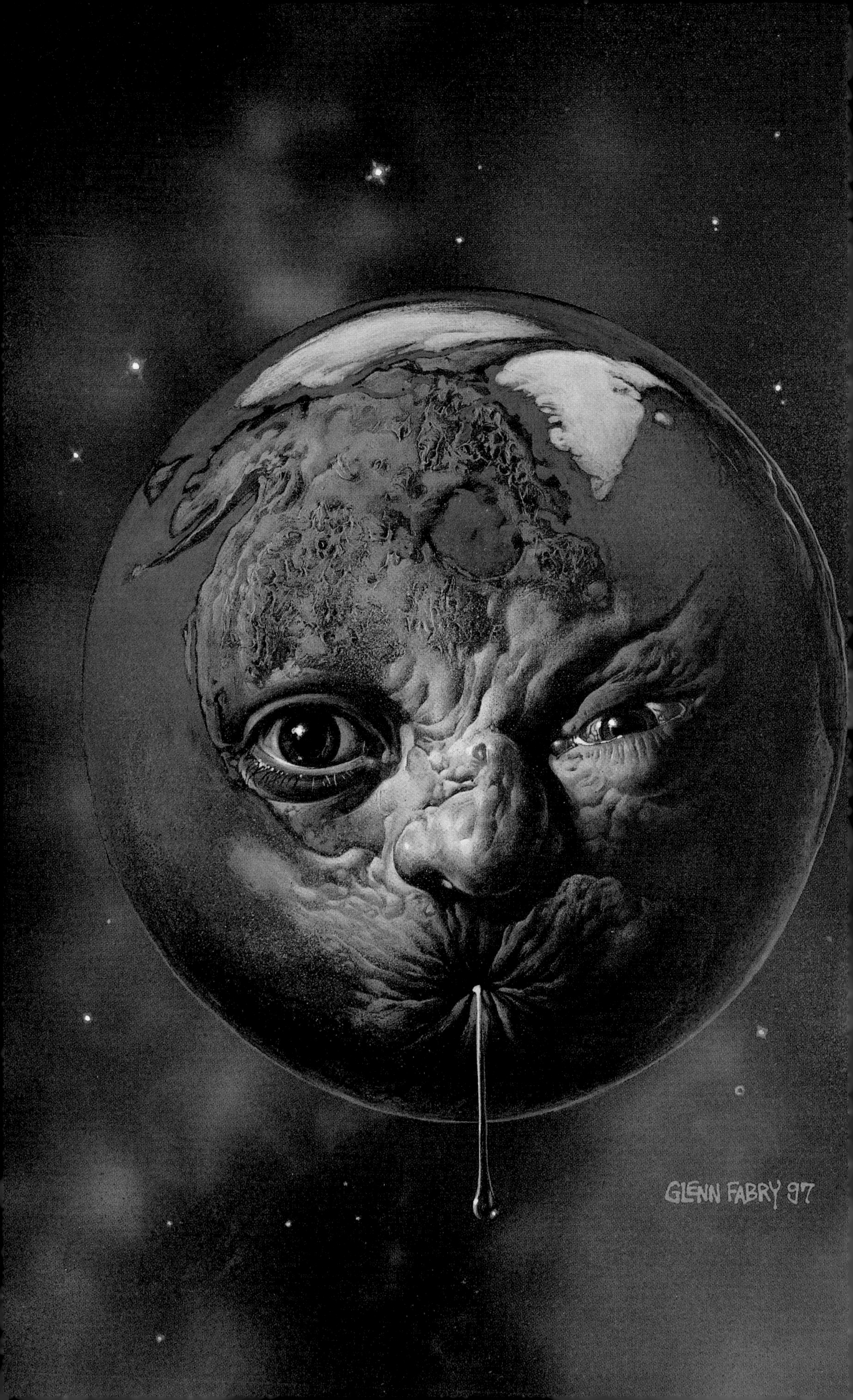
GLENN FABRY 97

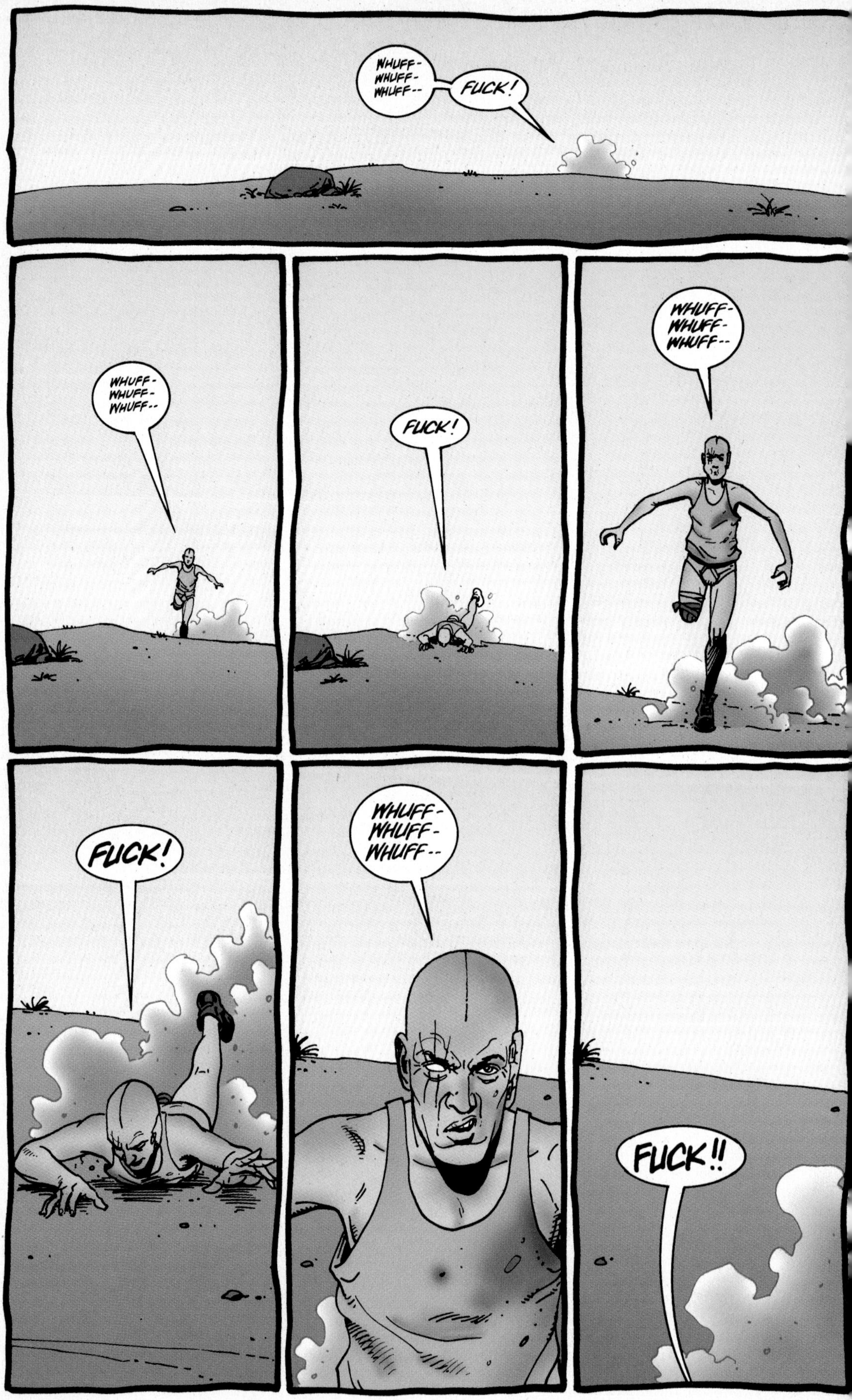
WHUFF-
WHUFF-
WHUFF--
FUCK!
WHUFF-
WHUFF-
WHUFF--
FUCK!
WHUFF-
WHUFF-
WHUFF--
FUCK!
WHUFF-
WHUFF-
WHUFF--
FUCK!!

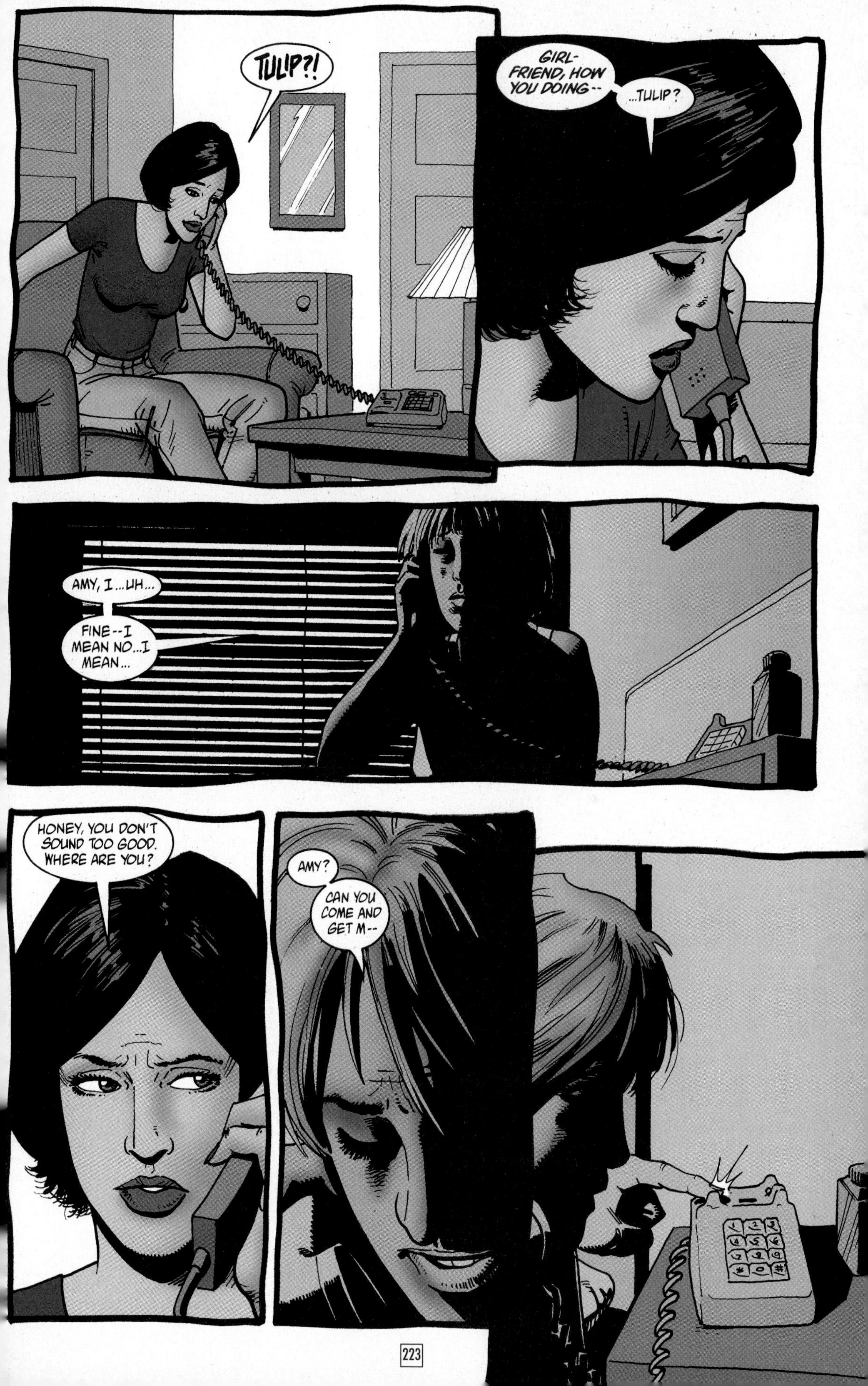
TULIP?!
GIRL-FRIEND, HOW YOU DOING--
...TULIP?
AMY, I...UH...
FINE--I MEAN NO...I MEAN...
HONEY, YOU DON'T SOUND TOO GOOD. WHERE ARE YOU?
AMY?
CAN YOU COME AND GET M--

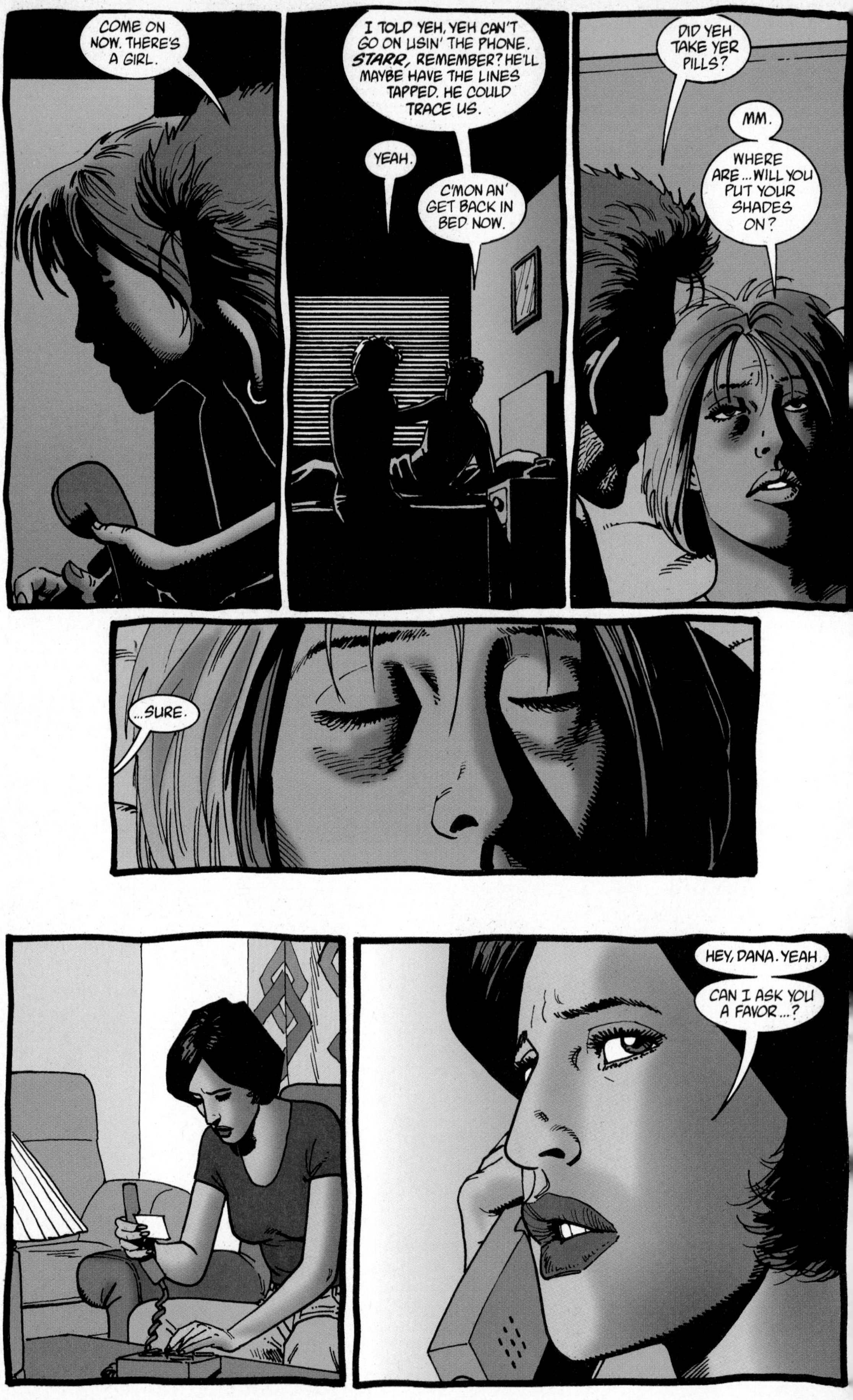
COME ON NOW. THERE'S A GIRL.
I TOLD YEH, YEH CAN'T GO ON USIN' THE PHONE. STARR, REMEMBER? HE'LL MAYBE HAVE THE LINES TAPPED. HE COULD TRACE US.
YEAH.
C'MON AN' GET BACK IN BED NOW.
DID YEH TAKE YER PILLS?
MM.
WHERE ARE ... WILL YOU PUT YOUR SHADES ON?
...SURE.
HEY, DANA. YEAH.
CAN I ASK YOU A FAVOR...?

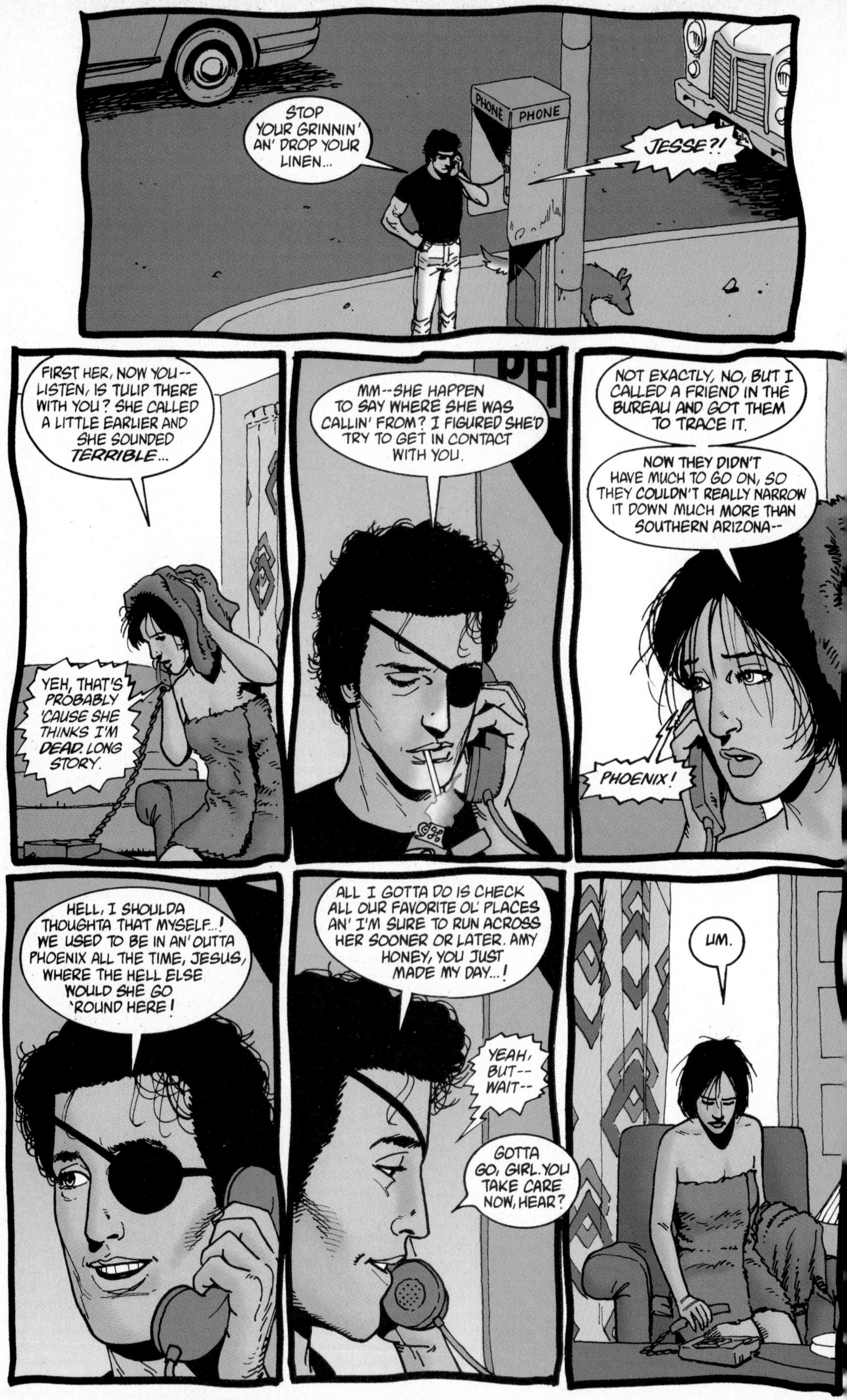

PHONE
PHONE
STOP YOUR GRINNIN' AN' DROP YOUR LINEN...
JESSE?!
FIRST HER, NOW YOU-- LISTEN, IS TULIP THERE WITH YOU? SHE CALLED A LITTLE EARLIER AND SHE SOUNDED TERRIBLE...
YEH, THAT'S PROBABLY 'CAUSE SHE THINKS I'M DEAD. LONG STORY.
MM--SHE HAPPEN TO SAY WHERE SHE WAS CALLIN' FROM? I FIGURED SHE'D TRY TO GET IN CONTACT WITH YOU.
NOT EXACTLY, NO, BUT I CALLED A FRIEND IN THE BUREAU AND GOT THEM TO TRACE IT.
NOW THEY DIDN'T HAVE MUCH TO GO ON, SO THEY COULDN'T REALLY NARROW IT DOWN MUCH MORE THAN SOUTHERN ARIZONA--
PHOENIX!
HELL, I SHOULDA THOUGHTA THAT MYSELF...! WE USED TO BE IN AN' OUTTA PHOENIX ALL THE TIME, JESUS, WHERE THE HELL ELSE WOULD SHE GO 'ROUND HERE!
ALL I GOTTA DO IS CHECK ALL OUR FAVORITE OL' PLACES AN' I'M SURE TO RUN ACROSS HER SOONER OR LATER. AMY HONEY, YOU JUST MADE MY DAY...!
YEAH, BUT-- WAIT--
GOTTA GO, GIRL. YOU TAKE CARE NOW, HEAR?
UM.

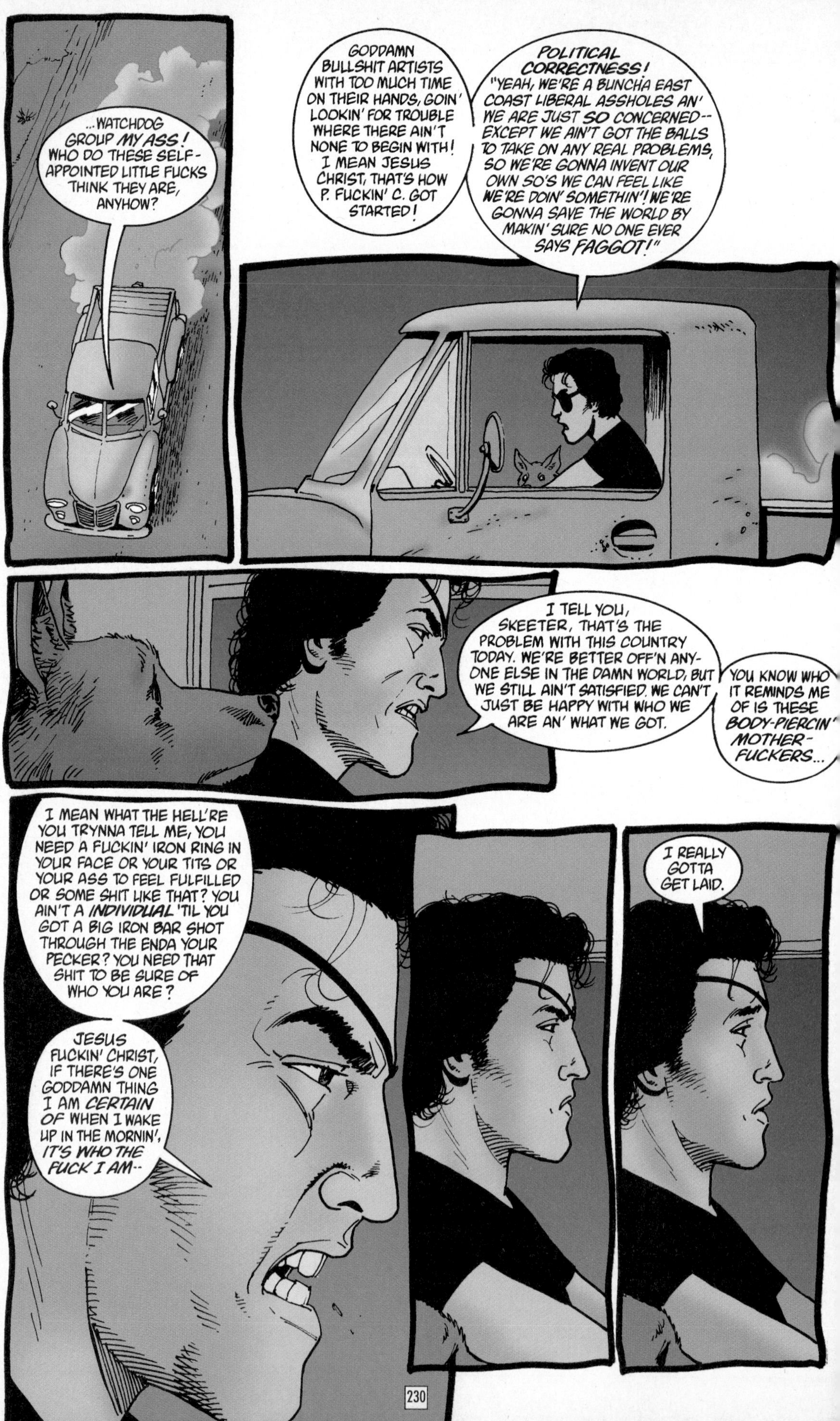

...WATCHDOG GROUP MY ASS! WHO DO THESE SELF-APPOINTED LITTLE FUCKS THINK THEY ARE, ANYHOW?
GODDAMN BULLSHIT ARTISTS WITH TOO MUCH TIME ON THEIR HANDS, GOIN' LOOKIN' FOR TROUBLE WHERE THERE AIN'T NONE TO BEGIN WITH! I MEAN JESUS CHRIST, THAT'S HOW P. FUCKIN' C. GOT STARTED!
POLITICAL CORRECTNESS! "YEAH, WE'RE A BUNCHA EAST COAST LIBERAL ASSHOLES AN' WE ARE JUST SO CONCERNED-- EXCEPT WE AIN'T GOT THE BALLS TO TAKE ON ANY REAL PROBLEMS, SO WE'RE GONNA INVENT OUR OWN SO'S WE CAN FEEL LIKE WE'RE DOIN' SOMETHIN'! WE'RE GONNA SAVE THE WORLD BY MAKIN' SURE NO ONE EVER SAYS FAGGOT!"
I TELL YOU, SKEETER, THAT'S THE PROBLEM WITH THIS COUNTRY TODAY. WE'RE BETTER OFF'N ANY-ONE ELSE IN THE DAMN WORLD, BUT WE STILL AIN'T SATISFIED. WE CAN'T JUST BE HAPPY WITH WHO WE ARE AN' WHAT WE GOT.
YOU KNOW WHO IT REMINDS ME OF IS THESE BODY-PIERCIN' MOTHER-FUCKERS...
I MEAN WHAT THE HELL'RE YOU TRYNNA TELL ME, YOU NEED A FUCKIN' IRON RING IN YOUR FACE OR YOUR TITS OR YOUR ASS TO FEEL FULFILLED OR SOME SHIT LIKE THAT? YOU AIN'T A INDIVIDUAL 'TIL YOU GOT A BIG IRON BAR SHOT THROUGH THE ENDA YOUR PECKER? YOU NEED THAT SHIT TO BE SURE OF WHO YOU ARE?
JESUS FUCKIN' CHRIST, IF THERE'S ONE GODDAMN THING I AM CERTAIN OF WHEN I WAKE UP IN THE MORNIN', IT'S WHO THE FUCK I AM--
I REALLY GOTTA GET LAID.

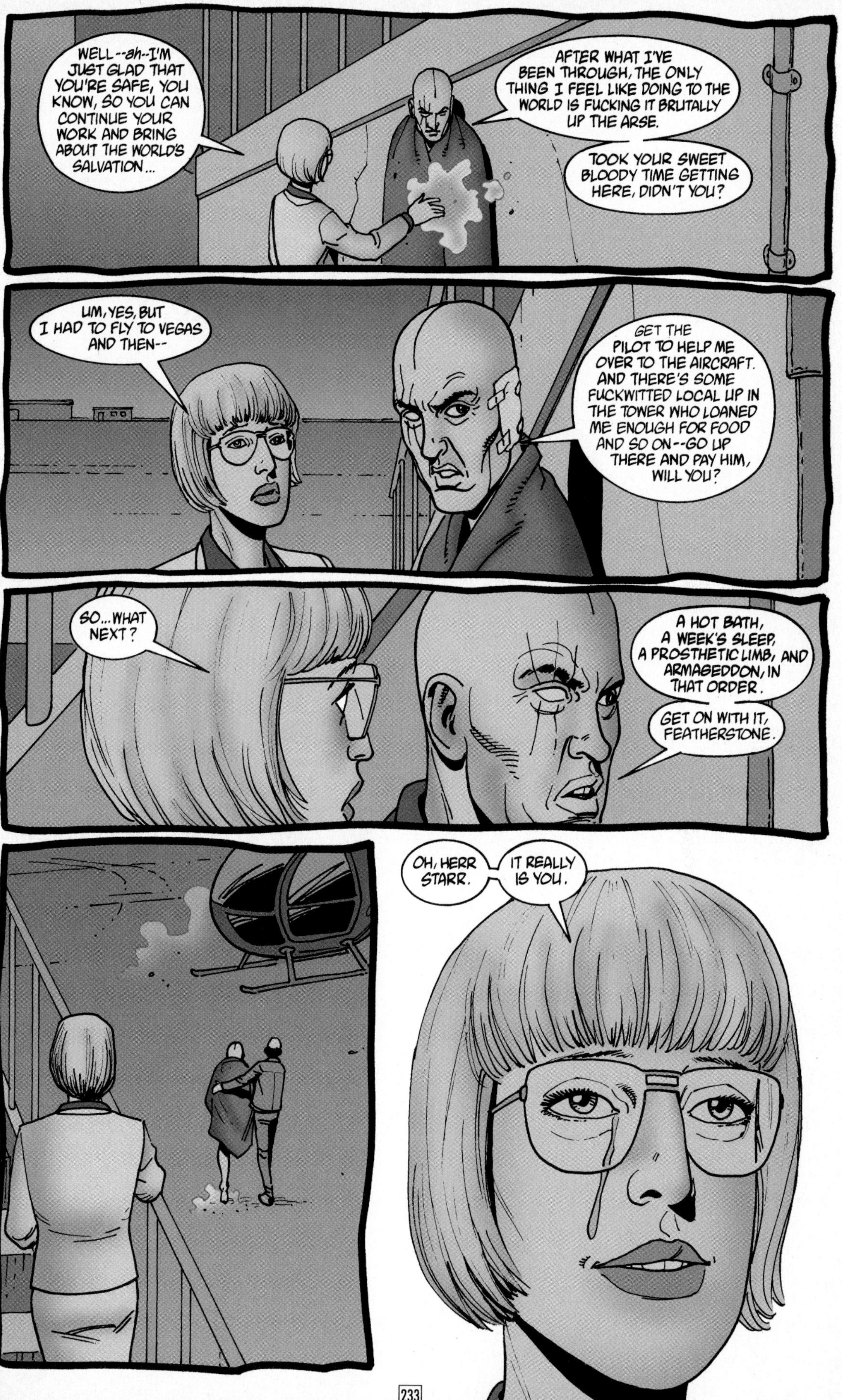
WELL--ah--I'M JUST GLAD THAT YOU'RE SAFE, YOU KNOW, SO YOU CAN CONTINUE YOUR WORK AND BRING ABOUT THE WORLD'S SALVATION...
AFTER WHAT I'VE BEEN THROUGH, THE ONLY THING I FEEL LIKE DOING TO THE WORLD IS FUCKING IT BRUTALLY UP THE ARSE.
TOOK YOUR SWEET BLOODY TIME GETTING HERE, DIDN'T YOU?
UM, YES, BUT I HAD TO FLY TO VEGAS AND THEN--
GET THE PILOT TO HELP ME OVER TO THE AIRCRAFT. AND THERE'S SOME FUCKWITTED LOCAL UP IN THE TOWER WHO LOANED ME ENOUGH FOR FOOD AND SO ON--GO UP THERE AND PAY HIM, WILL YOU?
SO...WHAT NEXT?
A HOT BATH, A WEEK'S SLEEP, A PROSTHETIC LIMB, AND ARMAGEDDON, IN THAT ORDER.
GET ON WITH IT, FEATHERSTONE.
OH, HERR STARR.
IT REALLY IS YOU.

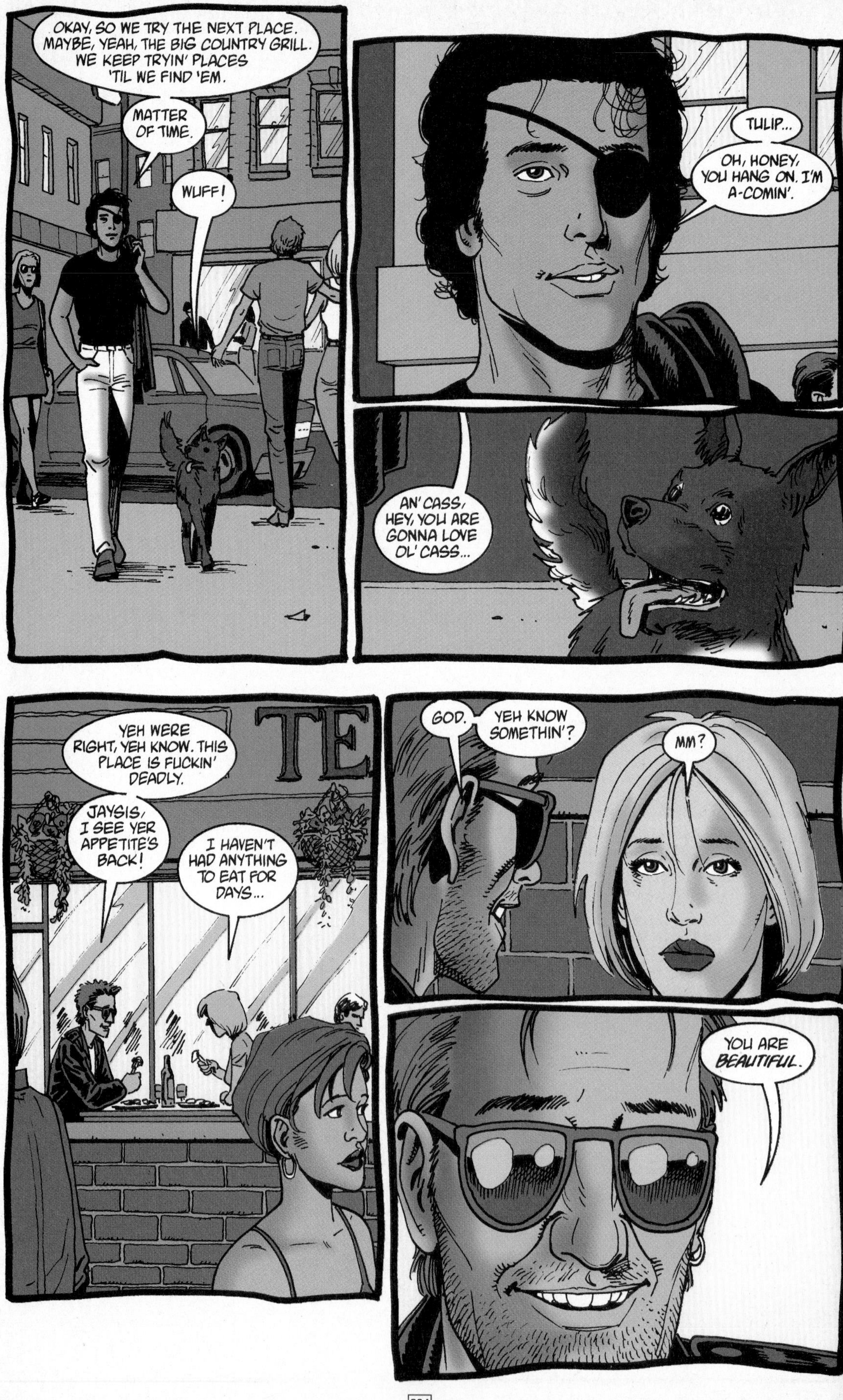
OKAY, SO WE TRY THE NEXT PLACE. MAYBE, YEAH, THE BIG COUNTRY GRILL. WE KEEP TRYIN' PLACES 'TIL WE FIND 'EM.
MATTER OF TIME.
WUFF!
TULIP...
OH, HONEY, YOU HANG ON. I'M A-COMIN'.
AN' CASS, HEY, YOU ARE GONNA LOVE OL' CASS...
TE
YEH WERE RIGHT, YEH KNOW. THIS PLACE IS FUCKIN' DEADLY.
JAYSIS, I SEE YER APPETITE'S BACK!
I HAVEN'T HAD ANYTHING TO EAT FOR DAYS...
GOD.
YEH KNOW SOMETHIN'?
MM?
YOU ARE BEAUTIFUL.

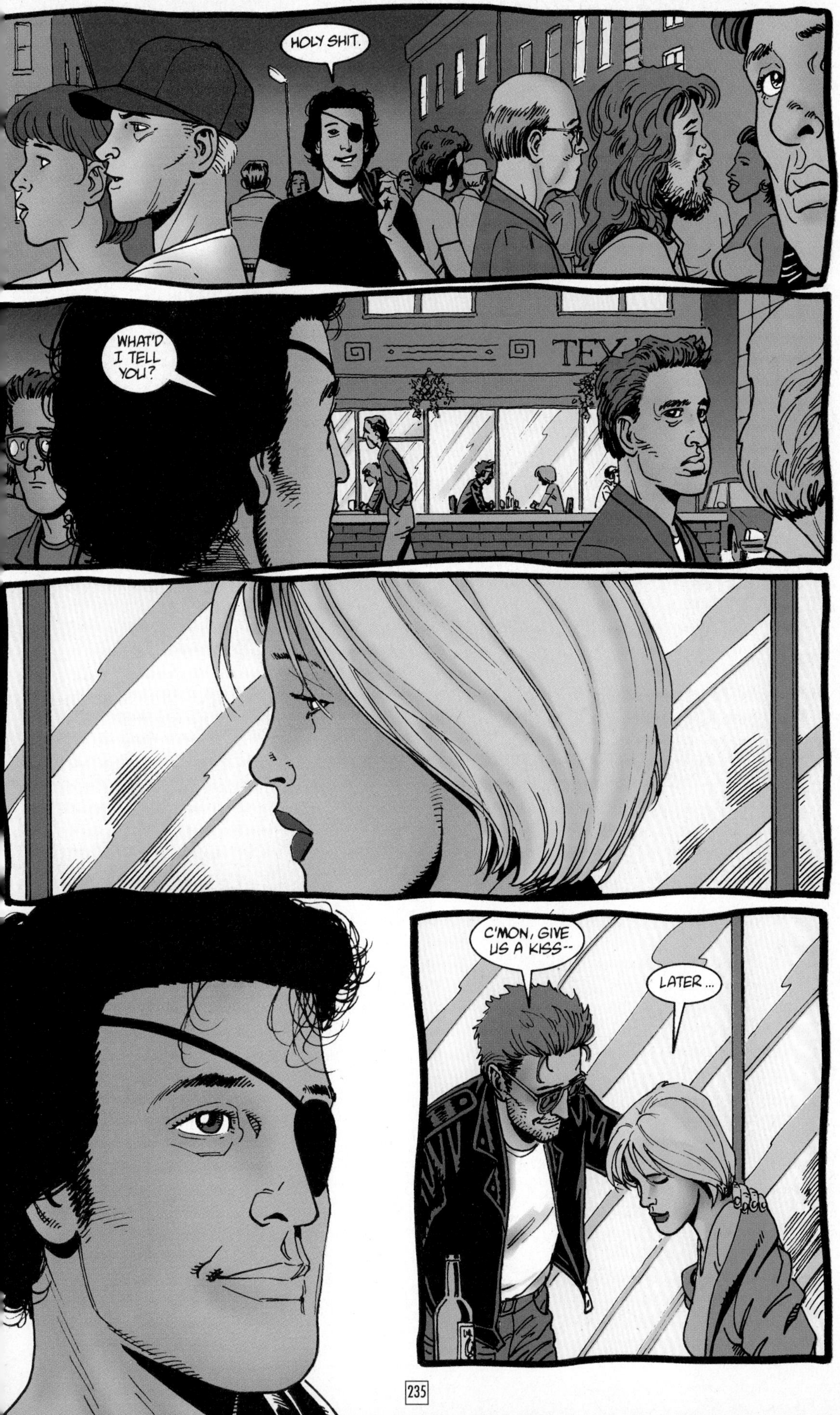
HOLY SHIT.
WHAT'D I TELL YOU?
TEX
C'MON, GIVE US A KISS--
LATER...

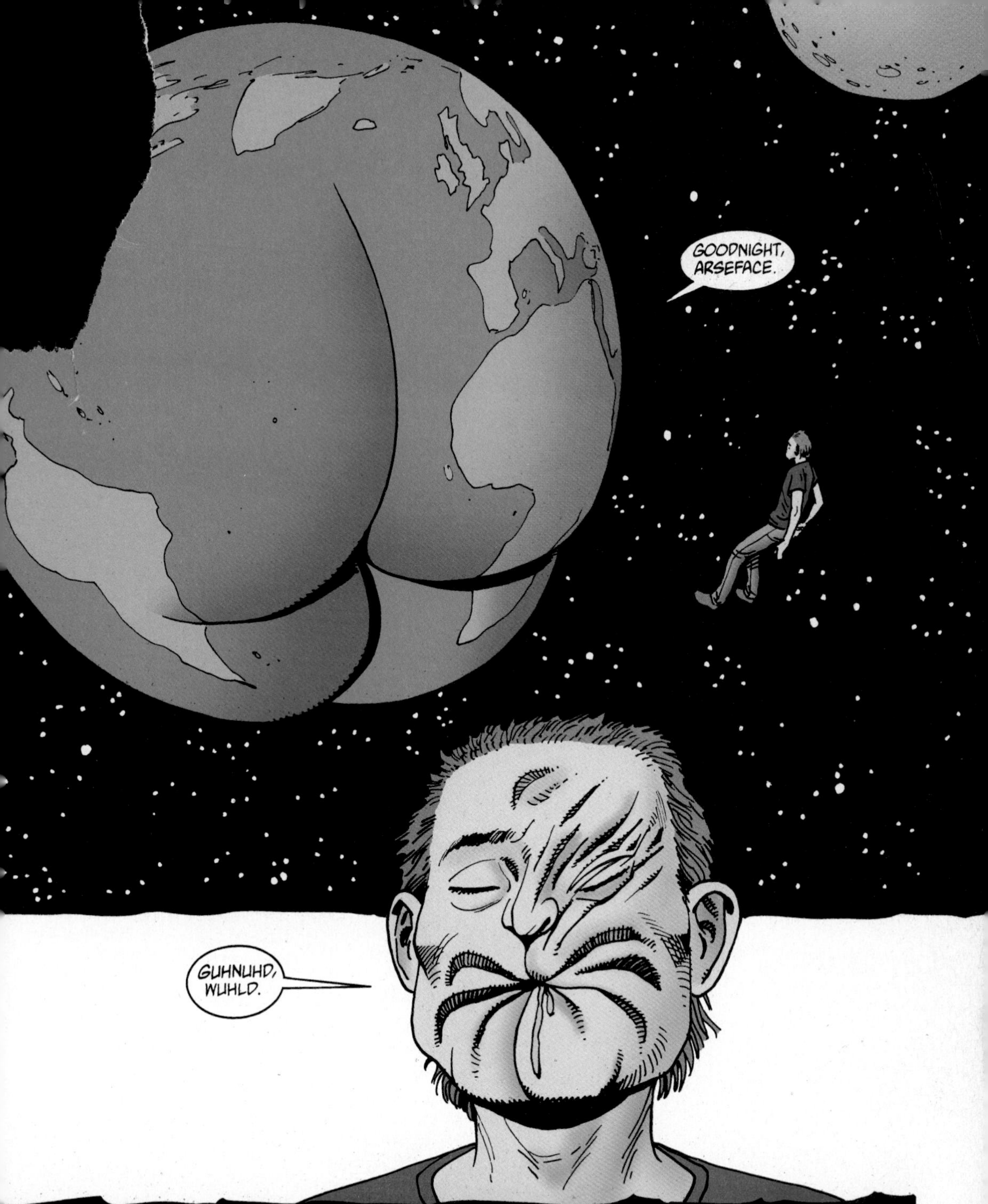
GOODNIGHT, ARSEFACE.
GUHNUHD, WUHLD.

ARSEFACED WORLD

GARTH ENNIS-Writer
STEVE DILLON-Artist

Pamela Rambo-Colorist, Clem Robins-Letterer,
Axel Alonso-Editor

PREACHER created by Garth Ennis and Steve Dillon